NEW POEMS

Rilke:
New Poems

translated from the German by

JOSEPH CADORA

and with a foreword by

ROBERT HASS

Copper Canyon Press
Port Townsend, Washington

Translations and introduction copyright 2014 by Joseph Cadora.
Foreword copyright 2014 by Robert Hass.

Printed in the United States of America

Cover art: Baladine Klossowska, Rilke Sketch, 1923-25.

Copper Canyon Press is in residence at Fort Worden State Park in Port Townsend,
Washington, under the auspices of Centrum. Centrum is a gathering place for
artists and creative thinkers from around the world, students of all ages and
backgrounds, and audiences seeking extraordinary cultural enrichment.

I would like to thank Michael Wiegers and Tonaya Thompson at Copper Canyon
Press. I would also like to acknowledge the help and support of my partner and
friend, Carol Chapman. Thanks also to Dan Gerber for his help with cover art.

LIBRARY OF CONGRESS CATALOGING-IN-PUBLICATION DATA

Rilke, Rainer Maria, 1875-1926.
[Neue Gedichte. English]
New poems / Rainer Maria Rilke; translated from the German
by Joseph Cadora.
pages cm
Includes index.
ISBN 978-1-55659-4243
I. Cadora, Joseph. II. Title.
PT2635.I65N49 2013
831'.912–dc23
2013010244

35798642
FIRST PRINTING

COPPER CANYON PRESS
Post Office Box 271
Port Townsend, Washington 98368

www.coppercanyonpress.org

This book is dedicated to my teacher and mentor,
Robert Hass.

Contents

Foreword

There are only a handful of books of poetry that define modernism in Europe–in the world, in fact–at the beginning of the twentieth century in the way that Picasso's *Les Demoiselles d'Avignon* does for painting or Stravinsky's *The Rite of Spring* for music. Or in the ways that the works of Joyce and Proust and Kafka do for fiction. *The Waste Land,* of course, is one of those books, and another is Rilke's two-volume *Neue Gedichte.* Or so I've always thought, and said so in a piece of writing some years ago when admiring the new translations of Rilke by Stephen Mitchell. I think I said that the great drama of Rilke's poetry was to drag the burden of the sublime, the intense longing for something ineffable and infinite in symbolist poetry–*der Ferne* was the word for it in German–down to earth and into the twentieth century. It was a project begun in *New Poems*–harder and plainer poems than he had ever before written, composed, he said, under the tutelage of his study of Rodin–and wrestled to a sort of conclusion in the ninth Duino Elegy. My friend Czesław Miłosz disagreed. *Almost* dragged it into the twentieth century, he said. Never quite got there.

Thirty years older than I, Miłosz was bound to have a different eye and ear, and he also had his reasons for not being in his youth an avid reader of German poetry. So our occasional argument about Rilke was qualified by the fact that we were neither of us fluent readers of the German language, and we talked a bit about how hard it was to know exactly what formal effects the poems were creating when you read them in translation, even with some knowledge of German and the original poem on the facing page. Especially when you were trying to make fine distinctions about the sources of Rilke's intensity. Miłosz was born in 1911, a few years after Rilke published those poems. Coming of age in the 1930s–during a worldwide depression and the uneasy aftermath of the Russian revolutions, having a more uneasy sense of impending and catastrophic war–his generation had no taste for the high tone of the symbolist poets and was inclined to think of turn-of-the-century Nietzscheanism as middle-class self-indulgence. I don't mean to put words in Miłosz's mouth, but he has written enough about the crisis brought on by the slow dissolution of religious faith in the European imagination for me to guess that for him the symbolist enterprise, Rilke's hushed diction, and perhaps the drama of the *Duino Elegies* were the work of writers who knew the cathedral was empty, but couldn't leave and were composing poems of great vertical longing to the empty air. I think he felt the same way about Mallarmé's *Un Coup de dés,* that it was melodrama, that the poets of imagination had better stop describing the vast, turbulent, boundaryless ocean they found themselves in and start swimming.

I guess I thought that in *New Poems* Rilke had started swimming. I came to Rilke, as an undergraduate, by reading the few famous poems that everyone reads: "Autumn Day" and "The Panther" and "Archaic Torso of Apollo" which I think I found in the early C.F. MacIntyre translations published by University of California Press, though I may have found them in the M.D. Herter Norton translations published by W.W. Norton. I know that the first Rilke poem I memorized was MacIntyre's translation of "Initiation," which I also memorized in German while I was at it. I loved the opening of that poem–

> Whoever you are, go out into the evening,
> leaving your room, of which you know each bit;
> your house is the last before the infinite,
> whoever you are.

Not long after I came across Herter Norton's translation–which barely gets the poem out of German–

> Whoever you are: at evening step forth
> out of your room, where all is known to you;
> last thing before the distance lies your house:
> whoever you are.

and it sent me across to Rilke's text:

> Wer du auch seist: am Abend tritt hinaus
> aus deiner Stube, drin du alles weißt;
> als letztes vor der Ferne liegt dein Haus:
> wer du auch seist.

And I began to understand the concept of "translation," not least because I was electrified by saying that third line, by the force and authority the regular iambic pentameter (not a concept I had at that moment) gave to *als letztes vor der Ferne liegt dein Haus.* This was –also something I didn't know–exactly the symbolist idea, one that Emily Dickinson would have been quite comfortable with, and one that was probably initiated in European literature by Charles Baudelaire. Here is a quiet, plainspoken voice setting out these vertical longings of the nineteenth century in a completely ordinary setting –*aus deiner Stube,* though I have learned since that *Stube* was in 1907 a slightly old-fashioned word for which the equivalent would be something like "quarters"–and then making a magic of it by the rhythm it is cast in. That magic is probably more or less what Miłosz was suspicious of and what attracted me, an adolescent beginning to approach modern poetry.

The other idea I had at the time was that the *Duino Elegies* was one of the masterworks of modernism–like *Ulysses* and *The Cantos* –one of the great adventures to be wandered into, and when I began on it, I started with a translation I found in a gift shop, a translation by one Harry Behn, published by something called Peter Pauper Press, and I read there the beginning of the first Elegy:

> Who, if I cried out, would heed me amid the host of the Angels?

Not a sentence you have to consciously memorize. It's in your head forever. I didn't know that it is a line problematic for translators. Rilke's first line goes like this:

> Wer, wenn ich schriee, hörte mich denn aus der Engel

That is, it's grammatically incomplete, enjambed. And so are the second line and the third. To complete the sense of the first line, you need the second:

> Wer, wenn ich schriee, hörte mich denn aus der Engel
> Ordnungen? und gesetzt selbst, es nähme

Here is Stephen Mitchell's translation:

> Who, if I cried out, would hear me among the angels'
> hierarchies? and even if one of them pressed me

Here is Galway Kinnell and Hannah Liebmann's :

> Who, if I screamed out, would hear among the hierarchies of
> angels? And if one suddenly did take me

And here is William Gass's:

> Who, if I cried, would hear me among the Dominions
> of Angels? And even if one of them suddenly

So I understood early on that to read Rilke meant, unless one was going to go live in Berlin or Vienna and acquire something like a native speaker's fluency, reading as many translations as I could get my hands on. (And that the same was true of reading Baudelaire and Neruda and Dostoyevsky.) The version of the *Duino Elegies* I carried around then was the Leishman/Spender translation published in 1939. Since then I've read W.H. Auden's review of it that same year in *The New Republic.* Auden had this to say:

> What a scholar's opinion of these translations may be I do not
> know and do not very much care. There is no such thing as a
> perfect translation; it is a job that has to be redone for every
> generation. But I am confident that this translation by Mr.
> Leishman and Mr. Spender will remain definitive for our own.

The translation for my generation was Steven Mitchell's, published by Random House in 1982. That was the book that set me finally to studying Rilke, set me to that great adventure I knew was out there. If, as Auden said, there was no perfect translation, and if, as he implied, I wouldn't have been competent to judge even if there were one, still Mitchell's Rilke, with the German on the facing page, seemed nearly perfect to me; that is, it seemed a book I could read on its own terms as a book of poems. Reading it, I came to know Rilke somewhat more fully. And then came Edward Snow's fresh, direct, straightforward translations of the *New Poems* in two volumes from North Point Press in 1984 and 1987, and Albert Poulin's translations of Rilke's French-language poems in 1986, and then, after an interval, Galway Kinnell's *The Essential Rilke* in 1999, especially interesting because his own *Book of Nightmares* seemed modeled on the *Duino Elegies,* and surprisingly in the same year the master novelist Gass's *Reading Rilke,* with *his* translation of the elegies.

What to conclude except that you could take down from the shelf different Rilkes in the way that you would different poets in English, or different books – early Yeats and late Yeats – by the same poet. Or that you might have as a touchstone Pablo Casals's recording of a Bach cello suite and come to know the music better by listening to other performances. I was just beginning to read Walter Benjamin's "The Task of the Translator," the great essay he wrote in 1923 out of his experience of attempting to translate Baudelaire, when Joseph Cadora told me that he had set about translating the *Neue Gedichte* into English in the original meters with the original rhyme scheme. It seemed to me, on the face of it, an impossible task, besides being an improbable one. Benjamin, curiously drawn both to Marxism and the Kabbalah, begins with what is a symbolist-era idea: the ideal version of the poem exists somewhere beyond the poem in its original language and any of its translations. Or, as he put it, "the original and the translation [are] recognizable as fragments of a greater language." Or: "It is the task of the translator to release in his own language that pure language which is under the spell of another, to liberate the language imprisoned in a work in his re-creation of that work." It is an almost Brechtian idea: the translation has, in a way, an advantage over the original by virtue of being a translation, because it heightens the reader's sense that it is not the absolute poem, that the absolute poem is out there, somewhere, just beyond our reach. Which is to say: your house is the last before the infinite.

My argument with Czesław Miłosz over the tone of *Neue Gedichte* probably can't be resolved. It was about a quite subtle thing buried in the music of the poems, in their formal qualities, where it can be quite difficult to get at and where even native speakers are apt to disagree. One of the spectacular things about Joseph Cadora's *New Poems,* the impossible task that he accomplished, is it allows English-language readers of Rilke to get that much closer to the tones and inflections of the young and maturing poet—Rilke was in his early thirties when he wrote these poems. It was, of course, impossible to make translation into English in meter and rhyme without taking liberties with the original—and Cadora takes plenty with nuances of meaning in the German, but on the whole it is surprising how few he takes, how often he stays on Rilke's ground. And when he doesn't, because he is, of course, giving us a Rilke for the ear, it is easily compensated for by the reader who has Snow's or Mitchell's Rilke to hand.

One of the *New Poems* that has haunted me is "Jugend-Bildnis meines Vaters," "Portrait of My Father as a Youth." It is a poem that initiated a genre—the poet's meditation on photographs of parents—which was not what I first noticed about it. What struck me had to do with tone and with trying to understand Rilke. Rilke had an intense, not easy relationship with his mother. His father, Josef Rilke, was a petty official in the Austro-Hungarian bureaucracy. That's the description of the father's employment given in all the accounts of him: "petty official." He'd been in the military and went to work for the railroad where officials also wore uniforms signifying their rank, a feature of Austrian life noticed by Franz Kafka and Joseph Roth. It was common, I suppose, to all of Eastern and Central Europe. In Chekhov's "The Lady with the Dog," the protagonist, Gurov, meets a beautiful and mysterious upper-class woman at a spa in Yalta. She is by herself, and she confesses to Gurov about her husband, who is at home in the town of S., "I don't know what it is he does at his office." And then, "But I know he's a flunky." When I read that recently, I thought of Rilke and his father. Here is the beginning of the poem in Edward Snow's crisp and direct translation:

> Dream in the eyes. The brow as if in touch
> with something far away. About the lips
> immense youth, unsmiling seductiveness,
> and across the full ornamental braids
> of the slim aristocratic uniform
> the saber's basket hilt and both the hands—
> waiting, calmly, urged toward nothing.

The infinite, which was next door in "Initiation," seems to touch the father's brow—*mit etwas Fernem*—in this poem. Here is the German, easy to read with Snow as a trot:

> Im Auge Traum. Die Stirn wie in Berührung
> mit etwas Fernem. Um den Mund enorm
> viel Jugend, ungelächelte Verführung,
> und vor der vollen schmückenden Verschnürung
> der schlanken adeligen Uniform
> der Säbelkorb und beide Hände—, die
> abwarten, ruhig, zu nichts hingedrängt.

The main formal feature of these lines is the strong triple rhyme of *Berührung* and *Verführung* and *Verschnürung. Enorm,* of course, rhymes with *Uniform,* and when we come to the end of this portrait, the devastating end, *die* and *hingedrängt* do not rhyme. They pick up rhymes later, but here they end a sequence in which all the rhyme invests and makes dreamy the portrait of the father's impotence in his full-dress uniform of a dashing young Hapsburg cavalier, and then seems abruptly to stop rhyming: what do his hands reach for? *Nichts.* Snow gets Rilke's distancing irony exactly, and without the rhyme, I think, he can't get the dreaminess. Here is Cadora's version of the same lines:

In the eyes, dream. The brow seems to ruminate
on something distant. Tremendous youth about
the mouth, though in a dour, seductive state,
and across the fully decorated plait
filling the slim, noble uniform out,
the basket-hilt sword and both hands resting,
as if compelled toward nothing, composed.

You can see the chances Cadora took. The brow touched by *der Ferne* ruminates on it. The *ungelächelte* mouth has become "dour" to keep the meter—"unsmiling" or "serious" is three syllables. But he gets other effects: "resting" anticipates "nothing" (the fierce *nichts* in the German) and gives it a little extra force. You can see Cadora's remarkable ingenuity at work and his almost stubborn loyalty to the idea of catching Rilke's sound.

This bears directly on the question of Rilke's relation to the symbolist inheritance because here, it's pretty clear, he has projected it onto his father. Josef Rilke's is the brow touched by the infinite. And the idea comes back in the second half of the poem. Here is Snow's version. He is still speaking of the father's hands:

And now scarcely visible: as if they would be
first, grasping the distant, to disappear.
And all the rest self-shrouded
and erased as if we didn't understand
and dimmed by something deep in its own depths–.

You swiftly fading daguerreotype
in my more slowly fading hands.

That "distant" in Snow is Rilke's *die Fernes.* Here is Rilke's German:

Und nun fast nicht mehr sichtbar: als ob sie
zuerst, die Fernes greifenden, verschwänden.
Und alles andre mit sich selbst verhängt
und ausgelöscht als ob wirs nicht verständen
und tief aus seiner eignen Tiefe trüb–.

Du schnell vergehendes Daguerreotyp
in meinen langsamer vergehenden Händen.

It is a portrait of his father's hiddenness to him, of a man whose inner life, insofar as it existed, is occluded. And also the portrait of a generation whose hands reaching for the infinite are the only real thing about them and the first to disappear. It's very striking, and so is the end of the poem, the sudden address to the image. In German there is that run on *verschwänden* and *verständen* and *Händen* and the curious polysyllabic rhyme of *Tiefe trüb* and *Daguerreotyp,* as well as the last phrase, one to make you think translation is basically impossible, *in meinen langsamer vergehenden Händen.* How do you get that sound into English? "We think by feeling," Theodore Roethke wrote. "What is there to know?" Rilke clearly enough is finding that out by letting the sound of the poem say what he understands about learning mortality from a parent. And in this case a parent, hands reaching into the distance, he can hardly see.

Here's Cadora with these lines:

And now barely visible, as if grasping
at distance in order not to be found.
And all else here seems self-imposed,
wiped away so we cannot understand
and clouded deep in its own sounding.

You daguerreotype rapidly fading
within my more slowly fading hand.

It's my impression that Snow's version gets Rilke's ironic distance from his father perfectly and that Cadora's gets his rhyme-haunted relation to his father's unreachableness. Again there is ingenuity and risk in Cadora: "deep in its own sounding" is a bit awkward, but it comes closest to mimicking the musical intricacy of Rilke's lines, and brings us a bit closer to the argument about Rilke that may or may not ever be resolved. Which may have been Walter Benjamin's thought. Another way to what he meant may be the mathematical observation that a circle is the limit of the polygon. For Benjamin, the half-symbolist, half-modernist literary critic, the circle is the fullness of the poem completely realized. The first polygon to inscribe it is the poet's text; the others reaching nearer and nearer to the circle are the readings and translations that press it forward. Cadora's versions, giving us a Rilke to hear, along with notes on what has helped him to listen so closely to the poems, constitute an enormous gift toward our understanding of *New Poems,* and Cadora's Rilke is deeply absorbing to read.

Robert Hass

Introduction

Rainer Maria Rilke ranks in German poetry with Goethe and Hölderlin, and no other German poet belongs in that company. Of the three, Rilke's verse is by far the most widely read, and his poetry has also been the source of musical compositions by Dmitry Shostakovich, Paul Hindemith, and others. The philosopher Martin Heidegger used Rilke as an example of the highest sort of intellect in his essay "What Are Poets For?" In the estimation of translator and critic William H. Gass, Rilke stands beside Valéry and Yeats as one of the greatest poets of the twentieth century. *Neue Gedichte* (*New Poems*) was published in two volumes, in 1907 and 1908, and the poet lived mainly in Paris during the period in which these pieces were composed, though he traveled intermittently. The verse in these volumes marks the maturity of a poetic talent that had been struggling toward emotional development and a unique artistic vision.

Barely into his third decade when he began *New Poems,* Rilke had already published several well-received volumes, including *Life and Songs, The Book of Images,* and *The Book of Hours.* He was at work on a minor epic, *The Lay of the Love and Death of Cornet Christoph Rilke,* and had written two monographs on aesthetics, one on Auguste Rodin and the other on the artists' colony at Worpswede, where he and his wife, Clara, had lived for a while. His letters on Cézanne, also written around the time of *New Poems,* would later become part of the critical canon on that artist. Already something of a minor celebrity, he was also composing his *Letters to a Young Poet,* a correspondence with an admirer named Franz Kappus. If all that were not enough, Rilke was also working on his only novel, *The Notebooks of Malte Laurids Brigge,* an early example of Expressionism. Young Malte, Rilke's complex protagonist, would become a model for such existential heroes as Sartre's Antoine Roquentin. It is not hard to make the case that the *New Poems* period of Rilke's life was his most intensely creative, although his two masterpieces, *Sonnets for Orpheus* and *Duino Elegies,* would appear later, after a long dry period.

In his youth, Rilke had been the protégé and lover of Lou Andreas-Salomé, an author in her own right and a friend of both Freud and Nietzsche. Fifteen years his senior, Lou was the one who got Rilke to change his Gallic, feminine-sounding birth name, René, to the more masculine and Germanic Rainer. She also took him to Russia and introduced him to Tolstoy. Lou eventually distanced herself from Rilke's affections, although their correspondence and friendship continued. In April 1901, the poet married Clara Westhoff, an aspiring sculptor who bore an uncanny resemblance to Lou. A daughter, Ruth, was born that December. Theirs was supposed to be a union of two artistic temperaments, but it was clear to both after just a few years of marriage that domesticity was incompatible with the life of the artist. Rainer and Clara soon gave Ruth over to the care of her Westhoff grandparents and thereafter maintained separate lives.

In September 1905, Rilke took up residence at Rodin's estate at Meudon-Val-Fleury in order to serve as his secretary. Rilke was awed by Rodin–the great man seemed to embody the very essence of the creative force to the young poet. In Rilke's letters of this period he describes Rodin as "beyond all measure," "incomparable," the one for whom "God makes the sun to rise and set." And so it was a great blow to the poet when a misunderstanding over his handling of Rodin's correspondence caused the sculptor to dismiss Rilke from his service, although the two reconciled shortly thereafter.

We can readily see what an accomplished thirty-year-old Rilke was when he began work on *New Poems.* Yet he had experienced a rather troubled childhood, and the scars of his early years would show through his verse and his relationships throughout his life. Rilke had grown up in Prague, only a bit older than Kafka, although the two did not travel in the same circles. His birth was premature, and there were health problems in early childhood. His mother had lost an earlier female child and desperately wanted a girl. Having given birth to a boy instead, she dressed him in girls' clothing and named him René Maria. Young Malte in Rilke's autobiographical novel is, not surprisingly, also raised as a girl by his mother. A photograph of Rilke in a girl's jumper at age three shows him with a somber face, his little brow knit as if questioning why he is dressed in such a ridiculous costume. René Maria became a sensitive boy, one attracted by and attractive to women, in whom he brought out the mothering instinct. By age eight we see him attired in a cadet's uniform and showing a much happier demeanor.

The poet's father, Josef, was a midlevel railway clerk who had failed at a military career. Josef Rilke was famously described by Max Brod, Kafka's confidante, as "a stylish ladies' man who looked like a dashing cavalry officer" in his rail clerk's uniform. The elder Rilke had served the Austro-Hungarian Empire in 1859 in its bid to continue the oppression of its Italian possessions. For a short time he had been head of the Austrian garrison at Brescia, until his unit was driven from the city by Garibaldi and his Redshirts. Josef Rilke was on the wrong side of history in this conflict, and his career in the officer corps was thwarted by this defeat.

The marriage of Josef and Phia Rilke was not a happy one. Phia was used to a certain level of luxury–her parents maintained a Baroque mansion in Prague's most elegant neighborhood. Moving into a modest, rented apartment on Heinrichsgasse, a much less fashionable address, must have been a great disappointment to her. René Maria could not have failed to notice the disparity in the lifestyles of his grandparents' and his parents'. And then there were the pretensions to title on the paternal side–the Rilkes had always maintained that they were descendants of the noble Rulike family. It is no wonder that Rilke felt like the scion of a dying branch, or that he sought shelter in the grand houses of the nobility in his constant quest for a roof over his head. His parents separated when he was nine years old, presaging his own break from Clara after only a few years of marriage. Unlike Josef and Phia, who had little to do with one another after splitting, Rainer and Clara maintained a close friendship until the poet's death in 1926.

The pieces in these two volumes are often referred to as *Dinggedichte* or "thing-poems." Only a few, however, portray inanimate objects. The term may refer more to the fact that the poet was approaching his art as another artist may approach a canvas or a block of stone–the poems are things, artifacts, in the same sense that a painting or a granite bust is. In Rilke's words, written to his lifelong correspondent Lou Andreas-Salomé, "The thing is definite, the art-thing must be more definite yet; aloof from all accident, drained of all obscurity; withdrawn from time and given over to space, it has become an endurance capable of eternity." Wolfgang Leppmann, in his fine biography of the poet, remarks that the words *I* and *my* seldom appear in *New Poems,* although they are much in evidence in Rilke's earlier verse. It seems as if Rilke had invented the thing-poem as an escape from the emotion and subjectivity of his earlier work. As he wrote later, the pieces in *New Poems* are supposed to evince "*non des sentiments, mais des choses que j'avais senties,*" "not the emotions, but the things I have felt." Rilke has cast himself in the guise of a recording instrument in these poems; he is a camera and has abandoned the more subjective stance of *The Book of Images*.

Reading these poems we find that art is a constant theme as well as an objective. We encounter pieces of art made from great cathedrals, from salons full of overblown paintings, from architectural angels and stained-glass windows. There are also scenes from zoos and pleasure parks alongside observations of life and death. Some poems dwell on quotidian objects: a dried-out hydrangea blossom, a ball in flight, an old piece of lace. Others plumb the depths of human experience: the interiority of a hopeless prisoner or the secret hand gestures of the insane. There is a series of poems from the Old and New Testaments in which David, Saul, Jeremiah, Esther, Jesus, and Mary Magdalene appear as characters or voices. Sappho, Buddha, Don Juan, Hokusai, and Orpheus make appearances as well. The animal kingdom is represented by flamingos, dolphins, parrots, a pet dog, and a black cat, while poems such as "Interior of a Rose," "Opium Poppy," and "Persian Heliotrope" examine the floral world. Rilke also explores the various masks of the poet, casting the maker of verse as Sibyl, Alchemist, Courtesan, Adventurer, and Hermit. It is as if Rilke had assumed the aspect of Shiva, in the god's manifestation as Lord of the Dance, in order to bring into being the infinite multiplicity of the world.

What is *new* for me in these poems is how Rilke is able to create complex images the way a cinematographer will, by using various angles and tricks of light. Thus we get the great rose window of the cathedral reflected in the eye of a caged panther. The panther reappears in his own poem, and we are shown the animal from the inside out–from deep within his eyes, which are myopic from the haze of bars that surround him. We see the grace of a gazelle in a girl's reflection in a pond, and we witness the process of dying in a swan's launching itself into the water. What we also experience is Rilke's immense compassion for the whole of creation. He gives us the pathos of houses squatting in the shadows of great cathedrals, of women going slowly blind or simply languishing unloved. He shows us Jesus's moment of doubt and the Magdalene's frustrated feelings for him. The poet's eye is everywhere and on everything–he draws portraits of himself and of his father, takes us into strange parks to read the gravestones there, shows us a young officer in the shadow of death or a Spanish dancer whirling like a dervish.

H.W. Belmore, in his remarkably thorough study of the poet's style, *Rilke's Craftsmanship,* maintains that most of the pieces in *New Poems* are permutations of the sonnet form, and this seems correct to me. Although only around a quarter of the almost two hundred poems in the two volumes are bona fide sonnets, an even larger number are three-stanza, twelve-line poems, and another large grouping are poems of either thirteen or fifteen lines that closely resemble Rilke's true sonnets in line length and meter. Some of the poems would be fourteen-line sonnets except for an extra line in parentheses. All of these show both the poet's skill at manipulating traditional forms and his refusal to hew to convention. Except for the long, unrhymed poems that close the first volume, *New Poems* can be seen as Rilke's Bach-like variations on the sonnet.

Throughout his career Rilke's shorter poems tended toward rhyme while his longer pieces relied on blank verse. But of the *New Poems,* only five are unrhymed, the rest being poems with an often elaborate rhyme scheme. Some of these pieces contain a single unrhymed line – perhaps reminiscent of the rough spots a sculptor sometimes leaves on the finished work. But Rilke was, in his mature period, never a haphazard craftsman, and the unrhymed lines are almost always there for emphasis. In "Lament for Jonathan," for example, the unrhymed line, *erzeugte, wenn sein Samen in ihm glänzt,* expresses the mourning of King David for his favorite in his wish that some father should come and create a new Jonathan by offering his seed. This unrhymed line exquisitely contains the essence of the entire poem as a single sperm cell contains the essence of a human being. In "Samuel's Visitation of Saul" the unrhymed word, *schrie,* echoes the scream of the witch of Endor, which is the turning point of the poem and prefigures Saul's downfall. The unrhymed line in "The Balcony" is the very first line of the poem, and the unrhymed word reflects both the piece's title and the visual frame of the entire poem.

Although Rilke's rhymes most often fall on the most significant words, he also, like Verlaine, sometimes employed simple articles and pronouns as rhyming words. These are strategically used in enjambed lines, where the rhyme would be de-emphasized anyway. Another of his techniques is to sustain two closely related rhymes over several stanzas, as he does at the end of "Parrot Park." This unusual piece also shows Rilke's bold use of rhyming quartets (AAAA BBBB), a trick very hard to pull off without sounding monotonous. It works here because it mimics the repetitive screech and speech of the parrots. Rilke's rhymes are occasionally paired with adjacent ones. This technique is used in "The Panther" (*Stäbe gäbe*), in "The Unicorn" (*leichten Gleichgewichten*), and in "Tombs of the Hetaerae" (*schnellen Wellen*), to emphasize an essential element in the poem—the endless bars surrounding the panther, the relaxed stance of the unicorn, the swift waves in which the lovers of the Hetaerae drown.

New Poems is also very rich in internal rhymes—again, usually employed for some strategic purpose or emphasis. The *Bangen und Verlangen* we find in "Abishag" underlines the young girl's fear and the old king's impotent longings, the two dominant emotions in the poem. A triple internal rhyme occurs in the last stanza of "Pietà," a poem in which Mary Magdalene mourns the dead Jesus in her arms. Three words rhyming on their stressed initial syllables —*dein, keine, meinem:* your, none, mine—these are a perfect encapsulation of the anguished mood of the poem. "Your love was never mine," the Magdalene seems to say, "and now there is no chance, none, that you will *ever* be mine." Internal rhymes are also encountered in "The Cathedral," "The Courtesan," "The Procession of the Virgin Mary," "Dolphins," "Absalom's Downfall," and many other pieces. And then there is the famous ending line of "Birth of Venus" where a dolphin washes up on the beach like an afterbirth, *tot, rot und offen.* The two adjacent rhymes here are closely followed by the strong assonance of another long *o,* a shocking aural effect meant to underscore the startling image of the dolphin, "dead, red, and open," a vision for which the reader is totally unprepared since everything that has come before has been an image of beauty.

Assonance is another frequently used brush in Rilke's paintbox. In the poem "Dolphins," Rilke does what for a less skillful poet might be considered too much—*die stumme, stumpfgemute / Zucht der Fische, Blut von ihrem Blute*—six more or less long *u* sounds in a row. They lead the reader to the most important idea in the poem:

even the early Greeks had realized that dolphins were unlike fish and more like us, "blood of their blood." Rilke will occasionally use the accumulation of vowel sounds through an entire stanza as a device to build tension. In the poem "The Resurrected," there are thirteen repetitions of the short *a:*

Aber da sie dann, um ihn zu salben,
an das Grab kam, Tränen im Gesicht,
war er auferstanden ihrethalben,
daß er seliger ihr sage: Nicht—

These vowel repetitions lead inexorably to the most important word in the poem: *Nicht,* translated in this context as "don't." It is Jesus, upon rising from his tomb, telling Mary Magdalene that she must not anoint or embrace him. The piece, after all, is about renunciation, not resurrection, and the single word *don't* summarizes its mood exquisitely. Rilke can sometimes sustain these flights of echoing vowels over a pair of stanzas as in "Prayer for the Lunatic and the Convict," in which he repeats the long *i* (German *ei*) eleven times in eight rather short lines. They all point to, and rhyme with, the three most important words in the poem—*Sein, Freiheit,* and *Zeit:* being, freedom, and time. For these are the concepts Rilke is coming to terms with in this prayer for the wretched, and by repeating these vowel sounds in a sustained rush of images he makes this clear to the reader.

  Rilke's use of meter in these poems establishes a rather loose framework, the way the time signature is used in syncopated music. Strictly followed meters are seldom encountered in *New Poems.* Instead, the poet establishes a rhythm over the meter that often comments on the action or the images in the poem itself. The most striking example of this type of cadence play is in "The Swan," where Rilke emphasizes the awkward walking of the creature with the awkward rhythm in a line: *gleicht dem ungeschaffnen Gang des Schwanes.* Three consecutive unstressed syllables establish a halting pace that perfectly conveys the swan's heavy limp, and perfectly sets up the more liquid rhythm of the poem once the swan enters the water and begins to glide gracefully. A similar trick occurs in "Washing the Corpse," where the poet breaks the strict iambic meter he has established, using an anapest to emphasize the flickering kitchen lamplight that illuminates the scene.

"The Carousel," a poem that could serve as the meat of an entire essay on Rilke's prosody, shows how idiosyncratic Rilke's use of rhythm can seem until we discover its purpose:

⏑ ⏑⏑ / ⏑ ⏑⏑ / ⏑ /

Mit einem Dach und seinem Schatten dreht

/ ⏑⏑ / ⏑ / ⏑⏑ ⏑ /

sich eine kleine Weile der Bestand

⏑ / ⏑ / ⏑ /⏑ / ⏑ /

von bunten Pferden, alle aus dem Land,

⏑ /⏑ /⏑ /⏑ /⏑ /

das lange zögert, eh es untergeht.

The first two lines read more like prose than poetry, and readers will sometimes hear false stresses in an attempt to make the lines scan. A common mistake here is to stress the first syllables of *einem* and *seinem* in order to get an iambic line. Stressing the first syllable of *einem,* however, changes the meaning and makes it read as if there is *one roof,* clearly not Rilke's intent, rather than simply *a roof.* And we can also tell that these repetitions of three unstressed syllables are deliberate since the final three, the set that precedes the second syllable of *Bestand,* cannot be read any other way. After these two very oddly measured lines, Rilke falls into a steady iambic meter. What is the poet doing here, and what is he pointing to? If we consider what a carousel does when it starts up, it will be obvious. The first two lines, with their repetition of unstressed syllables, are meant to convey the slow start of the machinery, the initial movement of rising and falling horses as the carousel gets up to speed. Once it is in full gear the carousel whirls in iambic pentameter, that is, until Rilke wants to underline something else in the poem – notably the young women in stanza five, who are almost too old for such fun and who swing distractedly to their own rhythms. Belmore comments that the irregular lines, set off by the "refrain-like repetition" of the line *Und dann und wann ein weißer Elefant,* lend a very musical sonority to the piece, "suggesting the perpetual gay circling of the merry-go-round."

Rilke is also not averse to using a rather singsong rhythm when that is precisely what the poem calls for, as he does in "Resurrection." This darkly comic poem is presented largely in iambic trimeter, and the odd meter perfectly complements this bizarre story of a deceased family waiting on Judgment Day for its youngest members to catch up. Another Rilke trick is to use a trochee or spondee like a speed bump after a few lines of relatively even iambic meter. He does this with beautiful precision in "The Flag Bearer," where after four marching lines of iambs that portray the other, somewhat banal, soldiers in his unit, the flag bearer himself is introduced with the line: *er aber trägt – als trüg er eine Frau.* There are three strong stresses on the first three words of this line, and they are no accident, for Rilke is introducing the subject of his poem, the stalwart man who protects the flag with his very life, the one who, as the last line says, is courage and glory personified to his fellows. In a similar vein, the very last line of "Landscape" uses the two stressed syllables that begin the word *Erzengel* (archangel) to present the sudden brilliant gleam of the moon through the clouds – a spectacular effect.

The pace of *New Poems* is rather slow – andante or larghetto versus allegro. And this seems a necessity since the poems are, for the most part, sonnet length or less, and the poet is trying to present a concise description in a few lines. But as with everything to be said about Rilke's prosody, there are notable exceptions. "The Last Count von Brederode Eludes Turkish Captivity," for example, begins at a furious pace, fast as the horseback escape of its hero. But by the third line, the pace begins to relax as the rider realizes he no longer needs to flee like a hunted animal. By the time he reaches the river, Rilke's heroic count is once more his noble self, and his haste is subsumed into his own strength of character. The pace of "A Doge" also seems quicker than most of the other poems here, perhaps indicative of the poem's subject, who is much quicker in intellect than Venices's Council of Ten.

Rilke sometimes controls the pace of a poem by varying line length, as he does in "Emigrant Ship." The first stanza here contains lines of seven, eight, nine, or ten syllables, and it is their irregularity that slows the action from the metaphoric level, that of a defeated army fleeing a battle, to the literal level of the poem, in which an inelegant tub full of poor emigrants is steaming out of Naples harbor. Of course these wretched passengers *were* defeated in something resembling a battle, but their flight is a much slower one, and by carefully managing his line length, Rilke gets to have it both ways.

One of the most obvious hallmarks of Rilke's style is his extensive use of clauses, a device usually used sparingly by other poets. "Corrida," a poem describing a bullfight, is a perfect example of Rilke's amazing skill at manipulating syntax for a poetic purpose. Starting with a prepositional clause, the verse proceeds through six stanzas and twenty-six lines before we encounter a period at its very end. The various clauses, participles, and other devices that Rilke uses here fill the poem with suspense, as if we are holding our breath until the end, until we are certain the bull has been slain and the matador is safe. Rilke's use of accumulated participles, a device that condenses action like a compressed spring that is suddenly released by a verb, is also noteworthy. In the poem "The Dog," Rilke uses six participles in seven lines in order to portray the dog's anxiety and to accumulate the tension that will be released at the very end in the words "for otherwise he would not exist." Rilke also employs extensive parenthetical phrases—seen much less often in the work of other poets of this period. "Night Journey," "The Parks," "A

Doge," "The Adventurer," "Don Juan's Selection," "The Sundial," and "The Abduction" are just a few of the poems where parentheses are used to great effect.

The problems of translating Rilke are many, and they are thoroughly catalogued by William H. Gass in his excellent book *Reading Rilke*. For one thing, the poet's rhyme schemes frame his verses, establishing their form—and this is especially evident in pieces such as "Spanish Dancer," in which the *bailaora*'s dance is actually shaped by the rhyme scheme. "The Lace" is another poem where the rhyme scheme shapes the whole—here the complex weaving of rhymes is meant to suggest the intricate pattern of lacework, an art of which Rilke was a great admirer. Rhymes on the last line of a poem often point back to a previous line and are meant to tie a poem's conclusion to another element within it. "A Woman's Fate" is an example of this: the rhymes on *gelten* and *selten* are meant to draw attention to the one word the two lines share in common: *kostbar* or "precious." An irony is unveiled in this pairing—a certain cup is precious and rare, so it is kept on a curio shelf, but a woman placed "on the shelf," as it were, is never precious and never rare.

So many translators have shied away from Rilke's rhyme that they have sometimes gone out of their way to avoid perfectly good English cognates that also rhyme. And so in "Pietà," where Rilke rhymes *wusch* and *Dornenbusch,* it seems strange to me that anyone would translate them as anything but "wash" and "thornbush," even though a slight manipulation of verb tense is necessary in order to pull this off. Similarly, where Rilke uses foreign (usually French) words, as he does in "In the Salon," it seems like an infidelity to translate the rhymes *Jabots* and *Bibelots* as "scarves" and "trinkets" when both these words are included in any good English dictionary. "Parrot Park" is another fine example where it would behoove the translator to stay out of Rilke's way. *Rasenrändern, Ständern,* and *Ländern* translate nicely into "strand," "stand," and "land"; while "parade" and "jade" are the same words in the English and the German. And without the quartets of rhyme that evoke the chattering parrots, the poem is just not the same. I am convinced that, without the rhyme schemes, Rilke would not be Rilke, and have endeavored to keep them exact where I could. Of course I have had to use a more modern and looser sense of rhyme, sometimes relying on slant rhyme, syllabic rhyme, eye rhyme, and the like, since English is nowhere near as rhyme-rich as German. I have included the rhyme schemes for the original German as an aid to the reader.

Rilke's extensive use of caesura and enjambment recalls the way bricklayers build a wall, locking it together with alternating courses. But his enjambment is often deliberately calculated to de-emphasize rhymes that would otherwise seem overused, and his use of caesura is meant to slow down the pace of certain lines. I've tried to keep these as often as possible. Rilke's meter is another matter altogether. I've attempted to keep line lengths and syllable counts as close to Rilke's as I could, and I've tried to duplicate some of his rhythmic tricks, such as the limping line in "The Swan." In many other cases, however, English and German are too far apart to match Rilke's meter, and keeping it would have introduced some awkward constructions in the English. In these cases I chose readability over fidelity to Rilke.

There are other aspects of Rilke's *New Poems* that are untranslatable but require a passing comment. Rilke often coins words, and his verbal play doesn't always translate into English. "Sacrifice," for example, contains an artificial ending added to the adjective *alt* in order to get *Altes,* a noun that at once suggests "the old" and "the all." In the poem "The Temptation" Rilke uses the word *Nichte,* which translates as "niece," but he uses the singular form where only a plural would be appropriate because he's chasing an internal rhyme while also trying to suggest the word *nichts* or "nothing." I have rendered this as "nothing-nieces," which fits well the poem's images of incestuous fantasy—but a lot of the subtlety of the wordplay is lost in translation. Idioms can also be problematic. Germans thread the *ear* of the needle, not the *eye,* and because of this small difference in language the translator of "Legend of the Three Living and the Three Dead," runs smack into a wall in trying to present all the nuances Rilke has stuffed into this parable of the senses. Still, it is a worthwhile effort to try to get as much Rilke as one can into the translations of his poems since nothing in them is accidental, and every tiny gear and escapement has a place in the clockwork of his verse.

It is now a little more than a century since these poems were first written and published, but their themes still echo in our world today. "Last Evening" can hardly be read without thinking of the endless deployments of soldiers to Iraq and Afghanistan. "The King" and his cold detachment as he signs a death warrant reminds us much of some contemporary leaders. "The Lace" echoes the sweatshops of cities where undocumented workers toil in obscurity. The poems are not for everyone, for Rilke's vision is sometimes bleak. His Christ has been forsaken, abandoned by his father, and shut out of his mother's womb. His Buddha does not see us, and does not care. His Joshua has abandoned the chosen people for the fastness of the mountains. Still there is so much to see in the poet's images, so much to hear in his rhythm and rhyme, so much to grasp that he will grant, not easily but with a bit of earnest effort.

I find myself reading each of these poems the way the narrator in "Tanagra" examines an ancient statuette–lifting and turning it, examining it from every angle to see what a different light will do. As part of this process I have read many fine translations, notably those of Edward Snow, Stephen Mitchell, Walter Arndt, and Galway Kinnell and Hannah Liebmann, though inevitably I find myself back with Rilke's German. I had no idea, on starting, what a formidable task translation would be, but I tried to stay true to a vision of Rilke that would invite the reader into *his* world, not mine. Rilke felt that the art of the Master, as he called Rodin, was a result of "handwork," the intense yet almost unintentional will to constantly perfect one's creations, and that is the steep path I have tried to follow. I was also lucky enough to get valuable and insightful feedback on some of these translations from Robert Hass's Poetry Translation Workshop at the University of California, Berkeley, and from Professor Hass himself.

A brief commentary on each poem has been included, mostly a result of reading the poet's letters, several biographies, and three other works of Rilke's that are contemporary with *New Poems: The Notebooks of Malte Laurids Brigge, The Lay of the Love and Death of Cornet Christoph Rilke,* and *Letters to a Young Poet.* All translations from these and other works are mine except where noted. Difficult as the crafting has been, translating *New Poems* has been a labor of love, and thus, no labor at all. I only hope I have conveyed a small part of the richness that Rainer Maria Rilke imagined for us in the early years of the last century. If I can lead a few more readers to such a poet, I will have done well.

Joseph Cadora
Berkeley

NEW POEMS

VOLUME ONE

Karl und Elisabeth von der Heydt in Freundschaft

Früher Apollo

Wie manches Mal durch das noch unbelaubte	A
Gezweig ein Morgen durchsieht, der schon ganz	B
im Frühling ist: so ist in seinem Haupte	A
nichts was verhindern könnte, daß der Glanz	B
aller Gedichte uns fast tödlich träfe;	C
denn noch kein Schatten ist in seinem Schaun,	D
zu kühl für Lorbeer sind noch seine Schläfe	C
und später erst wird aus den Augenbraun	D
hochstämmig sich der Rosengarten heben,	E
aus welchem Blätter, einzeln, ausgelöst	F
hintreiben werden auf des Mundes Beben,	E
der jetzt noch still ist, niegebraucht und blinkend	G
und nur mit seinem Lächeln etwas trinkend	G
als würde ihm sein Singen eingeflößt.	F

Early Apollo

As often through boughs bare and leaf lorn
the sunrise gazes, though Springtime looms,
thus nothing upon his head is worn
to prevent the blazing light of all poems

from striking us a blow almost fatal;
for in his glance there is still no shadow,
his temples are too cool for the laurel,
and only later, from over his brow,

will the tall-stemmed rose garden rise,
its petals fluttering, one by one, to fall
slowly upon those trembling lips of his,

which are still quiet, unused and glinting,
as though the infusion of his own song
were there in his barely sipping smile.

Rilke begins volume one of the *New Poems* with this piece and begins volume two
with "Archaic Torso of Apollo." Both poems can be seen as invocations to the god
of poetry, and thus each is placed as the frontispiece of its volume. Both evoke, to
a certain extent, Hölderlin's "Dem Sonnengott." Apollo's "barely sipping" smile
can be seen in Archaic period statues, in the male *kouroi* and the female *korai* who
share the enigmatic semi-smile so typical of the period. The Rilkean smile of sud-
den revelation will appear over and over again throughout these poems.

Mädchen-Klage

Diese Neigung, in den Jahren,　　　　　　　　　A
da wir alle Kinder waren,　　　　　　　　　　A
viel allein zu sein, war mild;　　　　　　　　B
andern ging die Zeit im Streite,　　　　　　　C
und man hatte seine Seite,　　　　　　　　　C
seine Nähe, seine Weite,　　　　　　　　　　C
einen Weg, ein Tier, ein Bild.　　　　　　　　B

Und ich dachte noch, das Leben　　　　　　　D
hörte niemals auf zu geben,　　　　　　　　　D
daß man sich in sich besinnt.　　　　　　　　E
Bin ich in mir nicht im Größten?　　　　　　F
Will mich Meines nicht mehr trösten　　　　　F
und verstehen wie als Kind?　　　　　　　　E

Plötzlich bin ich wie verstoßen,　　　　　　　G
und zu einem Übergroßen　　　　　　　　　　G
wird mir diese Einsamkeit,　　　　　　　　　H
wenn, auf meiner Brüste Hügeln　　　　　　　I
stehend, mein Gefühl nach Flügeln　　　　　　I
oder einem Ende schreit.　　　　　　　　　　H

A Girl's Lament

This inclination of ours
from back in our childhood years,
this wish to be alone was gentle;
others passed the time fighting,
and each of them had his own gang,
his near and his distant thing,
a picture, a path, an animal.

And still I believed that life
would never stop yielding if
oneself was what one beheld.
Is not what's within me my best?
Will not what is mine grant the trust
and understanding of a child?

Suddenly, as if disowned,
I feel a solitude so profound,
something too big to comprehend,
for here on these breast-hills my feelings
seem to be screaming to rise on wings
or merely cry out for an end.

This may be an answering poem to Hölderlin's "Da Ich ein Knabe War" ("Since I Was a Boy"). But where Hölderlin's young boy feels freedom in nature, Rilke's young girl feels penned in by her swelling breasts that signal the end of her independence.

Liebes-Lied

Wie soll ich meine Seele halten, daß	A
sie nicht an deine rührt? Wie soll ich sie	B
hinheben über dich zu andern Dingen?	C
Ach gerne möcht ich sie bei irgendwas	A
Verlorenem im Dunkel unterbringen	C
an einer fremden stillen Stelle, die	B
nicht weiterschwingt, wenn deine Tiefen schwingen.	C
Doch alles, was uns anrührt, dich und mich,	D
nimmt uns zusammen wie ein Bogenstrich,	D
der aus zwei Saiten *eine* Stimme zieht.	E
Auf welches Instrument sind wir gespannt?	F
Und welcher Geiger hat uns in der Hand?	F
O süßes Lied.	E

Love Song

How shall I maintain my soul in order
that it might not mix with yours? How shall
I lift it over you toward other things?
Ah, but I would gladly give it shelter
with something lost in the dapplings
of a strange and quiet place that will
not waver with your deepest shudder.
Yet all that brings the two of us low
takes us together like the stroke of a bow
that from two strings draws *one* harmony.
On what instrument are we splayed?
And what player's hand has played?
Oh sweet melody.

Rilke recognized that love was largely the province of women. As young Malte comments in *The Notebooks of Malte Laurids Brigge,* "For centuries now they have performed the whole of love; they have always played the full dialogue, both parts. For the man has only imitated them, badly. And this has made their learning difficult with his inattentiveness, with his negligence, with his jealousy, which is also a form of negligence."

Eranna an Sappho

O du wilde weite Werferin: A
Wie ein Speer bei andern Dingen B
lag ich bei den Meinen. Dein Erklingen B
warf mich weit. Ich weiß nicht *wo* ich bin. A
Mich kann keiner wiederbringen. B

Meine Schwestern denken mich und weben, C
und das Haus ist voll vertrauter Schritte. D
Ich allein bin fern und fortgegeben, C
und ich zittere wie eine Bitte; D
denn die schöne Göttin in der Mitte D
ihrer Mythen glüht und lebt mein Leben. C

Eranna to Sappho

O you savage, far-flinging one,
I lay among my own kith and kin,
a spear among common things. Your din
hurls me afar. I unknow myself and none
may ever bring me back again.

My sisters weave and remember me;
the house is full of familiar routine.
I alone am trembling like a plea,
I alone am distant and withdrawn,
for at the core of her myth the divine
goddess shines and lives my life for me.

W.H. Auden facetiously called Rilke "the greatest Lesbian poet since Sappho."
While that is an obvious overstatement, this piece and the two following poems
illustrate Auden's point. The three Sapphic poems might also be regarded as
invocations to Artemis, offered up after the invocation to her brother, Apollo,
that begins the first volume of these poems.

Sappho an Eranna

Unruh will ich über dich bringen,   A
schwingen will ich dich, umrankter Stab.   B
Wie das Sterben will ich dich durchdringen   A
und dich weitergeben wie das Grab   B
an das Alles: allen diesen Dingen.   A

Sappho to Eranna

Unrest to you would I bring,
wielding you like a staff entwined.
I would pierce you like death's sting,
deliver you like the grave, consigned
to the All, to everything.

Along with Anactoria, Andromeda, and Mnasidika, Eranna is one of the names
used by Sappho to refer to lovers or ex-lovers. There was a female poet named
Erinna who was reputed to have been a student of Sappho's, but since Eusebius
dates her around the fourth century B.C.E., two centuries after the poet of Les-
bos, this reference most likely refers to her poetic debt to Sappho.

Sappho an Alkaïos

FRAGMENT

Und was hättest du mir denn zu sagen,	A
und was gehst du meine Seele an,	B
wenn sich deine Augen niederschlagen	A
vor dem nahen Nichtgesagten? Mann,	B
sieh, uns hat das Sagen dieser Dinge	C
hingerissen und bis in den Ruhm.	D
Wenn ich denke: unter euch verginge	C
dürftig unser süßes Mädchentum,	D
welches wir, ich Wissende und jene	E
mit mir Wissenden, vom Gott bewacht,	F
trugen unberührt, daß Mytilene	E
wie ein Apfelgarten in der Nacht	F
duftete vom Wachsen unsrer Brüste–.	X
Ja, auch dieser Brüste, die du nicht	G
wähltest wie zu Fruchtgewinden, Freier	H
mit dem weggesenkten Angesicht.	G
Geh und laß mich, daß zu meiner Leier	H
komme, was du abhältst: alles steht.	I

Sappho to Alcaeus

FRAGMENT

And what could you have to say to me,
and why should I concern my soul then
if you turn your defeated eyes away
when the thing-not-spoken approaches, man.

See how we are transported to splendor,
enrapt by this thing that has been said.
When I think how among your kind comes the poor
annihilation of our sweet maidenhood,

which we, both I in my knowing way
and all those knowing with me, god shielded,
have borne unspoiled since Mytilene
like an orchard in the night yielded
the lingering scent of our swelling breasts.

Yes, even these breasts you do not embrace
as one might choose the fruit entwined,
suitor with your shrinking-from-me face.
Go, leave me, that in my lyre I might find
the thing that you hold back – all is as was.

Dieser Gott ist nicht der Beistand Zweier,   H
aber wenn er durch den Einen geht   I

This god does not succor two of our kind
except if he penetrates one of us

Mytilene with its magnificent harbor is the principal city of the island of Lesbos and, as archaeological excavations show, has been inhabited since the early Bronze Age. The city was also Sappho's home for most of her life. The Alcaeus referred to here was another poet of Mytilene, a contemporary of Sappho's and the reputed originator of Alcaic verse, which stands beside the Sapphic stanza as one of the most important forms of classical poetry. In a letter to Clara dated July 24, 1907, Rilke noted a fifth-century vase he had seen depicting Sappho and Alcaeus together. It was likely the red-figured *kalathos* from the Staatliche Antikensammlungen in Munich, and on it we can see Alaceus, lyre in hand, shyly averting his face from Sappho, as in the poem. In his *Rhetoric,* Aristotle references this very episode between Sappho and Alcaeus as an example of things that evoke shame. He quotes the fragment that Rilke mentions in the poem's subtitle, in which Alcaeus says, "I wish to tell you something, but shame will not permit me." Sappho replies that if what Alcaeus had to say were worthy and proper, he wouldn't have any qualms expressing himself, or looking her in the eye.

Grabmal eines jungen Mädchens

Wir gedenkens noch. Das ist, als müßte	A
alles dieses einmal wieder sein.	B
Wie ein Baum an der Limonenküste	A
trugst du deine kleinen leichten Brüste	A
in das Rauschen seines Bluts hinein:	B
–jenes Gottes.	X
Und es war der schlanke	C
Flüchtling, der Verwöhnende der Fraun.	D
Süß und glühend, warm wie dein Gedanke,	C
überschattend deine frühe Flanke	C
und geneigt wie deine Augenbraun.	D

Gravestone of a Young Girl

We can still recall. As if this must
all have to happen once more.
Like a tree on the Lemon Coast,
you bore your small, subtle breasts,
into his blood's surging roar

–that god's.
         And it was the snake-slender
fugitive, that spoiler of women.
Warm as your thoughts, glowing and tender,
overshadowing your fresh-flanked splendor,
arching as your brows did then.

The Lemon Coast refers to the area south of Sorrento, although today it is more often called the Amalfi Coast. The variety of lemons grown there, known as Sfusato Amalfitano, have been known since antiquity. They feature a prominent "nipple" on the end and are used here to evoke the small breasts of a young girl.

Opfer

O wie blüht mein Leib aus jeder Ader   A
duftender, seitdem ich dich erkenn;   B
sieh, ich gehe schlanker und gerader,   A
und du wartest nur–: wer bist du denn?   B

Sieh: ich fühle, wie ich mich entferne,   C
wie ich Altes, Blatt um Blatt, verlier.   D
Nur dein Lächeln steht wie lauter Sterne   C
über dir und bald auch über mir.   D

Alles was durch meine Kinderjahre   E
namenlos noch und wie Wasser glänzt,   F
will ich nach dir nennen am Altare,   E
der entzündet ist von deinem Haare   E
und mit deinen Brüsten leicht bekränzt.   F

Sacrifice

Oh how my body blooms from every vein
more fragrantly since I've held you within;
see what a narrow, direct gait I maintain,
and you alone wait there–who are you then?

As I lose all these old things, blade by blade,
I feel withdrawn from myself completely,
only the pure stars of your smile arrayed
over you and soon, as well, over me.

Everything still without a name
that glittered in childhood as water did,
will I name for you here on the altar flame
that is ignited by your hair's gleam
and by your breasts softly garlanded.

C.F. MacIntyre, J.B. Leishman, and others have pointed out Rilke's cult of
childhood–which is briefly touched on in the last stanza here. Other poems in
this volume that explore this magical and frightening territory are "A Girl's
Lament," "Childhood," "The Grown-up," "Before the Summer Rain," and
"The Carousel."

Östliches Taglied

Ist dieses Bette nicht wie eine Küste,	A
ein Küstenstreifen nur, darauf wir liegen?	B
Nichts ist gewiß als deine hohen Brüste,	A
die mein Gefühl in Schwindeln überstiegen.	B
Denn diese Nacht, in der so vieles schrie,	C
in der sich Tiere rufen und zerreißen,	D
ist sie uns nicht entsetzlich fremd? Und wie:	C
was draußen langsam anhebt, Tag geheißen,	D
ist das uns denn verständlicher als sie?	C
Man müßte so sich ineinanderlegen	E
wie Blütenblätter um die Staubgefäße:	F
so sehr ist überall das Ungemäße	F
und häuft sich an und stürzt sich uns entgegen.	E
Doch während wir uns aneinander drücken,	G
um nicht zu sehen, wie es ringsum naht,	H
kann es aus dir, kann es aus mir sich zücken:	G
denn unsre Seelen leben von Verrat.	H

Eastern Day Song

Is this bed not like a kind of coast,
only a strip of seacoast where we sprawl?
Nothing is certain but your high breasts
that my feelings transcend by a swindle.

For this night, within which so much screams,
in which beasts bellow and tear their prey,
is it not ghastly strange? And how looms
that thing that slowly rises there, called day,
is it any more knowable than night seems?

One would have to lie interwoven there,
tightly as the petals of budding flowers,
so much the immoderate is everywhere,
heaping itself, slumped against us and ours.

Yet only while we cling together as one
in order to ignore what encircles us two
can it draw itself out of me or you,
for our souls are living on treason.

Compare this bleak love poem with Goethe's "May Song," singing lightly as it does of bright sunbeams and bursting blooms. Rilke despaired of ever knowing the lover. As his alter ego, Malte, expresses it in *The Notebooks of Malte Laurids Brigge,* "Then for the first time did it strike me that one cannot say anything about a woman; I noticed when they spoke of her, how much they left blank, how they named and described other people, surroundings, localities."

Abisag

I

Sie lag. Und ihre Kinderarme waren	A
von Dienern um den Welkenden gebunden,	B
auf dem sie lag die süßen langen Stunden,	B
ein wenig bang vor seinen vielen Jahren.	A

Und manchmal wandte sie in seinem Barte	C
ihr Angesicht, wenn eine Eule schrie;	D
und alles, was die Nacht war, kam und scharte	C
mit Bangen und Verlangen sich um sie.	D

Die Sterne zitterten wie ihresgleichen,	E
ein Duft ging suchend durch das Schlafgemach,	F
der Vorhang rührte sich und gab ein Zeichen,	E
und leise ging ihr Blick dem Zeichen nach–.	F

Aber sie hielt sich an dem dunkeln Alten	G
und, von der Nacht der Nächte nicht erreicht,	H
lag sie auf seinem fürstlichen Erkalten	G
jungfräulich und wie eine Seele leicht.	H

II

Der König saß und sann den leeren Tag	A
getaner Taten, ungefühlter Lüste	B
und seiner Lieblingshündin, der er pflag–.	A
Aber am Abend wölbte Abisag	A
sich über ihm. Sein wirres Leben lag	A
verlassen wie verrufne Meeresküste	B
unter dem Sternbild ihrer stillen Brüste.	B

Abishag

I

She lay. And her childish arms were tied
by the servants around the wilting king,
whom she spent the long, sweet hours warming,
whose many years left her a bit afraid.

Sometimes she sought his beard with her face
when an owl had screamed from someplace near;
and all that was night came to embrace
her with a terrible longing, with fear.

The stars shivered through the night as did she
while through the room came a seeking fragrance,
the stirring curtains gave a sign, and slowly
toward the sign she turned her glance.

But to that murky old man she still clung,
that night of nights he could not consummate,
upon his princely frigidness the young
girl lay, light as a soul, inviolate.

II

The old king sat and mused the empty day
of deeds accomplished, of life without zest,
of the dear pup with whom he used to play.
But evenings Abishag would come and splay
herself above him. His tangled life lay
abandoned as an ill-starred seacoast
beneath the constellation of her nursing breast.

Und manchmal, als ein Kundiger der Frauen,   c

erkannte er durch seine Augenbrauen   c

den unbewegten, küsselosen Mund;   d

und sah: ihres Gefühles grüne Rute   e

neigte sich nicht herab zu seinem Grund.   d

Ihn fröstelte. Er horchte wie ein Hund   d

und suchte sich in seinem letzten Blute.   e

And sometimes, as a knower of women's ways,
he recognized through bushy eyebrows
that mouth of hers, never kissed, restrained,
and he saw that her passion's slim, green rod
never bent itself down toward his ground.
It chilled him. He pricked his ears like a hound,
and sought himself within his final blood.

Abishag was the young girl who was chosen to warm King David's bed when the
monarch was old and feeble (1 Kings 1:4). It is interesting to contrast the old and
decrepit David shown here with the young harpist in the very next poem of this
volume, "David Sings before Saul."

David singt vor Saul

I

König, hörst du, wie mein Saitenspiel   A
Fernen wirft, durch die wir uns bewegen: B
Sterne treiben uns verwirrt entgegen,   B
und wir fallen endlich wie ein Regen,   B
und es blüht, wo dieser Regen fiel.   A

Mädchen blühen, die du noch erkannt,   C
die jetzt Frauen sind und mich verführen;   D
den Geruch der Jungfraun kannst du spüren,   D
und die Knaben stehen, angespannt   C
schlank und atmend, an verschwiegnen Türen.   D

Daß mein Klang dir alles wiederbrächte.   E
Aber trunken taumelt mein Getön: F
Deine Nächte, König, deine Nächte–,   E
und wie waren, die dein Schaffen schwächte,   E
o wie waren alle Leiber schön.   F

Dein Erinnern glaub ich zu begleiten,   G
weil ich ahne. Doch auf welchen Saiten   G
greif ich dir ihr dunkles Lustgestöhn?–   F

II

König, der du alles dieses hattest   A
und der du mit lauter Leben mich   B
überwältigest und überschattest: A
komm aus deinem Throne und zerbrich   B
meine Harfe, die du so ermattest.   A

David Sings before Saul

I

King, do you hear the way my string-play
slings the distances through which we move;
against us the bewildered stars shove,
and we fall like a deluge from above,
and it blooms where fallen raindrops lie.

Young girls bloom, whom you've already possessed,
who are women now, to me like a snare;
you sense the fragrance of virgins in the air,
and the young boys linger, fraught and stressed,
lean and breathing at the secret door.

That my sound should bring it all back to you now.
But my drunken music may seem to stagger:
your nights, O King, your nights—and how,
those who sapped your creative spark, oh,
how beautiful all those bodies were.

I can play along to your memories,
which I can imagine. Still, on which of these
strings shall I pluck their dark groans of desire?

II

King, oh you who possessed everything,
you who with your blatant life overpower
and overshadow this underling,
come down from your high throne and shatter
my harp, which you weary till it cannot sing.

Sie ist wie ein abgenommner Baum: C
durch die Zweige, die dir Frucht getragen,   D
schaut jetzt eine Tiefe wie von Tagen   D
welche kommen –, und ich kenn sie kaum.   C

Laß mich nicht mehr bei der Harfe schlafen;   E
sieh dir diese Knabenhand da an: F
glaubst du, König, daß sie die Oktaven   E
eines Leibes noch nicht greifen kann?   F

III

König, birgst du dich in Finsternissen,   A
und ich hab dich doch in der Gewalt.   B
Sieh, mein festes Lied ist nicht gerissen,   A
und der Raum wird um uns beide kalt.   B
Mein verwaistes Herz und dein verworrnes   C
hängen in den Wolken deines Zornes,   C
wütend ineinander eingebissen   A
und zu einem einzigen verkrallt.   B

Fühlst du jetzt, wie wir uns umgestalten?   D
König, König, das Gewicht wird Geist.   E
Wenn wir uns nur aneinander halten,   D
du am Jungen, König, ich am Alten,   D
sind wir fast wie ein Gestirn das kreist.   E

It is like a tree that stands quite bare—
through the twigs that had once been fruitful
a profound wisdom peers out, as from all
those days that arise, I hardly know from where.

Let my harp no longer share my bed;
behold the hand of this young boy;
do you suppose, King, that it cannot spread
to grasp the octaves of a body?

III

King, you wall yourself within this gloom,
and I have you yet within my hold.
See, my constant song has no cunning aim,
and the space around us both grows cold.
My orphaned heart and your confounded one
hang in the clouds of your raging passion,
both furiously chewed up together whom
fate clawed and scraped into a single mold.

Do you feel how we reshape each other?
King, this heavy weight becomes spiritual
if only each to each we cling together,
you to youth, King, I to age, we are
almost like a star moving in a circle.

The young David in this poem has not yet become corrupted into the very thing he abhors in Saul. The story of David singing before Saul can be read in 1 Samuel 16:23. Viewed from another angle this poem may portray a bit of the strained relationship between Rilke and Rodin. Rilke was the Rodin's protégé just as David was Saul's, and the story of the poet and the sculptor also contains a betrayal and a break.

Josuas Landtag

So wie der Strom am Ausgang seine Dämme A
durchbricht mit seiner Mündung Übermaß, B
so brach nun durch die Ältesten der Stämme A
zum letzten Mal die Stimme Josuas. B

Wie waren die geschlagen, welche lachten, C
wie hielten alle Herz und Hände an, D
als hübe sich der Lärm von dreißig Schlachten C
in einem Mund; und dieser Mund begann. D

Und wieder waren Tausende voll Staunen E
wie an dem großen Tag vor Jericho, F
nun aber waren in ihm die Posaunen, E
und ihres Lebens Mauern schwankten so, F

daß sie sich wälzten von Entsetzen trächtig G
und wehrlos schon und überwältigt, eh H
sie's noch gedachten, wie er eigenmächtig G
zu Gibeon die Sonne anschrie: steh: H

Und Gott ging hin, erschrocken wie ein Knecht, I
und hielt die Sonne, bis ihm seine Hände J
wehtaten, ob dem schlachtenden Geschlecht, I
nur weil da einer wollte, daß sie stände. J

Und das war dieser; dieser Alte wars, K
von dem sie meinten, daß er nicht mehr gelte L
inmitten seines hundertzehnten Jahrs. K
Da stand er auf und brach in ihre Zelte. L

Joshua's Council

Just as the estuary, with the blast
of its excessive mouth, breaks the silted wall,
so through the tribe's elders, for the last
time now, broke the sound of Joshua's call.

How those laughing ones received that stroke,
as if all their hearts and hands were halted:
from one mouth the sound of thirty battles broke,
all at once on all sides they were assaulted.

And once more the thousand were astonished
as on that great day before Jericho,
but now the trumpets in the man admonished,
and the ramparts of their lives tottered so,

that they themselves trembled, pregnant with fright,
overwhelmed, defenseless, in disarray,
before they had yet recalled that self-born might
with which he ordered Gibeon's sun to stay.

And God came undone like a fearful servant;
till his hands were scorched he held back the sun
over the nation's murderous battle count
merely because it was willed by this one.

And that was this one, this old man here,
whom they counted someone who mattered no more
in the midst of his hundred and tenth year.
Then he stood up, and into their tents he tore.

Er ging wie Hagel nieder über Halmen: M
Was wollt ihr Gott versprechen? Ungezählt   N
stehn um euch Götter, wartend daß ihr wählt.   N
Doch wenn ihr wählt wird euch der Herr zermalmen.   M

Und dann, mit einem Hochmut ohnegleichen: O
Ich und mein Haus, wir bleiben ihm vermählt.   N

Da schrien sie alle: Hilf uns, gieb ein Zeichen   O
und stärke uns zu unserer schweren Wahl.   P

Aber sie sahn ihn, wie seit Jahren schweigend,   Q
zu seiner festen Stadt am Berge steigend;   Q
und dann nicht mehr. Es war das letzte Mal.   P

Like a hailstorm over the grass he rushed:
What would ye pledge to God? Numberless
gods surround you, all awaiting your choice.
Yet if ye choose, by the Lord ye shall be crushed.

And he, with unique and arrogant pride:
We are wedded to him, I and my house.

Then help us, give us a sign, they all cried,
brace us for the difficult choice to come.

But they watched him, as if for years ascending,
to the fastness of his mountain city wending
and then nevermore. It was the last time.

Joshua abandoned the Israelites after issuing a warning to the tribes at Shechem
(Joshua, chapters 23–24).

Der Auszug des verlorenen Sohnes

Nun fortzugehn von alledem Verworrnen,   A
das unser ist und uns doch nicht gehört,   B
das, wie das Wasser in den alten Bornen,   A
uns zitternd spiegelt und das Bild zerstört;   B
von allem diesen, das sich wie mit Dornen   A
noch einmal an uns anhängt–fortzugehn   C
und Das und Den,   C
die man schon nicht mehr sah   D
(so täglich waren sie und so gewöhnlich),   E
auf einmal anzuschauen: sanft, versöhnlich   E
und wie an einem Anfang und von nah;   D
und ahnend einzusehn, wie unpersönlich,   E
wie über alle hin das Leid geschah,   D
von dem die Kindheit voll war bis zum Rand–:   F
Und dann doch fortzugehen, Hand aus Hand,   F
als ob man ein Geheiltes neu zerrisse,   G
und fortzugehn: wohin? Ins Ungewisse,   G
weit in ein unverwandtes warmes Land,   F
das hinter allem Handeln wie Kulisse   G
gleichgültig sein wird: Garten oder Wand;   F
und fortzugehn: warum? Aus Drang, aus Artung,   H
aus Ungeduld, aus dunkler Erwartung,   H
aus Unverständlichkeit und Unverstand: F

The Departure of the Prodigal Son

Now to go forth from all this confusion
that is ours, yet does not belong to us,
which like a fountain's flowing reflection
shows our trembling image as dubious,
from all this—like a thorn's connection
that once again clings to us—forth to go,
and the This and the That to finally know
that one already could no longer see
(so trivial they seemed and so everyday),
at last to look in a kind, forgiving way,
from beginning and from close proximity,
and to realize with some dismay
how sorrow came to all impersonally
to fill up childhood to the brim, and
still to go forth, hand slipping from hand,
as if ripping a wound where a scab had grown,
and to go forth—where? Into the unknown,
far into an unfamiliar, balmy land
that looms like a stage set behind the action,
garden or wall, no matter in the end,
to go forth—why? Because of one's nature,
impatience, dark expectations, ardor,
or an obscure failure to understand.

Dies alles auf sich nehmen und vergebens   I
vielleicht Gehaltnes fallen lassen, um   J
allein zu sterben, wissend nicht warum –   J

Ist das der Eingang eines neuen Lebens?   I

To take this upon yourself, this vain persistence,
perhaps to lose everything you had thereby,
to die alone yet never knowing why –

is this the doorway to a new existence?

Jesus relates the Parable of the Prodigal Son in Luke 15:11–32. In the New Testa-
ment version the son is tearfully received back into the fold despite his wander-
ings from the straight and narrow. Rilke offers no such sentimentality or rec-
onciliation, only admonition. Rilke was also probably thinking of Rodin's 1884
sculpture, *L'Enfant prodigue,* in which the Prodigal Son kneels, naked on a jag-
ged rock, arms flung up to heaven in supplication.

Der Ölbaum-Garten

Er ging hinauf unter dem grauen Laub   A
ganz grau und aufgelöst im Ölgelände   B
und legte seine Stirne voller Staub   A
tief in das Staubigsein der heißen Hände.   B

Nach allem dies. Und dieses war der Schluß.   C
Jetzt soll ich gehen, während ich erblinde,   D
und warum willst Du, daß ich sagen muß   C
Du seist, wenn ich Dich selber nicht mehr finde.   D

Ich finde Dich nicht mehr. Nicht in mir, nein.   E
Nicht in den andern. Nicht in diesem Stein.   E
Ich finde Dich nicht mehr. Ich bin allein.   E

Ich bin allein mit aller Menschen Gram,   F
den ich durch Dich zu lindern unternahm,   F
der Du nicht bist. O namenlose Scham...   F

Später erzählte man: ein Engel kam–.   F

Warum ein Engel? Ach es kam die Nacht   G
und blätterte gleichgültig in den Bäumen.   H
Die Jünger rührten sich in ihren Träumen.   H
Warum ein Engel? Ach es kam die Nacht.   G

Die Nacht, die kam, war keine ungemeine;   I
so gehen hunderte vorbei.   J
Da schlafen Hunde und da liegen Steine.   I
Ach eine traurige, ach irgendeine,   I
die wartet, bis es wieder Morgen sei.   J

The Olive Orchard

He went up under gray-leaved bough,
all drained and gray in the olive lands,
and there he laid his dust-powdered brow
deep in the dustiness of burning hands.

After everything this. And this was the end.
Now must I go, although I go blind,
and why do You insist I must pretend
You exist, if You I can no longer find.

I find You no more. From me You are gone.
Not in the others. Not in this stone.
I find You no more. I am alone.

I am alone with all mankind's grief,
although through You I had sought its relief,
You who do not exist. Oh nameless shame...

Later, they recount, an angel came.

Why an angel? Ah, what came was the night.
Indifferently through the trees it browsed,
stirring the disciples' dreams as they drowsed.
Why an angel? Ah, what came was the night.

Nothing unusual was the night that came;
the dogs sleep and the stones just lie there.
So hundreds of nights pass by just the same.
Alas, a sad one, any night that might come,
waiting till morning is once again here.

Denn Engel kommen nicht zu solchen Betern,   K
und Nächte werden nicht um solche groß.   L
Die Sich-Verlierenden läßt alles los,   L
und sie sind preisgegeben von den Vätern   K
und ausgeschlossen aus der Mütter Schooß.   L

For angels do not come to such praying ones,
and great nights around such ones never loom.
Forsaking all, the self-losing are those whom
even their fathers abandon–these sons,
each shut out of his mother's very womb.

Luke 22:39–46 details Christ's agony in the Garden of Gethsemane. The name
is a Greek form of the Hebrew *gat shemanim,* meaning "oil press." It was tra-
ditionally thought to be on the western slope of the Mount of Olives, and olives
still grow there. This was also the location of Judas's betrayal.

Pietà

So seh ich, Jesus, deine Füße wieder,   A
die damals eines Jünglings Füße waren,   B
da ich sie bang entkleidete und wusch;   C
wie standen sie verwirrt in meinen Haaren   B
und wie ein weißes Wild im Dornenbusch.   C

So seh ich deine niegeliebten Glieder   A
zum erstenmal in dieser Liebesnacht.   D
Wir legten uns noch nie zusammen nieder,   A
und nun wird nur bewundert und gewacht.   D

Doch, siehe, deine Hände sind zerrissen –:   E
Geliebter, nicht von mir, von meinen Bissen.   E
Dein Herz steht offen und man kann hinein: F
das hätte dürfen nur mein Eingang sein.   F

Nun bist du müde, und dein müder Mund   G
hat keine Lust zu meinem wehen Munde –.   H
O Jesus, Jesus, wann war unsre Stunde?   H
Wie gehn wir beide wunderlich zugrund.   G

Pietà

So I see your feet again, that flesh,
dear Jesus, of you who were so young,
those feet I anxiously unclothed to wash–
entangled there where my long hair hung
they were like a white beast caught in a thornbush.

Now over your unloved limbs I stand watch,
my first sight of them in this love-night so still.
We never lay down to each other's touch,
and now there is only this adoring vigil.

But how your tender hands are torn, oh see,
but never, beloved, were they bitten by me.
Your heart stands open; one can see to its core–
that should have been for me alone, that door.

Now your spent body and mouth so weary
have no desire for these sore lips that moan:
Oh Jesus, Jesus, when was our hour alone?
How our ruin is so extraordinary.

Traditionally the Pietà was a representation of the dead Christ in the arms of his
mother, Mary, as in Michelangelo's famous example. Rilke's twist on this has
Jesus in the arms of a different Mary, the Magdalene, who laments that she and
the Savior were never lovers. Rodin had already sculpted Jesus and Mary Mag-
dalene together in a Pietà, and it is likely that his piece had inspired Rilke's. The
Magdalene washed the feet of Jesus in John 12:1–8.

Gesang der Frauen an den Dichter

Sieh, wie sich alles auftut: so sind wir; A

denn wir sind nichts als solche Seligkeit. B

Was Blut und Dunkel war in einem Tier, A

das wuchs in uns zur Seele an und schreit B

als Seele weiter. Und es schreit nach dir. A

Du freilich nimmst es nur in dein Gesicht C

als sei es Landschaft: sanft und ohne Gier. A

Und darum meinen wir, du bist es nicht, C

nach dem es schreit. Und doch, bist du nicht der, D

an den wir uns ganz ohne Rest verlören? E

Und werden wir in irgend einem *mehr?* D

Mit uns geht das Unendliche *vorbei.* F

Du aber sei, du Mund, daß wir es hören, E

du aber, du Uns-Sagender: du sei. F

Song of the Women to the Poet

See how it all looms – so are we all,
since except for such rapture we are nothing.
What were blood and darkness in the animal
in us grew into the soul, and screaming

out yet remains soul. And it screams for you.
Indeed, you bear it in your face only,
like a gentle, selfless landscape you do.
And so we assume it isn't really

you for which it screams. Yet are you not still
the one for whom we lose ourselves entire?
Do we become anything more at all?

With us the unending goes right past.
But you exist, you mouth, that we might hear;
you however, you Us-Sayer, you last.

This may be Rilke's fantasy of how the women in his life–Clara Rilke, Lou Andreas-Salomé, Ellen Key, and Paula Becker–should regard him. In Rilke's universe it is the poet who attributes value to women, for the world certainly did not. Without the poet, the "Us-Sayer," the emotional contribution of women would go largely unnoticed and unappreciated.

Der Tod des Dichters

Er lag. Sein aufgestelltes Antlitz war   A
bleich und verweigernd in den steilen Kissen,   B
seitdem die Welt und dieses von-ihr-Wissen,   B
von seinen Sinnen abgerissen,   B
zurückfiel an das teilnahmslose Jahr.   A

Die, so ihn leben sahen, wußten nicht,   C
wie sehr er Eines war mit allem diesen;   D
denn Dieses: diese Tiefen, diese Wiesen   D
und diese Wasser *waren* sein Gesicht.   C

O sein Gesicht war diese ganze Weite,   E
die jetzt noch zu ihm will und um ihn wirbt;   F
und seine Maske, die nun bang verstirbt,   F
ist zart und offen wie die Innenseite   E
von einer Frucht, die an der Luft verdirbt.   F

The Death of the Poet

His pale face lay upon the funeral bier,
propped on steep pillows in a lawless thrall,
now that the world and his sense of it all
had been torn away from him, only to fall
back upon the ever-uncaring year.

Those who had seen him alive could not trace
how fully he had become one with these,
for these: these meadows, these deep valleys,
and these flowing waters *were* his face.

Oh how his face was this entire breadth
that now seeks him out and woos him there;
and his mask, which now lies in dreadful death,
is as delicate and bare as the fair
flesh of a fruit that spoils in the open air.

This poem may have been inspired by Rodin's sculpture *La Mort du poète,* according to Theodore Ziolkowski's notes to Leishman's translation. Rilke's evocation of the death mask recalls Malte's description of the mask-maker's shop in *The Notebooks of Malte Laurids Brigge,* where a young girl's death mask hangs in the *mouleur*'s window.

Buddha

Als ob er horchte. Stille: eine Ferne...   A
Wir halten ein und hören sie nicht mehr.   B
Und er ist Stern. Und andre große Sterne,   A
die wir nicht sehen, stehen um ihn her.   B

O er ist Alles. Wirklich, warten wir,   C
daß er uns sähe? Sollte er bedürfen?   D
Und wenn wir hier uns vor ihm niederwürfen,   D
er bliebe tief und träge wie ein Tier.   C

Denn das, was uns zu seinen Füßen reißt,   E
das kreist in ihm seit Millionen Jahren.   F
Er, der vergißt was wir erfahren   F
und der erfährt was uns verweist.   E

Buddha

As if he listened. Silence, something far...
We hold ourselves back and cease to hear.
And he is star. And many a great star
that we cannot see surrounds him there.

Oh, he is all. Truly, do we wait
so that he might see us? Is that his need?
And even if we throw ourselves down to plead,
he remains like a beast, deep and sedate.

For what draws us directly to his feet
has spun within him for a million years.
He who forgets what we experience here
and experiences that which casts us out.

Rilke includes two pieces named "Buddha" in the *New Poems,* volume one, and another, "Buddha in Glory," concludes the second volume. They are at least partly inspired by the Buddha statue in Rodin's garden at Meudon-Val-Fleury, which Rilke describes in a letter to his wife, Clara, of September 1905; "*C'est le centre du monde,*" he says of it. Rilke's other model for Buddha is Rodin himself. In consecutive letters of the same month Rilke tells Clara that Rodin "moves like a star" and is "beyond all measure." Concerning the Master, as Rilke often called him, the poet writes: "He is everything, everything far and wide." Compare this to the language in the poem.

L'Ange du Méridien

Chartres

Im Sturm, der um die starke Kathedrale	A
wie ein Verneiner stürzt der denkt und denkt,	B
fühlt man sich zärtlicher mit einem Male	A
von deinem Lächeln zu dir hingelenkt:	B
lächelnder Engel, fühlende Figur,	C
mit einem Mund, gemacht aus hundert Munden:	D
gewahrst du gar nicht, wie dir unsre Stunden	D
abgleiten von der vollen Sonnenuhr,	C
auf der des Tages ganze Zahl zugleich,	E
gleich wirklich, steht in tiefem Gleichgewichte,	F
als wären alle Stunden reif und reich.	E
Was weißt du, Steinerner, von unserm Sein?	G
und hältst du mit noch seligerm Gesichte	F
vielleicht die Tafel in die Nacht hinein?	G

L'Ange du Méridien

Chartres

In the storm swelling round the stout cathedral
like a denier who sits to ponder,
one feels fondly, in just a moment's wander,
drawn to you, in thrall to your tender smile:

sensitive creature, beaming angel,
your mouth reflects a hundred such,
don't you know how our temporal
moments slip from your sundial's touch;

counting the numbers of the day, the shadow
marks them as if they stood in balance,
as if all of our hours were rich and mellow.

Thing of stone, what do you know of our plight?
And does your face show a more blessed glance
as you hold your slate far into the night?

In a letter to Clara in January 1906, Rilke mentions his visit to Chartres with the Master. He remarks on the fact that the cathedral at Chartres seems more weather-beaten than Notre Dame and mentions the angel "holding a sundial which is exposed to the day's circling of hours... infinitely beautiful." When Rilke seemed nervous about an approaching storm, Rodin noted that cathedrals are often surrounded by a downdraft—"the storm swelling round the stout cathedral"—because of the great height of their towers. Rodin's *Le Penseur,* which was first presented to the public in 1904, may be the model for the "denier who sits to ponder."

Die Kathedrale

In jenen kleinen Städten, wo herum — A
die alten Häuser wie ein Jahrmarkt hocken, — B
der *sie* bemerkt hat plötzlich und, erschrocken, — B
die Buden zumacht und, ganz zu und stumm, — A

die Schreier still, die Trommeln angehalten, — C
zu ihr hinaufhorcht aufgeregten Ohrs –: — D
dieweil sie ruhig immer in dem alten — C
Faltenmantel ihrer Contreforts — D
dasteht und von den Häusern gar nicht weiß: — E

in jenen kleinen Städten kannst du sehn, — F
wie sehr entwachsen ihrem Umgangskreis — E
die Kathedralen waren. Ihr Erstehn — F
ging über alles fort, so wie den Blick — G
des eignen Lebens viel zu große Nähe — H
fortwährend übersteigt, und als geschähe — H
nichts anderes; als wäre Das Geschick, — G
was sich in ihnen aufhäuft ohne Maßen, — I
versteinert und zum Dauernden bestimmt, — J
nicht Das, was unten in den dunkeln Straßen — I
vom Zufall irgendwelche Namen nimmt — J
und darin geht, wie Kinder Grün und Rot — K
und was der Krämer hat als Schürze tragen. — L
Da war Geburt in diesen Unterlagen, — L
und Kraft und Andrang war in diesem Ragen — L
und Liebe überall wie Wein und Brot, — K
und die Portale voller Liebesklagen. — L

The Cathedral

In those small towns in which the old houses
squat like booths around a fair, noticing *her,*
suddenly and fearfully they shutter
their shops, until only stillness browses,

the criers dumb and the drums now mute
to the upward-harking, excited ear;
in the meanwhile, calmly in the suit
of pleated stone that her buttresses wear,
she stands there, and of houses knows not:

in those small towns you can clearly see
how beyond their bounds, how overwrought
the cathedrals once grew. Rising steeply
they overtook all, looming there in space,
as our own life, when seen from too near,
exceeds our view, as if nothing else happens here;
as if fate were mounded up in some place
where without moderation it grows,
petrified and eternally decided,
not like the traffic in the dark street goes,
taking any name from chance, guided
along like the children, green and red,
or by what the shopkeeper has in stock.
Birth was in this foundation's every block,
its surging strength rose upward like smoke,
and love was everywhere, like wine and bread,
and the doors with love's lamenting spoke.

Das Leben zögerte im Stundenschlagen,
und in den Türmen, welche voll Entsagen
auf einmal nicht mehr stiegen, war der Tod.

Life hesitated on the hour's stroke,
and in the towers, when abdication broke
their sudden, swift ascent, there was death instead.

"The Cathedral" bears the unmistakable influence of Hölderlin's monumen-
tal poem "Brot und Wein," which, among other things, is a plea for the return
to the ancient Orphic religion. Particularly, the closing of the shops reflects the
first stanza of Hölderlin's long poem, and the mention of wine and bread toward
the end seems to be a homage. The idea that the Christian religion had outlived
its time is also repeated in "God in the Middle Ages," and in the poem that fol-
lows this one, "The Portal."

Das Portal

Da blieben sie, als wäre jene Flut A
zurückgetreten, deren großes Branden B
an diesen Steinen wusch, bis sie entstanden; B
sie nahm im Fallen manches Attribut A

aus ihren Händen, welche viel zu gut A
und gebend sind, um etwas festzuhalten. C
Sie blieben, von den Formen in Basalten C
durch einen Nimbus, einen Bischofshut, A

bisweilen durch ein Lächeln unterschieden, D
für das ein Antlitz seiner Stunden Frieden D
bewahrt hat als ein stilles Zifferblatt; E

jetzt fortgerückt ins Leere ihres Tores, F
waren sie einst die Muschel eines Ohres F
und fingen jedes Stöhnen dieser Stadt. E

II

Sehr viele Weite ist gemeint damit: A
so wie mit den Kulissen einer Szene B
die Welt gemeint ist; und so wie durch jene B
der Held im Mantel seiner Handlung tritt:– A

so tritt das Dunkel dieses Tores handelnd C
auf seiner Tiefe tragisches Theater, D
so grenzenlos und wallend wie Gott-Vater D
und so wie Er sich wunderlich verwandelnd C

The Portal

There they remain, as if that ocean wave
had fallen back whose massive tidal flows
overflowed these stones until they rose;
many a tidal attribute they gave

with hands too generous and excellent,
so these might stand here firm as rock.
There they remain, once basalt block,
now mitered bishop or haloed saint,

sometimes distinguished only by a smile,
for the one face their peaceful hours compile
continues like the clock's most tranquil stare;

now upon this portal they disappear
but once they framed the seashell of an ear
to hear the groaning city's every prayer.

II

Here there's a broader meaning to assume,
just as on a proscenium's painted screen
a world is supposed, and through the scene
the hero goes, dressed in action's costume:

in such action strides the darkness of this gate
down into the depths of tragic theater,
as borderless and seething as God the Father,
as if he, in a transformed and wondrous state,

in einen Sohn, der aufgeteilt ist hier E

auf viele kleine beinah stumme Rollen, F

genommen aus des Elends Zubehör. G

Denn nur noch so entsteht (das wissen wir) E

aus Blinden, Fortgeworfenen und Tollen F

der Heiland wie ein einziger Akteur. G

III

So ragen sie, die Herzen angehalten, A

(sie stehn auf Ewigkeit und gingen nie); B

nur selten tritt aus dem Gefäll der Falten A

eine Gebärde, aufrecht, steil wie sie, B

und bleibt nach einem halben Schritte stehn C

wo die Jahrhunderte sie überholen. D

Sie sind im Gleichgewicht auf den Konsolen, D

in denen eine Welt, die sie nicht sehn, C

die Welt der Wirrnis, die sie nicht zertraten, E

Figur und Tier, wie um sie zu gefährden, F

sich krümmt und schüttelt und sie dennoch hält: G

weil die Gestalten dort wie Akrobaten E

sich nur so zuckend und so wild gebärden, F

damit der Stab auf ihrer Stirn nicht fällt. G

One of Rilke's architectural poems, along with "L'Ange du Méridien," "The Cathedral," and "The Capital." The statues of bishops and saints described here line the portal of one of the great Gothic cathedrals the poet was studying under Rodin's tutelage. In the first sonnet of the triptych, Rilke compares them to the crags of rock from which they came—they are so weathered by time that they appear to be natural shapes. In the second sonnet the statues are contrasted with scenes from the life of Christ, portrayed not with freestanding statues like the

becomes the Son, divided many times here,
playing many a mute and minor role
selected from misfortune's repertoire.

For (as we know) it is only from the sphere
of the mad, the blind, and the ignoble
that the Savior might appear, a lone actor.

III

So they loom above, their hearts now still,
they stand upon the ages, going nowhere;
only seldom from their garment folds will
a gesture step, erect and steep as they are,

remaining in mid-stride, each effigy,
where the centuries overtake them all.
And each of them balances on a console
in which there is a world they never see,

that world of chaos on which they trample
consisting of beasts and human figures,
the warped and wobbling ones on which they tread:

like an acrobat is each of this ensemble,
each of them trembling with such frantic gestures,
for fear the bishop's staff might strike his head.

looming bishops but in bas-reliefs enclosed in carved consoles. The third sonnet
deals with the consoles depicting the lives of humble folk and animals. These
serve as pedestals for the bishops and saints, a juxtaposition that also indicates
the strict hierarchy of the Catholic Church. The irony is that Christ appears like
"the mad, the blind, and the ignoble," not like the bishop or the saint. And not
only must the humble folk live trembling beneath the boot of the bishop, they
must also constantly worry about his staff falling on their heads.

Die Fensterrose

Da drin: das träge Treten ihrer Tatzen A
macht eine Stille, die dich fast verwirrt; B
und wie dann plötzlich eine von den Katzen A
den Blick an ihr, der hin und wieder irrt, B

gewaltsam in ihr großes Auge nimmt, – C
den Blick, der, wie von eines Wirbels Kreis D
ergriffen, eine kleine Weile schwimmt C
und dann versinkt und nichts mehr von sich weiß, D

wenn dieses Auge, welches scheinbar ruht, E
sich auftut und zusammenschlägt mit Tosen F
und ihn hineinreißt bis ins rote Blut –: E

So griffen einstmals aus dem Dunkelsein G
der Kathedralen große Fensterrosen F
ein Herz und rissen es in Gott hinein. G

The Rose Window

There within: the languid, silent pace
of their paws lulls, almost bewilders you,
then one of the cats quickly turns its face
and captures your gaze and its straying view

violently in its magnificent eye,
and as if seized in a maelstrom's clasp,
it swims for a while, but by and by
abandons itself, slips from its own grasp,

as this eye with its apparent stillness
suddenly opens, then shuts with a roar
and snatches the gaze into its own red blood,

just so one time, out of utter darkness,
the cathedral's soaring rose window tore
a heart and plunged it deeply into God.

The vortex appears over and over in *New Poems*—it is in the panther's tightly
turning circle, in the motion of the carousel, and in the storm swelling around
the cathedral. In "The Rose Window" the vortex is at its most specific, *eines
Wirbels Kreis,* a maelstrom that can suck one's gaze and one's very existence
into the maw of oblivion. It is that to which all things return—the black hole at
the center of a galaxy, the very eye of God.

Das Kapitäl

Wie sich aus eines Traumes Ausgeburten	A
aufsteigend aus verwirrendem Gequäl	B
der nächste Tag erhebt: so gehn die Gurten	A
der Wölbung aus dem wirren Kapitäl	B
und lassen drin, gedrängt und rätselhaft	C
verschlungen, flügelschlagende Geschöpfe:	D
ihr Zögern und das Plötzliche der Köpfe	D
und jene starken Blätter, deren Saft	C
wie Jähzorn steigt, sich schließlich überschlagend	E
in einer schnellen Geste, die sich ballt	F
und sich heraushält–: alles aufwärtsjagend,	E
was immer wieder mit dem Dunkel kalt	F
herunterfällt, wie Regen Sorge tragend	E
für dieses alten Wachstums Unterhalt.	F

The Capital

Spawn of itself, as if born of a dream,
swelling from torment's bewildering squall
the next day rises; so these marble ribs seem
to raise the tangled vault of the capital

and leap from there, each cryptic, crowded shape,
like intricate, wing-beating creatures
with wavering, sudden heads, and the features
of those stout leaves, whose welling sap

springs like anger, overturning their own flow
in a swift gesture, like some combative
fist, thrusting high, driven up from below:

that which the darkness will finally give
back, falling cold, as rain begets sorrow,
in order to keep this old growth alive.

Compare this architectural poem (especially the last two stanzas) to the fol-
lowing passage in *The Notebooks of Malte Laurids Brigge:* "Consummator of
the world: as that which falls down in rain over the earth... rises again out of all
things, more visible and more joyous in its law, and ascends and floats and forms
the heavens: so the ascent of our precipitations rose out of you and domed the
world about with music."

Gott im Mittelalter

Und sie hatten Ihn in sich erspart	A
und sie wollten, daß er sei und richte,	B
und sie hängten schließlich wie Gewichte	B
(zu verhindern seine Himmelfahrt)	A
an ihn ihrer großen Kathedralen	C
Last und Masse. Und er sollte nur	D
über seine grenzenlosen Zahlen	C
zeigend kreisen und wie eine Uhr	D
Zeichen geben ihrem Tun und Tagwerk.	E
Aber plötzlich kam er ganz in Gang,	F
und die Leute der entsetzten Stadt	G
ließen ihn, vor seiner Stimme bang,	F
weitergehn mit ausgehängtem Schlagwerk	E
und entflohn vor seinem Zifferblatt.	G

God in the Middle Ages

And within themselves they locked him away,
and they wanted him just to judge and to be,
and hung weights upon him finally–
to prevent his rising on Ascension Day–

freighting him with the great cathedral's mass.
And they thought he should only be allowed
to rule the unending numbers that pass,
and run in circles as a clock would,

to be the measure of their days and labor.
But suddenly he got into full swing,
and in the town the fearful populace

let him go on with the terrible clanging
of the unhinged and hanging bell clapper;
and all of them have fled from his clockface.

The most dramatic image here is the one of the *ausgehängtem Schlagwerk,* the unhinged clapper of the clockwork-god that Rilke describes. It conveys the sense of an irrational deity and, at the same time, of something with its guts hanging out–hence the fear and flight of the townspeople. In a letter to another irrational deity, dated May 1906, Rilke discusses the recent falling out with Rodin, telling the Master, "You have... become invisible to me, as though by some ascension carried upward to skies of your own." *Himmelfahrt* is translated by others simply as ascension, but there are many other German words for the act of rising, and this is the specific term used by German-speaking Catholics for Ascension Day. Rilke labels his letter to Baroness Uexküll of May 24, 1906, *Himmelfahrt,* Ascension Day.

Morgue

Da liegen sie bereit, als ob es gälte,   A
nachträglich eine Handlung zu erfinden,   B
die mit einander und mit dieser Kälte   A
sie zu versöhnen weiß und zu verbinden;   B

denn das ist alles noch wie ohne Schluß.   C
Wasfür ein Name hätte in den Taschen   D
sich finden sollen? An dem Überdruß   C
um ihren Mund hat man herumgewaschen: D

er ging nicht ab; er wurde nur ganz rein.   E
Die Bärte stehen, noch ein wenig härter,   F
doch ordentlicher im Geschmack der Wärter,   F

nur um die Gaffenden nicht anzuwidern.   G
Die Augen haben hinter ihren Lidern   G
sich umgewandt und schauen jetzt hinein.   E

Morgue

There they lie ready, as if it might matter
to plan some endeavor this late in the game
that with this cold and with one another
would reconcile and perhaps unite them;

for it is all still without any closure.
What kind of name might someone have found
in those pockets? The tedious composure
of their mouths that someone had washed around,

it wouldn't come off; it just became clean.
The beards remain, only stiffer and darker,
but neater, at least to the taste of the warder,

if only not to sicken those who must stare.
The eyes are hiding behind eyelids where
they turn themselves round and now look within.

In *The Notebooks of Malte Laurids Brigge,* Rilke has Malte pass a mask-maker's shop every day on his rounds. In the window are two masks—one is of a young girl whose death mask was taken in the morgue, "because it was beautiful, because it smiled, smiled so deceptively, as though it knew." The other mask is of the mask-maker himself "which did know." As is clear in this poem, and in other depictions of death in *New Poems,* most particularly in the characterization of Eurydice, the dead know only about death and nothing else. Their eyes "turn themselves round and now look within."

Der Gefangene

I

Meine Hand hat nur noch eine	A
Gebärde, mit der sie verscheucht;	B
auf die alten Steine	A
fällt es aus Felsen feucht.	B
Ich höre nur dieses Klopfen	C
und mein Herz hält Schritt	D
mit dem Gehen der Tropfen	C
und vergeht damit.	D
Tropften sie doch schneller,	E
käme doch wieder ein Tier.	F
Irgendwo war es heller –.	E
Aber was wissen wir.	F

II

Denk dir, das was jetzt Himmel ist und Wind,	A
Luft deinem Mund und deinem Auge Helle,	B
das würde Stein bis um die kleine Stelle	B
an der dein Herz und deine Hände sind.	A
Und was jetzt in dir morgen heißt und: dann	C
und: späterhin und nächstes Jahr und weiter –	D
das würde wund in dir und voller Eiter	D
und schwäre nur und bräche nicht mehr an.	C
Und das was war, das wäre irre und	E
raste in dir herum, den lieben Mund	E
der niemals lachte, schäumend von Gelächter.	F

The Prisoner

I

My hand has just one gesture,
meant to warn and shoo away;
upon the ancient stone floor,
dampness falls from masonry.

I hear only this knocking,
and my heart keeps pace
with these drops, dropping,
and it dies when they cease.

If only they fell faster,
if some creature came again.
Somewhere once it was brighter,
but what do we know then.

II

Imagine that what is now wind and sky,
to your eye, brightness, to your mouth, air,
became stone right up to that small place where
your heart beats and your hands lie.

And suppose what you call *tomorrow* and *then*
and *later on* and *next year* and *furthermore*
became full of pus in you, a raw sore
that festered and would not break and drain.

And that what had once been was now quite mad,
raging in you, your tender mouth that had
never laughed now foaming with insane laughter.

Und das was Gott war, wäre nur dein Wächter   F

und stopfte boshaft in das letzte Loch   G

ein schmutziges Auge. Und du lebtest doch.   G

And what had been God was now just your jailer
and stuffed his filthy eye, vicious and furtive,
into the last hole. And still you seemed to live.

Rilke's notion of God transformed into the Cosmic Turnkey echoes the sentiments of young Malte in *The Notebooks of Malte Laurids Brigge:* "Left a good deal to myself, I passed early through a series of developments which I did not until much later, in a period of despair, connect with God; and then, indeed, with such violence that God took shape and was shattered for me almost in the same moment." In a sense the poem also reflects Rilke's disillusionment with Rodin, who once had been his god and had now seemed to turn into his jailer.

Der Panther

Im Jardin des Plantes, Paris

Sein Blick ist vom Vorübergehn der Stäbe A
so müd geworden, daß er nichts mehr hält. B
Ihm ist, als ob es tausend Stäbe gäbe A
und hinter tausend Stäben keine Welt. B

Der weiche Gang geschmeidig starker Schritte, C
der sich im allerkleinsten Kreise dreht, D
ist wie ein Tanz von Kraft um eine Mitte, C
in der betäubt ein großer Wille steht. D

Nur manchmal schiebt der Vorhang der Pupille E
sich lautlos auf–. Dann geht ein Bild hinein, F
geht durch der Glieder angespannte Stille– E
und hört im Herzen auf zu sein. F

The Panther

Jardin des Plantes, Paris

From endless passing of the bars his gaze
has wearied–there is no more it can hold.
There seem to be a thousand bars always,
and past those thousand bars there is no world.

The soft pad of his brawny, rippling pace
turns itself in a tightening circle till,
like a mighty dance around a tiny space,
it centers a numb but still enormous will.

But at times the shades of his pupils rise,
grasping an image he cannot resist;
through his tense, unmoving limbs it flies,
and within his heart it ceases to exist.

This piece was first published in the Prague periodical *Deutsche Arbeit* in September 1903. *Der Vorhang der Pupille* (in the last stanza) refers to the nictitating membrane, a transparent film that protects the eyes of certain species of animals. In cats and dogs the nictitating membrane is not usually evident, and its being visible is a sign of poor physical condition—as might be the case with this tightly caged panther. The constricted circling of the panther suggests a vortex, a recurring image in these poems.

Die Gazelle

Gazella Dorcas

Verzauberte: wie kann der Einklang zweier   A
erwählter Worte je den Reim erreichen,   B
der in dir kommt und geht, wie auf ein Zeichen.   B
Aus deiner Stirne steigen Laub und Leier,   A

und alles Deine geht schon im Vergleich   C
durch Liebeslieder, deren Worte, weich   C
wie Rosenblätter, dem, der nicht mehr liest,   D
sich auf die Augen legen, die er schließt: D

um dich zu sehen: hingetragen, als   E
wäre mit Sprüngen jeder Lauf geladen   F
und schösse nur nicht ab, solang der Hals   E

das Haupt ins Horchen hält: wie wenn beim Baden   F
im Wald die Badende sich unterbricht: G
den Waldsee im gewendeten Gesicht.   G

The Gazelle

Gazella dorcas

Enchanted one: how could two words avow,
resound together, reach the rhyming line
that moves through you as in some cryptic sign.
Leaf and lyre rise from above your brow,

and all of you already moves in accord
through songs of love whose soft-spoken word
settles on the eyes like the petals of a rose
on one no longer reading, whose eyes close

in order to observe you–taken aback,
as if those legs were a loaded gun barrel
and only kept from firing while the neck

tilts the head to hear–like a bathing girl,
interrupted in a woodland place,
the lake's reflection in her turning face.

In a letter of June 1907, Rilke writes to Clara about a morning spent in the Jardin des Plantes and his observation of the gazelles. He comments that their legs are "like guns, from which leaps are fired." The image of the rose petals fluttering down repeats one already used in "Early Apollo." Rilke also comments in one of his letters how pleasant it is to let a rose petal rest on one's eyes until it loses its coolness.

Das Einhorn

Der Heilige hob das Haupt, und das Gebet   A
fiel wie ein Helm zurück von seinem Haupte: B
denn lautlos nahte sich das niegeglaubte,   B
das weiße Tier, das wie eine geraubte   B
hülflose Hindin mit den Augen fleht.   A

Der Beine elfenbeinernes Gestell   C
bewegte sich in leichten Gleichgewichten,   D
ein weißer Glanz glitt selig durch das Fell,   C
und auf der Tierstirn, auf der stillen, lichten,   D
stand, wie ein Turm im Mond, das Horn so hell,   C
und jeder Schritt geschah, es aufzurichten.   D

Das Maul mit seinem rosagrauen Flaum   E
war leicht gerafft, so daß ein wenig Weiß   F
(weißer als alles) von den Zähnen glänzte;   G
die Nüstern nahmen auf und lechzten leis.   F
Doch seine Blicke, die kein Ding begrenzte,   G
warfen sich Bilder in den Raum   E
und schlossen einen blauen Sagenkreis.   F

The Unicorn

The saint raised his face until his prayer
fell backward like a helmet from his head,
for there the incredible silently stood
like a helpless hind with eyes that pled,
like a dispossessed white beast it stood there.

The legs resembled an ivory frame
and moved with an easy, balanced gait,
through its coat slid a white and blessed gleam,
and on the beast's brow, shining and sedate,
stood the horn, a tower lit by a moonbeam,
that every step seemed to elevate.

The creature's mouth with its rose-gray fleece,
drew back its lips till a portion of white
that was whiter than anything gleamed,
the nostrils flaring slightly, moist and bright.
Yet its glance, so unrestricted, seemed
to hurl its own image into space,
closing a blue saga-cycle with this rite.

The mythical beast referred to here was seen by Rilke in one of the unicorn tapestries in the Cluny Museum in Paris. They were commissioned (ca. 1509) by Jean de Chabannes Vandenesse in honor of his fiancée. In *The Notebooks of Malte Laurids Brigge,* Malte describes these very tapestries in great detail. The unicorn reappears in the *Sonnets to Orpheus,* 2, 4.

Sankt Sebastian

Wie ein Liegender so steht er; ganz A
hingehalten von dem großen Willen. B
Weitentrückt wie Mütter, wenn sie stillen, B
und in sich gebunden wie ein Kranz. A

Und die Pfeile kommen: jetzt und jetzt C
und als sprängen sie aus seinen Lenden, D
eisern bebend mit den freien Enden. D
Doch er lächelt dunkel, unverletzt. C

Einmal nur wird seine Trauer groß, E
und die Augen liegen schmerzlich bloß, E
bis sie etwas leugnen, wie Geringes, F
und als ließen sie verächtlich los E
die Vernichter eines schönen Dinges. F

Saint Sebastian

He stands like one reclining on the ground,
anticipating a great inner will
and absent as a nursing mother until
wrapped in himself, as a wreath is bound.

And then the arrows fly, now and now,
and as if they sprang from out of his hips
the iron bolts tremble to their feather-tips.
Yet darkly he smiles, unwounded somehow.

Only once does he nearly seem to despair,
and his eyes shine, painfully aware,
until they deny something so trifling
and scornfully let pass what they cannot bear:
these destroyers of a beautiful thing.

In *Death in Venice,* Thomas Mann names the "Sebastian Figure" as the supreme
emblem of Apollonian beauty and proportion. Many paintings on the subject,
which Rilke would have seen in his frequent visits to museums, portray the
martyr slouching in a curve against the tree or post to which he is tied—*in
sich gebunden wie ein Kranz.* Botticelli, Mantegna, Perugino, and El Greco all
painted versions of Sebastian's martyrdom.

Der Stifter

Das war der Auftrag an die Malergilde.   A
Vielleicht daß ihm der Heiland nie erschien;   B
vielleicht trat auch kein heiliger Bischof milde   A
an seine Seite wie in diesem Bilde   A
und legte leise seine Hand auf ihn.   B

Vielleicht war dieses alles: *so* zu knien   B
(so wie es alles ist was wir erfuhren):   C
zu knien: daß man die eigenen Konturen,   C
die auswärtswollenden, ganz angespannt   D
im Herzen hält, wie Pferde in der Hand.   D

Daß wenn ein Ungeheueres geschähe,   E
das nicht versprochen ist und nieverbrieft,   F
wir hoffen könnten, daß es uns nicht sähe   E
und näher käme, ganz in unsre Nähe,   E
mit sich beschäftigt und in sich vertieft.   F

The Donor

That was the commission to the painters' guild.
Perhaps there was no Savior's advent;
perhaps no holy bishop ever called,
as in this painting, and softly held
a hand upon that head so piously bent.

To kneel like *that,* perhaps his only intent,
as if that is all we experience—
to kneel, that one might check the expanse
of one's own contours, tightly reined,
held back by the heart like horses by the hand.

So if there should come some monstrosity,
something unpromised and never specified,
we could at least hope that it would not see
us, and thus would approach our vicinity
consumed with itself and preoccupied.

Anyone familiar with European painting has seen a work similar to the one
described here. The donor, who has paid for the painting, is portrayed kneeling
in prayer while the local bishop rests a hand upon him, signifying the donor's
hope for salvation. In Rilke's version it is *ein Ungeheueres* that may come
instead, something monstrous that the donor hopes will not notice him—per-
haps sickness or financial ruin. And in kneeling the donor seeks to make him-
self smaller, hoping that misfortune will simply pass by.

Der Engel

Mit einem Neigen seiner Stirne weist A

er weit von sich was einschränkt und verpflichtet; B

denn durch sein Herz geht riesig aufgerichtet B

das ewig Kommende das kreist. A

Die tiefen Himmel stehn ihm voll Gestalten, C

und jede kann ihm rufen: komm, erkenn–. D

Gieb seinen leichten Händen nichts zu halten C

aus deinem Lastenden. Sie kämen denn D

bei Nacht zu dir, dich ringender zu prüfen, E

und gingen wie Erzürnte durch das Haus F

und griffen dich als ob sie dich erschüfen E

und brächen dich aus deiner Form heraus. F

The Angel

With a quick nod of his brow he expels
anything likely to oblige or constrict,
for through his heart, which is hugely erect,
the eternal Coming One circles.

To him the deep heavens are full of shapes,
and each may summon him: come, realize.
Do not burden his buoyant hands, for perhaps
those very hands might materialize

to painfully examine you by night,
to go raging through the household,
clutching as if they created you, and might
in this manner break you out of your mold.

Rilke's angels appear often, and often appear to have little to do with Christian angels. They are the angels who forsake Christ in his hour of desperation, as in "The Olive Orchard." The "sensitive creature" of "L'Ange du Méridien," that stone figure who misapprehends us, is bookended here with this more threatening seraph, who might break us out of our molds. Rilke's *Duino Elegies* begins with the famous invocation "Who, if I cried out, would hear me among the ranks of the angels? and even if one pressed me suddenly to his heart, I would perish before that mighty presence." *Jeder Engel ist schrecklich,* Rilke tells us in the second of these elegies—every angel is terrible.

Römische Sarkophage

Was aber hindert uns zu glauben, daß	A
(so wie wir hingestellt sind und verteilt)	B
nicht eine kleine Zeit nur Drang und Haß	A
und dies Verwirrende in uns verweilt,	B
wie einst in dem verzierten Sarkophag	C
bei Ringen, Götterbildern, Gläsern, Bändern,	D
in langsam sich verzehrenden Gewändern	D
ein langsam Aufgelöstes lag–	C
bis es die unbekannten Munde schluckten,	E
die niemals reden. (Wo besteht und denkt	F
ein Hirn, um ihrer einst sich zu bedienen?)	G
Da wurde von den alten Aquädukten	E
ewiges Wasser in sie eingelenkt–:	F
das spiegelt jetzt und geht und glänzt in ihnen.	G

Roman Sarcophagi

But what keeps us from reckoning our fate
(as we are placed here and divided)
that for a long time only hunger and hate
and this confusion in us have abided,

as once in these sarcophagi, ornate
with icons, glasswork, ribbons and rings,
something in slowly self-consuming wrappings
lay in a languidly dissolving state –

until swallowed by silent jaws undreamed.
(Where does there exist a mind that knows
or even once makes use of this knowing?)

Then from the old aqueducts there streamed
eternal water into them, which flows
through them now, sparkling and reflecting.

Rilke may have encountered these sarcophagi at Aliscamps, the ancient ceme-
tery near Arles, where Roman sarcophagi stand empty and uncovered around
the grounds. There is a painting by Van Gogh that shows tourists strolling an
avenue in Aliscamps lined with these stone coffins. The elements of this poem
are reprised in the *Sonnets to Orpheus* (1, 10). Roman sarcophagi with eternal
waters running through them are there, but the later poem strikes a more hope-
ful note, regarding the dead as those who have been "released from doubt." The
silent jaws of the poem refer to the sarcophagus itself, since the word, in Greek,
means "flesh eater." During the Renaissance, Popes Sixtus v and Paulus v reno-
vated some of the old Roman aqueducts, and many Roman citizens used old sar-
cophagi as stone tanks to hold the newly running waters—thus the ending image
of the poem. The Palazzo Patrizi, the Palazzo Mattei di Giove, and many other
elegant buildings incorporated ancient sarcophagi into their elaborate water
fountains, and these can be seen to this day.

Der Schwan

Diese Mühsal, durch noch Ungetanes   A
schwer und wie gebunden hinzugehn,   B
gleicht dem ungeschaffnen Gang des Schwanes.   A

Und das Sterben, dieses Nichtmehrfassen   C
jenes Grunds, auf dem wir täglich stehn,   B
seinem ängstlichen Sich-Niederlassen –:   C

in die Wasser, die ihn sanft empfangen   D
und die sich, wie glücklich und vergangen,   D
unter ihm zurückziehn, Flut um Flut;   E
während er unendlich still und sicher   F
immer mündiger und königlicher   F
und gelassener zu ziehn geruht.   E

The Swan

This struggling through what is still undone,
awkward as trying to walk while bound,
recalls the ungainly gait of the swan.

And the dying, this abandonment
of the ground on which we daily stand,
is like his apprehensive descent

into waters gently greeting him,
glad and already past him, that seem,
wave upon wave, to go flowing on;
while ceaselessly quiet and secure,
ever more royal and mature,
he calmly lets himself be drawn.

In a letter to Clara dated September 1905, Rilke mentions the three pet swans that have the run of Rodin's garden at Meudon-Val-Fleury. He must have seen their awkward waddling through the grass and also the way they are instantly transformed into gracefully gliding creatures once in the water. The swan portrayed here is both life and death. On land, out of its element, it is the struggle of life bound in the ropes of mortality. Once it enters the water it has been freed, launched into eternity.

Kindheit

Es wäre gut viel nachzudenken, um A
von so Verlornem etwas auszusagen, B
von jenen langen Kindheit-Nachmittagen, B
die so nie wiederkamen – und warum? A

Noch mahnt es uns – : vielleicht in einem Regnen, C
aber wir wissen nicht mehr was das soll; D
nie wieder war das Leben von Begegnen, C
von Wiedersehn und Weitergehn so voll D

wie damals, da uns nichts geschah als nur E
was einem Ding geschieht und einem Tiere: F
da lebten wir, wie Menschliches, das Ihre F
und wurden bis zum Rande voll Figur. E

Und wurden so vereinsamt wie ein Hirt G
und so mit großen Fernen überladen H
und wie von weit berufen und berührt G
und langsam wie ein langer neuer Faden H
in jene Bilder-Folgen eingeführt, G
in welchen nun zu dauern uns verwirrt. G

Childhood

Best to often recall–before we try
to search among such abandoned ruins–
those lingering childhood afternoons
that will never return, and then to ask why.

Still they call out to us, perhaps in the rain,
but what this might mean we no longer know;
meetings, comings and goings–never again
with these things did life seem to overflow,

since nothing ever happened to us then
except what happens to animals or things,
and we felt then, as something quite human,
what was theirs–filled to the brim with imaginings.

And we were prone to a shepherd's loneliness,
and so filled with great distances then,
summoned from afar and rapturous
while, slowly as a growing thread of yarn,
into that picture sequence we were drawn–
which, when we dwell on it now, baffles us.

Another of Rilke's visits to "that land / that dallies here then ceases to be," as it
is described in "The Carousel." The child dwells in a country of long afternoons
that will never come again. In the Rilkean cult of childhood, a child's experience
is identical to "what happens to animals or things," and this echoes the line "a
picture, a path, an animal" from "A Girl's Lament."

Der Dichter

Du entfernst dich von mir, du Stunde.   A
Wunden schlägt mir dein Flügelschlag.   B
Allein: was soll ich mit meinem Munde?   A
mit meiner Nacht? mit meinem Tag?   B

Ich habe keine Geliebte, kein Haus,   C
keine Stelle auf der ich lebe.   D
Alle Dinge, an die ich mich gebe,   D
werden reich und geben mich aus.   C

The Poet

Your beating wings have wounded me,
you hour–you have flown away.
What use is my mouth when I'm lonely?
What for my night? What for my day?

No lover or home–my predicament,
not a place in which I may live.
And all those things to which I give
myself grow rich while I am spent.

This short poem of Rilke's bears the unmistakable stamp of Schiller's "Die Teilung der Erde," a canonical German lyric in which the poet, of all human-kind, is disinherited of the gifts of the earth but promised a divine reward. In Schiller's poem God asks the impoverished poet, "Where were you when I met mankind's demand?" The poet answers, "With Thee." Whereupon God assures him that he will always have a place in heaven. Rilke emphasizes the disinheri-tance and solitude of the poet, not the promise.

Die Spitze

I

Menschlichkeit: Namen schwankender Besitze,	A
noch unbestätigter Bestand von Glück:	B
ist das unmenschlich, daß zu dieser Spitze,	A
zu diesem kleinen dichten Spitzenstück	B
zwei Augen wurden? – Willst du sie zurück?	B

Du Langvergangene und schließlich Blinde,	C
ist deine Seligkeit in diesem Ding,	D
zu welcher hin, wie zwischen Stamm und Rinde,	C
dein großes Fühlen, kleinverwandelt, ging?	D

Durch einen Riß im Schicksal, eine Lücke	E
entzogst du deine Seele deiner Zeit;	F
und sie ist so in diesem lichten Stücke,	E
daß es mich lächeln macht vor Nützlichkeit.	F

II

Und wenn uns eines Tages dieses Tun	A
und was an uns geschieht gering erschiene	B
und uns so fremd, als ob es nicht verdiene,	B
daß wir so mühsam aus den Kinderschuhn	A
um seinetwillen wachsen –: Ob die Bahn	C
vergilbter Spitze, diese dichtgefügte	D
blumige Spitzenbahn, dann nicht genügte,	D
uns hier zu halten? Sieh: sie ward *getan*.	C

Ein Leben ward vielleicht verschmäht, wer weiß?	E
Ein Glück war da und wurde hingegeben,	F
und endlich wurde doch, um jeden Preis,	E

The Lace

Humanity, an unsteady possession,
if anything just an unverified luck—
is it inhuman that this lace, this one
small, intricate piece of lacework, took
two eyes as its price? Do you want them back?

You long-deceased one, you at long last blind,
is your bliss still in this thing you produced,
in which, as between the fruit's root and its rind,
your great passion, wrought so small, was lost?

Through the fabric of Fate you made a hole—
so it seems in this shimmering piece—
and out of the thread of time you drew your soul,
so that I smile at the word *usefulness.*

II

And if to us one day our efforts should
seem slight, moving us less than they ought,
or estranged from us, as if they matter not,
so that we, weary in the shoes of childhood,
mature because of it, could the course begun
in this yellowed lace, this elaborate, precise,
blooming length of lacework, not then suffice
to hold us here? Look at what once was *done.*

Perhaps it meant a life afflicted, who knows?
A happiness was there, surrendered for a while,
and finally, at any price one might impose,

dies Ding daraus, nicht leichter als das Leben F
und doch vollendet und so schön als sei's E
nicht mehr zu früh, zu lächeln und zu schweben. F

no easier than life, this thing emerged from toil,
and yet consummate and perfect it arose,
in time for us to hover and to smile.

Rilke had a great interest in and understanding of different lace patterns, as he
demonstrates in his precise descriptions of Venetian needlepoint, point d'Alençon,
and Binche in *The Notebooks of Malte Laurids Brigge.* The Rilkean "smile" that
concludes this poem is not the ordinary expression of pleasure that appears on the
human face, but a deep understanding, a grasp of the underlying artistic truth.
This smile appears in volume two of the *New Poems,* in "Archaic Torso of Apollo,"
where it runs through the turning loins of the headless statue, and it is also evi-
dent in "Tanagra" and "The Flag Bearer" where it is clearly linked to revelation.

Ein Frauen-Schicksal

So wie der König auf der Jagd ein Glas A
ergreift, daraus zu trinken, irgendeines, – B
und wie hernach der welcher es besaß A
es fortstellt und verwahrt als wär es keines: B

so hob vielleicht das Schicksal, durstig auch, C
bisweilen Eine an den Mund und trank, D
die dann ein kleines Leben, viel zu bang D
sie zu zerbrechen, abseits vom Gebrauch C

hinstellte in die ängstliche Vitrine, E
in welcher seine Kostbarkeiten sind F
(oder die Dinge, die für kostbar gelten). G

Da stand sie fremd wie eine Fortgeliehne E
und wurde einfach alt und wurde blind F
und war nicht kostbar und war niemals selten. G

A Woman's Fate

Just as the king on a hunt picks up
a drinking cup, any whatsoever,
and afterward the owner of the cup
puts it away, values it like no other:

so Fate perhaps, thirsty as well, once raised
a woman up like a cup of water,
then fearful that so small a thing might shatter,
it set aside the life it so appraised,

locked it away in the anxious showcase,
which often shelters treasures of that kind
(at least those things that pass as precious there).

As if on loan she remained strange in that place
and simply grew old and became blind
and was not precious and was never rare.

Rilke's grasp of the world that women were forced to inhabit by his society is understandable, given that little René Maria (it was Lou Andreas-Salomé who suggested he change his name to the more masculine Rainer) was dressed as a girl by his mother during his earliest years. His alter ego, Malte, was also dressed as a girl by his mother, and was called Sophie. In his "Self-Portrait from the Year 1906" Rilke describes himself as somewhat feminine, further identifying himself with the feminine gender. Compare this poem to the following passage in *The Notebooks of Malte Laurids Brigge:* "Sometimes a piece of real lace will fall into a child's drawer and please and no longer please and finally lie there among torn and dismembered things."

Die Genesende

Wie ein Singen kommt und geht in Gassen   A
und sich nähert und sich wieder scheut,   B
flügelschlagend, manchmal fast zu fassen   A
und dann wieder weit hinausgestreut: B

spielt mit der Genesenden das Leben;   C
während sie, geschwächt und ausgeruht,   D
unbeholfen, um sich hinzugeben,   C
eine ungewohnte Geste tut.   D

Und sie fühlt es beinah wie Verführung,   E
wenn die hartgewordne Hand, darin   F
Fieber waren voller Widersinn,   F
fernher, wie mit blühender Berührung,   E
zu liebkosen kommt ihr hartes Kinn.   F

The Convalescent

As a song might come and go through the streets,
approaching, shying away to hide,
wavering, at times it almost penetrates,
then once again the sound seems scattered wide:

so life plays with the convalescent
while she lies there, frail in her repose;
awkwardly she makes herself complaisant
as she assumes an unaccustomed pose.

And she feels it an almost seductive thing
when her stiffened hand, whose skin
recently held fever's nonsense within,
from some great distance, as if flowering,
plants a caress upon her steady chin.

Rilke's childhood was marked by a series of illnesses, and he occasionally speaks, in his own voice and in that of Malte Laurids Brigge, of how illness distorts our view of reality. Two adjectives in the poem, *hartgewordne* and *hartes,* are difficult to translate. The root adjective, *hart,* can mean callous, grim, severe, stiff, firm, or steady, as well as its cognate, hard. I have given the convalescent a "stiffened hand" and "steady chin," but other translations run the gamut of meanings, although it is unlikely that Rilke meant "hardened hand" or "hard chin."

Die Erwachsene

Das alles stand auf ihr und war die Welt	A
und stand auf ihr mit allem, Angst und Gnade,	B
wie Bäume stehen, wachsend und gerade,	B
ganz Bild und bildlos wie die Bundeslade	B
und feierlich, wie auf ein Volk gestellt.	A
Und sie ertrug es; trug bis obenhin	C
das Fliegende, Entfliehende, Entfernte,	D
das Ungeheuere, noch Unerlernte	D
gelassen wie die Wasserträgerin	C
den vollen Krug. Bis mitten unterm Spiel,	E
verwandelnd und auf andres vorbereitend,	F
der erste weiße Schleier, leise gleitend,	F
über das aufgetane Antlitz fiel	E
fast undurchsichtig und sich nie mehr hebend	G
und irgendwie auf alle Fragen ihr	H
nur eine Antwort vage wiedergebend:	G
In dir, du Kindgewesene, in dir.	H

The Grown-up

That it all stood upon her, all of creation,
and stood upon her with yearning and grace,
as trees stand erect and growing in place,
like the Ark of God, all image and imageless,
as if solemnly bestowed upon a nation.

And she bore this, quite casually she bore
the flying, the fleeing, the great propensity
to distance, the yet-unlearned, the immensity—
calmly on her head as the water bearer
her brimming jug. Until in the midst of play,
remade, preparing for some other thing,
the first white veil came gently gliding,
fell upon her, and over her open face lay,

nevermore lifting, almost opaque,
and for every question thereunto
leaving one vague answer in its wake:
in you, you child-that-has-been, in you.

In Rilke's land of childhood the veil that is "almost opaque" falls upon us all as
we mature, and afterward we are no longer able to experience things as an ani-
mal or a thing experiences them. Hölderlin, portraying a child's view of Nature
in "Da ich ein Knabe war," writes: "Yet I knew you better / Than ever I knew
mankind. / I understood your weather's whisper / As never I have the words of
men." Another aspect of childhood is evident in Maman's words to young Malte
in *The Notebooks of Malte Laurids Brigge:* "There are no classes in life for begin-
ners; it is always the most difficult thing that is asked of one right away."

Tanagra

Ein wenig gebrannter Erde,   A
wie von großer Sonne gebrannt.   B
Als wäre die Gebärde   A
einer Mädchenhand   B
auf einmal nicht mehr vergangen;   C
ohne nach etwas zu langen,   C
zu keinem Dinge hin   D
aus ihrem Gefühle führend,   E
nur an sich selber rührend   E
wie eine Hand ans Kinn.   D

Wir heben und wir drehen   F
eine und eine Figur;   G
wir können fast verstehen   F
weshalb sie nicht vergehen, –   F
aber wir sollen nur   G
tiefer und wunderbarer   H
hängen an dem was war   I
und lächeln: ein wenig klarer   H
vielleicht als vor einem Jahr.   I

Tanagra

A small bit of baked clay,
perhaps fired by a great sun.
As if the gesture seen today
in the hand of this maiden
were suddenly ancient no more,
without a thing to reach for,
lost to nothing, driven
only by its emotion,
touching itself alone,
like a hand upon the chin.

We lift and turn them on end,
each and every figure,
yet we barely comprehend
why these things still endure,
but we should only adhere,
more deeply and more in wonder,
to all these things that were,
and smile, perhaps a bit more clear
than we were a year before.

The title refers to a Greek town near Thebes, which is of archaeological significance. Tanagra is known for its terra-cotta figurines from the fourth century B.C.E. onward, which were mold-cast, mass-produced, and often polychromed. Again, the Rilkean "smile" in the last stanza is a gesture of understanding, not of simple pleasure. It is the Aha! moment.

Die Erblindende

Sie saß so wie die anderen beim Tee.   A
Mir war zuerst, als ob sie ihre Tasse   B
ein wenig anders als die andern fasse.   B
Sie lächelte einmal. Es tat fast weh.   A

Und als man schließlich sich erhob und sprach   C
und langsam und wie es der Zufall brachte   D
durch viele Zimmer ging (man sprach und lachte),   D
da sah ich sie. Sie ging den andern nach,   C

verhalten, so wie eine, welche gleich   E
wird singen müssen und vor vielen Leuten;   F
auf ihren hellen Augen die sich freuten   F
war Licht von außen wie auf einem Teich.   E

Sie folgte langsam und sie brauchte lang   G
als wäre etwas noch nicht überstiegen;   H
und doch: als ob, nach einem Übergang,   G
sie nicht mehr gehen würde, sondern fliegen.   H

One Going Blind

She sat as the others did, at tea.
The first thing I noticed, her teacup,
how peculiarly she held it up.
She smiled, and it almost hurt to see.

And as they all got up and talked,
and slowly then, as chance might loom,
chatted and laughed through many a room;
I saw her. At the rear she walked,

restrained as one who must this night
sing before some great audience,
her glad eyes full of radiance,
like a pond reflecting an outer light.

She followed slowly, with hesitation,
as if to surmount some one last thing,
and yet, as if after transformation,
instead of walking she would soon take wing.

The surmounting of "one last thing" seems to suggest that the woman in the poem, who is going blind, is also near death. Alternatively, it may indicate the enhancement of the power of the singer who, once completely blind, may be able to concentrate her entire soul in her voice. Or it may simply refer to the impending performance. But since this poem begins what seems to be a cycle of five pieces that dwell on death in one form or another, which ends with "Blue Hydrangea," it is more likely that the blind woman has not long to live.

In einem fremden Park

Borgeby-Gård

Zwei Wege sinds. Sie führen keinen hin. A
Doch manchmal, in Gedanken, läßt der eine B
dich weitergehn. Es ist, als gingst du fehl; C
aber auf einmal bist du im Rondel C
alleingelassen wieder mit dem Steine B
und wieder auf ihm lesend: Freiherrin A
Brite Sophie – und wieder mit dem Finger D
abfühlend die zerfallne Jahreszahl –. E
Warum wird dieses Finden nicht geringer? D

Was zögerst du ganz wie zum ersten Mal E
erwartungsvoll auf diesem Ulmenplatz, F
der feucht und dunkel ist und niebetreten? G

Und was verlockt dich für ein Gegensatz, F
etwas zu suchen in den sonnigen Beeten, G
als wärs der Name eines Rosenstocks? H

Was stehst du oft? Was hören deine Ohren? I
Und warum siehst du schließlich, wie verloren, I
die Falter flimmern um den hohen Phlox. H

In a Strange Park

Borgeby-gård

There are two paths. They lead you no place.
Yet as you ponder, one of them guides you on.
It's as if somehow you've missed your mark,
but suddenly you're in that roundel of the park,
once again left alone with nothing but this stone,
once more reading the words there—Baroness
Britt-Sophia—and your fingers skim again,
feeling for the moldering year and day.
Why does this obsession still remain?

Just as the first time, what makes you delay,
rapt in expectation, standing in this elm wood
that drips dampness and is dark and unvisited?

And what kind of seductive contradiction could
send you after something in that sun-drenched bed,
as if to seek the rose's botanical name?

Why do you stop so often? What do you hear?
And why do you finally see, as if lost there,
the moths flittering around the phlox's tall flame?

The park is in Flädie, Sweden. Rilke was there, as we know from the eighth of his
Letters to a Young Poet, on August 12, 1904. The poet writes his correspondent,
the young Mr. Kappus, "That which we name destiny comes from within peo-
ple, not from without. Only because so many of them have not absorbed their
destinies and transformed them within themselves… have they not recognized
what they have lost." This obsession with destiny is reflected in the compulsions
of the visitor to the park above—returning repeatedly to the same gravestone as
the moths return repeatedly to the phlox flowers. Rilke was translating Kierke-
gaard's letters to his fiancée around the time this was written, and some of that
Dane's melancholy is evident in this piece.

Abschied

Wie hab ich das gefühlt was Abschied heißt.   A
Wie weiß ichs noch: ein dunkles unverwundnes   B
grausames Etwas, das ein Schönverbundnes   B
noch einmal zeigt und hinhält und zerreißt.   A

Wie war ich ohne Wehr, dem zuzuschauen,   C
das, da es mich, mich rufend, gehen ließ,   D
zurückblieb, so als wärens alle Frauen   C
und dennoch klein und weiß und nichts als dies: D

Ein Winken, schon nicht mehr auf mich bezogen,   E
ein leise Weiterwinkendes –, schon kaum   F
erklärbar mehr: vielleicht ein Pflaumenbaum,   F
von dem ein Kuckuck hastig abgeflogen.   E

Farewell

How I have felt what *farewell* expresses.
How I still know—a dark, unwounded thing,
a cruelty where a beautiful coupling
is once more shown, held back, torn to pieces.

How I was defenseless watching that process,
because it beckoned me, and then let go again,
and stayed behind, as if it were all women,
though it was small and white and nothing but this:

a wave, no longer for me alone,
a gentle waving on, no more to be
explained: perhaps it is a plum tree
from which a cuckoo has now quickly flown.

Although Rilke was notorious for leaving others, it was only Lou Andreas-Salomé who left *him,* and she did it while he was still in her thrall. Perhaps this poem evokes her memory and Rilke's sorrow at the loss. One of her poems, "Du heller Himmel über mir," contains a line that is key to understanding her abandonment of Rilke, to whom she was not only a lover but a surrogate mother: "I need only one thing, room, just room." There is a famous photograph of Lou, sitting in a donkey-cart and wielding a little whip while the writer Paul Rée and the philosopher Friedrich Nietzsche pose as if they are harnessed to the cart's single-tree. Lou Andreas-Salomé was the kind of woman who could get even Nietzsche to act the ass.

Todes-Erfahrung

Wir wissen nichts von diesem Hingehn, das	A
nicht mit uns teilt. Wir haben keinen Grund,	B
Bewunderung und Liebe oder Haß	A
dem Tod zu zeigen, den ein Maskenmund	B

tragischer Klage wunderlich entstellt.	C
Noch ist die Welt voll Rollen, die wir spielen.	D
Solang wir sorgen, ob wir auch gefielen,	D
spielt auch der Tod, obwohl er nicht gefällt.	C

Doch als du gingst, da brach in diese Bühne	E
ein Streifen Wirklichkeit durch jenen Spalt	F
durch den du hingingst: Grün wirklicher Grüne,	E
wirklicher Sonnenschein, wirklicher Wald.	F

Wir spielen weiter. Bang und schwer Erlerntes	G
hersagend und Gebärden dann und wann	H
aufhebend; aber dein von uns entferntes,	G
aus unserm Stück entrücktes Dasein kann	H

uns manchmal überkommen, wie ein Wissen	I
von jener Wirklichkeit sich niedersenkend,	J
so daß wir eine Weile hingerissen	I
das Leben spielen, nicht an Beifall denkend.	J

This piece was written at Capri in memory of Louise Countess Schwerin on the first anniversary of her death. It was Countess Schwerin's sister, Alice Faehndrich, Baroness von Nordeck zur Rabenau, who invited Rilke to stay at their villa on Capri in the winter of 1906–07. The first six lines of the poem are carved into the memorial stone for the countess's daughter, who died some sixty

Death Experience

We have no knowledge of this departure
so strange to us, no grounds for regard,
nor to show either love or hate toward
Death, whom a mask's mouthing gesture

of tragic grief so queerly creases.
Still the world is full of roles we must take on.
So long as we fret and try to please everyone,
Death also acts, though he never pleases.

Still a ray of reality lit the scene
upon your leaving this stage; from the crack
through which you left, a green of true green,
real sunshine, and real forest have come back.

We play on. Anxious over hard-learned lines,
declaiming and posturing now and then,
but your exit from existence resigns
those remaining to the distance; and when

sometimes overcome, our thoughts are captured
by a reality that sinks in and gives us pause,
so that for a little while at least, enraptured,
we play at life, yet never thinking of applause.

years later. At the Villa Discopoli, which looked out onto the sea, Rilke shared
his evenings with Alice, her stepmother, Frau Nonna (who figures in the dedi-
cation of another poem in this volume), and with the young countess Manon zu
Solms-Laubach.

Blaue Hortensie

So wie das letzte Grün in Farbentiegeln   A
sind diese Blätter, trocken, stumpf und rauh,   B
hinter den Blütendolden, die ein Blau   B
nicht auf sich tragen, nur von ferne spiegeln.   A

Sie spiegeln es verweint und ungenau,   B
als wollten sie es wiederum verlieren,   C
und wie in alten blauen Briefpapieren   C
ist Gelb in ihnen, Violett und Grau;   B

Verwaschnes wie an einer Kinderschürze,   D
Nichtmehrgetragnes, dem nichts mehr geschieht: E
wie fühlt man eines kleinen Lebens Kürze.   D

Doch plötzlich scheint das Blau sich zu verneuen   F
in einer von den Dolden, und man sieht   E
ein rührend Blaues sich vor Grünem freuen.   F

Blue Hydrangea

Like the last bit of green in a pan of paint,
dull, dry and coarse, these leaves peep through
the blossoms that seem a shade of blue
they do not carry, its reflection faint.

They mirror in a vague and tear-stained way,
as if they would fade repeatedly,
and like a sheet of old, blue stationery,
there is yellow in them, violet and gray;

the pallid colors of a child's apron
that is no longer worn, a thing outgrown—
how short, one feels, a small life's span.

Yet suddenly the blue takes on a freshness
in a single blossom, and one is shown
a poignant blue rejoicing in greenness.

Anyone who knows the hydrangea knows that its blossoms start out green and
slowly take on color according to the pH of the soil. Acid soil produces a blue
flower, more alkaline soil produces the pink to red hues. The flowers reflect the
faded colors of a child's apron—perhaps one belonging to Rilke's daughter, Ruth,
who would have been about six at the time of this poem's composition. This jux-
taposition of childhood and the fading colors of death produces a jarring effect.
Yet in the last stanza there is a resurrection, "a poignant blue rejoicing in green-
ness." A companion piece, "Pink Hydrangea," appears in the second volume
of *New Poems*.

Vor dem Sommerregen

Auf einmal ist aus allem Grün im Park   A
man weiß nicht was, ein Etwas, fortgenommen;   B
man fühlt ihn näher an die Fenster kommen   B
und schweigsam sein. Inständig nur und stark   A

ertönt aus dem Gehölz der Regenpfeifer,   C
man denkt an einen Hieronymus: D
so sehr steigt irgend Einsamkeit und Eifer   C
aus dieser einen Stimme, die der Guß   D

erhören wird. Des Saales Wände sind   E
mit ihren Bildern von uns fortgetreten,   F
als dürften sie nicht hören was wir sagen.   G

Es spiegeln die verblichenen Tapeten   F
das ungewisse Licht von Nachmittagen,   G
in denen man sich fürchtete als Kind.   E

Before the Summer Rain

Suddenly, out of all the green in the park,
something, one knows not what, has gone;
one feels it approaching the window then
and notes its silence. Imploring and stark,

out of the grove stirs the song of the plover,
and one thinks of Saint Jerome in his cell,
so much does loneliness seem to wash over
this voice of fervor, which the sudden spell

of rain will answer. Salon walls that beguiled
us with pictures have now withdrawn from us,
as if they were not to hear what we say.

The sun-faded tapestries mirror the dubious
light of afternoons, that same light today
in which one grew so frightened as a child.

This poem, the result of a visit to Chantilly in June 1906, evokes the changing light and atmosphere of an approaching summer rainstorm—something everyone has experienced. Rilke wrote to his wife, Clara: "Yesterday we saw the approach of this rain from out in the country… through the windows of an old château." The identification of the plover with the hermit and the way the walls of the salon seem to recede with the impending weather are masterful. And in the last stanza Rilke returns to the world of the child that he so often visits.

Im Saal

Wie sind sie alle um uns, diese Herrn	A
in Kammerherrentrachten und Jabots,	B
wie eine Nacht um ihren Ordensstern	A
sich immer mehr verdunkelnd, rücksichtslos,	B
und diese Damen, zart, fragile, doch groß	B
von ihren Kleidern, eine Hand im Schooß,	B
klein wie ein Halsband für den Bologneser:	C
wie sind sie da um jeden: um den Leser,	C
um den Betrachter dieser Bibelots,	B
darunter manches ihnen noch gehört.	D
Sie lassen, voller Takt, uns ungestört	D
das Leben leben wie wir es begreifen	E
und wie sie's nicht verstehn. Sie wollten blühn,	F
und blühn ist schön sein; doch wir wollen reifen,	E
und das heißt dunkel sein und sich bemühn.	F

In the Salon

How all encompassing these painted lords are
in their chamberlain's liveries, their jabots,
like night surrounding their order's star,
growing darker here in a cavalier pose,
and these fragile ladies, who in their clothes
seem large, one hand in the lap, in repose,
small as the collar of a tiny Bolognese—
how they now enfold the reader like a haze,
and surround the beholder of these bibelots,
many of which their families still possess.

Full of tact, they allow us to address
life and firmly live it as we grasp its plan,
as *they* never did. They wanted to bloom,
and to bloom is fine, but we want to ripen,
and that requires effort, and sometimes gloom.

In Rilke's frequent visits to museums he encountered the great art of Europe, which must have stood in stark contrast to some of the private collections he saw in salons such as this one. The paintings in these great halls are often commissioned portraits of the Baroque period, and probably seemed either banal or overwrought compared to what the poet was able to examine at the Cluny or the Louvre. "They wanted to bloom," he says—meaning the now-outmoded aristocracy. The beginning image is complex: the painted lords' surrounding their order's star like night probably indicates the ranks of nobility with the monarchy at its center, but also describes the way their clothes surround them—note that the ladies are also lost in big clothes. Or it might refer simply to the brilliance of a medallion against dark cloth. The order's star could also refer to the "us" in the poem, for the painted lords surround us, the viewers, as well. "Chamberlain's liveries" is a rare instance of sarcasm from the poet, and alludes to the fact that well into modern times some servants were still dressed in the clothes of the eighteenth-century upper class, powdered wigs included.

Letzter Abend

(*Aus dem Besitze Frau Nonnas*)

Und Nacht und fernes Fahren; denn der Train	A
des ganzen Heeres zog am Park vorüber.	B
Er aber hob den Blick vom Clavecin	A
und spielte noch und sah zu ihr hinüber	B
beinah wie man in einen Spiegel schaut:	C
so sehr erfüllt von seinen jungen Zügen	D
und wissend, wie sie seine Trauer trügen,	D
schön und verführender bei jedem Laut.	C
Doch plötzlich wars, als ob sich das verwische:	E
sie stand wie mühsam in der Fensternische	E
und hielt des Herzens drängendes Geklopf.	F
Sein Spiel gab nach. Von draußen wehte Frische.	E
Und seltsam fremd stand auf dem Spiegeltische	E
der schwarze Tschako mit dem Totenkopf.	F

Last Evening

(*with the permission of Frau Nonna*)

And night and distant din, for the train roared
quickly past the park with its entire corps.
But lifting his eyes from the clavichord
he played on and gazed across to her once more,

nearly as one might peer into a mirror—
so filled he was with his fine, young aspect,
and knowing how it carried his mournful affect,
with each note more seductive and fairer.

Yet suddenly, as if he'd faded away,
she stood wearily within the window bay
and held back her heartbeat's insistent moans.

His playing stopped. Outside the wind gusted.
And weirdly on the pier table rested
the black shako with the white skull and bones.

The Frau Nonna referred to here is Baroness Julie von Nordeck zur Rabenau, who had lost a husband during the Austro-Prussian War, and her permission is needed since Rilke copied the poem into her guestbook on Capri in March 1907. The piece is a brilliant observation of the differing attitudes of men and women to impending war. The young officer at the keyboard is caught up in the romance of the moment, while his companion senses his imminent death on the battle-field. The *Totenkopf,* the skull and crossbones insignia on the young Prussian officer's military cap, was later adopted by Hitler's elite SS troops, lending an even more sinister note for modern readers.

Jugend-Bildnis meines Vaters

Im Auge Traum. Die Stirn wie in Berührung	A
mit etwas Fernem. Um den Mund enorm	B
viel Jugend, ungelächelte Verführung,	A
und vor der vollen schmückenden Verschnürung	A
der schlanken adeligen Uniform	B
der Säbelkorb und beide Hände–, die	C
abwarten, ruhig, zu nichts hingedrängt.	D
Und nun fast nicht mehr sichtbar: als ob sie	C
zuerst, die Fernes greifenden, verschwänden.	E
Und alles andre mit sich selbst verhängt	D
und ausgelöscht als ob wirs nicht verständen	E
und tief aus seiner eignen Tiefe trüb–.	F
Du schnell vergehendes Daguerreotyp	F
in meinen langsamer vergehenden Händen.	E

Portrait of My Father as a Youth

In the eyes, dream. The brow seems to ruminate
on something distant. Tremendous youth about
the mouth, though in a dour, seductive state,
and across the fully decorated plait
filling the slim, noble uniform out,
the basket-hilt sword and both hands resting,
as if compelled toward nothing, composed.
And now barely visible, as if grasping
at distance in order not to be found.
And all else here seems self-imposed,
wiped away so we cannot understand
and clouded deep in its own sounding.

You daguerreotype rapidly fading
within my more slowly fading hand.

There is a certain type of father who seems to fade away even in life, as the old photograph of Rilke's father does here. Josef Rilke became a petty railroad official after an unsuccessful career in the military, and one can imagine that the photograph of his father in military uniform evoked a sense of failure for the poet, who was also unsuccessful during his years at military school. His parents' marriage ended in 1884 when the boy was barely nine years old, and his mother, Phia, always loomed larger in his life than Josef Rilke did. The poem neglects to mention the grandiose Emperor Franz Joseph side-whiskers that the senior Rilke cultivated, another token of his dashed ambition. Max Brod described Rilke's father as a "ladies' man" who affected the look of a cavalry officer even though he wore the uniform of a railroad clerk. Josef died in 1906, around the time the poem was written.

Selbstbildnis aus dem Jahre 1906

Des alten lange adligen Geschlechtes   A
Feststehendes im Augenbogenbau.   B
Im Blicke noch der Kindheit Angst und Blau   B
und Demut da und dort, nicht eines Knechtes   A
doch eines Dienenden und einer Frau.   B
Der Mund als Mund gemacht, groß und genau,   B
nicht überredend, aber ein Gerechtes   A
Aussagendes. Die Stirne ohne Schlechtes   A
und gern im Schatten stiller Niederschau.   B

Das, als Zusammenhang, erst nur geahnt;   C
noch nie im Leiden oder im Gelingen   D
zusammgefaßt zu dauerndem Durchdringen,   D
doch so, als wäre mit zerstreuten Dingen   D
von fern ein Ernstes, Wirkliches geplant.   C

Self-Portrait from the Year 1906

The old and long-noble dynasty
established in the shape of the brow.
Childhood's angst lingers in the blue eyes now,
and here and there, not a slave's humility
but a servant's, perhaps somewhat feminine.
The mouth as it should be, large and genuine,
not persuasive, but full of equanimity.
The forehead completely lacking duplicity
and glad in the shadow of its downward ken.

This combination, scarcely guessed firsthand;
nor yet in any success or affliction
assembled for lasting penetration,
but as if from afar with this collection
a real and earnest thing were being planned.

The "old and long-noble dynasty" is not his mother's family, the Entz-Kinzel-bergers: though they maintained a large palazzo on Prague's Herrengasse, they were of the merchant class. It refers to the long-claimed nobility of the Rilke family, pressed by the poet's uncle, Jaroslav, who adopted a coat of arms in 1873 when Emperor Franz Joseph granted him the title Ritter von Rüliken, the equivalent of a British knighthood. Rilke's reference to himself as having the humility of a servant probably has to do with his being constantly obligated to wealthier friends and acquaintances who allowed him the use of their country and city homes in various European locations. He acted the part of the obsequious family retainer in return for their charity and hospitality.

Der König

Der König ist sechzehn Jahre alt.   A
Sechzehn Jahre und schon der Staat.   B
Er schaut, wie aus einem Hinterhalt,   A
vorbei an den Greisen vom Rat   B

in den Saal hinein und irgendwohin   C
und fühlt vielleicht nur dies: D
an dem schmalen langen harten Kinn   C
die kalte Kette vom Vlies.   D

Das Todesurteil vor ihm bleibt   E
lang ohne Namenszug.   F
Und sie denken: wie er sich quält.   G

Sie wüßten, kennten sie ihn genug,   F
daß er nur langsam bis siebzig zählt   G
eh er es unterschreibt.   E

The King

The king is sixteen years of age.
Sixteen years and already the state.
As if from ambush his eyes engage
the gray-haired men of his cabinet,

glancing into the hall beyond them,
perhaps all he can feel are these:
beneath his chin, long, hard, and slim,
the cold links of the Golden Fleece.

Before him lies the writ of death;
still unsigned it lingers there.
How he agonizes, they suppose.

Knowing him they would be aware
his slow count to seventy in those
moments before he signs in a breath.

The Hapsburg Order of the Golden Fleece, referred to here, is in the form of
a gold medallion and chain. It is unclear which Hapsburg king, if any, Rilke
is referring to, although a good guess would be Leopold ii, the butcher of the
Congo, had he not been older than sixteen at his accession. More likely, Rilke
encountered this king in a museum or on the walls of some château.

Auferstehung

Der Graf vernimmt die Töne,	A
er sieht einen lichten Riß;	B
er weckt seine dreizehn Söhne	A
im Erb-Begräbnis.	B
Er grüßt seine beiden Frauen	C
ehrerbietig von weit–;	D
und alle, voll Vertrauen,	C
stehn auf zur Ewigkeit	D
und warten nur noch auf Erich	E
und Ulriken Dorotheen,	F
die, sieben- und dreizehnjährig,	E
(sechzehnhundertzehn)	F
verstorben sind im Flandern,	G
um heute vor den andern	G
unbeirrt herzugehn.	F

Resurrection

The count picks up the sounds,
he sees a brightening cave;
he wakes his thirteen sons
in their ancestral grave.

He welcomes both his wives
from afar, respectfully;
believers all their lives,
they rise for eternity.

For only Eric do they hold
and for Ulrica Dorothy–
who, seven and thirteen years old
    (sixteen-hundred-and-ten A.D.),
rest in far-away Flanders–
so that today, with the others,
the children might go peacefully.

In a letter to Hedwig von Boddien dated August 10, 1913, Rilke explained some of what goes on in this darkly comic poem. Eric and Ulrica are young children who have died prematurely, at seven and thirteen years old, as the poem indicates. They were not buried at home but at a church in Flanders, and thus they are not with their family when the firmament cracks open on Judgment Day. The children may be confused by the situation unless their family waits for them. Eric might bear some relation to Malte's bizarre cousin Erik in *The Notebooks of Malte Laurids Brigge,* who spoke to the dead and who was based on Rilke's own cousin, Egon. Both of them, the character and the cousin, died in childhood.

Der Fahnenträger

Die Andern fühlen alles an sich rauh   A
und ohne Anteil: Eisen, Zeug und Leder.   B
Zwar manchmal schmeichelt eine weiche Feder,   B
doch sehr allein und lieb-los ist ein jeder;   B
er aber trägt – als trüg er eine Frau –   A
die Fahne in dem feierlichen Kleide.   C
Dicht hinter ihm geht ihre schwere Seide,   C
die manchmal über seine Hände fließt.   D

Er kann allein, wenn er die Augen schließt,   D
ein Lächeln sehn: er darf sie nicht verlassen. –   E

Und wenn es kommt in blitzenden Kürassen   E
und nach ihr greift und ringt und will sie fassen –:   E

dann darf er sie abreißen von dem Stocke   F
als riß er sie aus ihrem Mädchentum,   G
um sie zu halten unterm Waffenrocke.   F

Und für die Andern ist das Mut und Ruhm.   G

The Flag Bearer

The others feel the ill-proportioned outfit
rough against them: iron, wool, and leather.
True, some are flattered by a cap feather,
yet how alone and unloved they all are;
but he, as if it were a woman he bears it—
this banner in her ceremonial clothes—
just behind him her heavy silk blows,
and often draping over his hands she lies.

He sees just a smile when he shuts his eyes—
he will not ever give her over.

And when they come in blazing armor
and grasp and struggle and try to capture

his banner, from its staff he must hack it,
as if he were tearing her very
maidenhead, to hide it under his jacket.

And for the others this is courage and glory.

The forty-year-old Rilke was drafted into the Austro-Hungarian reserves in 1916.
Though he saw no combat and was soon exempt from service, he mentions his
brief stint in the Great War as "witness to the world's disgrace." On the other
hand, Rilke had already created the dashing character Cornet Rilke in his small
epic, *The Lay of the Love and Death of Cornet Christoph Rilke.* The cornet or
ensign was the officer who carried the flag. The poet's ambivalence to things
military is evident elsewhere in his work. He loves the uniform, the tradition and
ceremony, but he abhors conflict in any form. The smile in the second stanza is,
again, not a grin but the Rilkean smile of realization.

Der letzte Graf von Brederode entzieht sich türkischer Gefangenschaft

Sie folgten furchtbar; ihren bunten Tod   A
von ferne nach ihm werfend, während er   B
verloren floh, nichts weiter als: bedroht.   A
Die Ferne seiner Väter schien nicht mehr   B

für ihn zu gelten; denn um so zu fliehn,   C
genügt ein Tier vor Jägern. Bis der Fluß   D
aufrauschte nah und blitzend. Ein Entschluß   D
hob ihn samt seiner Not und machte ihn   C

wieder zum Knaben fürstlichen Geblütes.   E
Ein Lächeln adeliger Frauen goß   F
noch einmal Süßigkeit in sein verfrühtes   E

vollendetes Gesicht. Er zwang sein Roß,   F
groß wie sein Herz zu gehn, sein blutdurchglühtes: E
es trug ihn in den Strom wie in sein Schloß.   F

The Last Count von Brederode Eludes Turkish Captivity

Formidably they followed, their painted death
flung his way from afar while he fled, lost,
but nothing worse than threatened. In that breath
thoughts of his father's ancestral past

seemed not to matter, for in order to flee
that way, one must act like a hunter's prey.
Until the rushing, flashing river lay
before him. Resolve and this adversity

raised the boy's spirit and made him embrace
his royal blood. The smile of a noble breed
of women again poured sweetness into his face,

too-young, yet consummate. Pressing his steed—
keen as his blood-gleaming heart for the chase—
into the stream as if into his keep he sped.

This poem could be a description of a romantic painting or of a short story by
Tolstoy—so much it echoes the drama of a certain type of martial exploit. Rilke
himself seems caught up in this drama and definitely sides with the young
count, who seems a counterpart of Cornet Rilke.

Die Kurtisane

Venedigs Sonne wird in meinem Haar   A
ein Gold bereiten: aller Alchemie   B
erlauchten Ausgang. Meine Brauen, die   B
den Brücken gleichen, siehst du sie   B

hinführen ob der lautlosen Gefahr   A
der Augen, die ein heimlicher Verkehr   C
an die Kanäle schließt, so daß das Meer   C
in ihnen steigt und fällt und wechselt. Wer   C

mich einmal sah, beneidet meinen Hund,   D
weil sich auf ihm oft in zerstreuter Pause   E
die Hand, die nie an keiner Glut verkohlt,   F

die unverwundbare, geschmückt, erholt–.   F
Und Knaben, Hoffnungen aus altem Hause,   E
gehn wie an Gift an meinem Mund zugrund.   D

The Courtesan

The Venetian sun shall soon prepare
a gold in my hair–all alchemy
and its famed effect. My brow's symmetry
evokes the city's bridges; you can see

how it leads to the eyes' silent danger,
to their secret commerce with canals,
until it seems the sea rises and falls
and changes in them. And he who recalls

me even once envies my little hound,
since often in distracted pauses my hand
rests on him, a hand never burned by desire,

relaxing there, bejeweled and secure.
And boys in whom the hopes of great houses stand
die at my kiss as by a poison compound.

This courtesan's more Apollonian sister can be found in the second volume of
the *New Poems* in the piece "The Lute." That poem mentions Tullia (Tullia
d'Aragona) a sixteenth-century courtesan and musician, and displays the more
worthy side of the profession. The irony here is that Rilke himself was a kind of
courtesan–often sustained by women of "great houses," who supported the
poet by offering him refuge. And it is interesting to note that this is one of the
few poems in this volume voiced entirely in the first-person singular, aside from
the Sapphic poems and several of the love poems.

Die Treppe der Orangerie

Versailles

Wie Könige die schließlich nur noch schreiten   A
fast ohne Ziel, nur um von Zeit zu Zeit   B
sich den Verneigenden auf beiden Seiten   A
zu zeigen in des Mantels Einsamkeit–:   B

so steigt, allein zwischen den Balustraden,   C
die sich verneigen schon seit Anbeginn,   D
die Treppe: langsam und von Gottes Gnaden   C
und auf den Himmel zu und nirgends hin;   D

als ob sie allen Folgenden befahl   E
zurückzubleiben,–so daß sie nicht wagen   F
von ferne nachzugehen; nicht einmal   E
die schwere Schleppe durfte einer tragen.   F

The Stairs of the Orangery

Versailles

Like kings who at last seem almost to stride
without purpose, appearing time and again
to the courtiers bowing on either side
in the loneliness that royal robes contain,

alone between the balustrades of this place,
which have bowed since they were constructed there,
the stairs ascend, slowly and by God's grace,
and upward to heaven and leading nowhere,

as if they ordered those attendants
to not be presumptuous, to remain,
or to follow behind at some distance –
never might even one bear the heavy train.

Rilke mentions a visit to an orangery in a letter to Clara dated May 1906. He was looking for nightingales in the old, neglected parks outside Meudon-Val-Fleury and briefly recounts the old orangery and the houses in its vicinity "whose walls are gradually caving in, as though the cannons of time were aimed at them." Although the orangery of the poem is in Versailles, and presumably much grander than the one mentioned in the letter, it seems to have been a lonely place as well. The Versailles Orangerie is located right behind the great château next to the large pool named the Pièce d'eau des Suisses.

Der Marmor-Karren

Paris

Auf Pferde, sieben ziehende, verteilt,	A
verwandelt Niebewegtes sich in Schritte;	B
denn was hochmütig in des Marmors Mitte	B
an Alter, Widerstand und All verweilt,	A
das zeigt sich unter Menschen. Siehe, nicht	C
unkenntlich, unter irgend einem Namen,	D
nein: wie der Held das Drängen in den Dramen	D
erst sichtbar macht und plötzlich unterbricht:	C
so kommt es durch den stauenden Verlauf	E
des Tages, kommt in seinem ganzen Staate,	F
als ob ein großer Triumphator nahte	F
langsam zuletzt; und langsam vor ihm her	G
Gefangene, von seiner Schwere schwer.	G
Und naht noch immer und hält alles auf.	E

The Marble Wagon

Paris

Its weight divided among seven horses,
the unmovable transforms itself in stages;
for the marble's pride, fixed by the ages,
by inertia, by the All, rehearses

itself in mankind. Look, and it's plain as day,
under whatever name or depiction,
as the hero first shows the surge of action,
then suddenly interrupts the play:

thus, through the jam of traffic, its coming,
coming in the full regalia of state,
like a triumph granted to someone great,

slowly nearing. And struggling before this one,
the captives oppressed by this heavy burden.
And it keeps approaching, halting everything.

In 1906 Rodin's huge sculpture, *Le Penseur,* was moved to an installation near the Pantheon, and that operation may have provided Rilke with the kernel of this piece. However, something more complicated than the heavy movement of a marble wagon is going on here. Although Rodin's artistic advice to Rilke was "work, always work," it was Rodin's constant demands on him that made work for Rilke almost impossible while he was with the Master. The huge blocks of marble in Rodin's studio and garden must have seemed like concrete manifestations of "writer's block" to the poet, and the great man's requirements kept on "halting everything." It was only when Rilke got away from Rodin that he was able to consistently create.

Buddha

Schon von ferne fühlt der fremde scheue   A
Pilger, wie es golden von ihm träuft;   B
so als hätten Reiche voller Reue   A
ihre Heimlichkeiten aufgehäuft.   B

Aber näher kommend wird er irre   C
vor der Hoheit dieser Augenbraun: D
denn das sind nicht ihre Trinkgeschirre   C
und die Ohrgehänge ihrer Fraun.   D

Wüßte einer denn zu sagen, welche   E
Dinge eingeschmolzen wurden, um   F
dieses Bild auf diesem Blumenkelche   E

aufzurichten: stummer, ruhiggelber   G
als ein goldenes und rundherum   F
auch den Raum berührend wie sich selber.   G

Buddha

The shy, foreign pilgrim, before he draws nigh,
already feels how it drips golden from him,
as if secrets had been heaped up high
by many a penitent kingdom.

But on coming nearer he grows delirious
before the splendor that from this brow springs,
for it is not in any precious chalice
of theirs, nor in the women's earrings.

Is there anyone who could tell us
what sort of things were once melted down,
recast into this image on this lotus:

more a peaceful, muted yellow surface
round about it than a golden one,
verging on both itself and on space.

Rodin's presence is evident in this second Buddha poem, as it is in the first
one contained in this volume. Rilke is the "shy, foreign pilgrim," who decided
to offer himself to the Master while he and Clara were at the artists' colony at
Worpswede. Traveling to Paris and finally meeting Rodin, Rilke indeed grew
"delirious / before the splendor that from this brow springs."

Römische Fontäne

Borghese

Zwei Becken, eins das andre übersteigend	A
aus einem alten runden Marmorrand,	B
und aus dem oberen Wasser leis sich neigend	A
zum Wasser, welches unten wartend stand,	B
dem leise redenden entgegenschweigend	A
und heimlich, gleichsam in der hohlen Hand,	B
ihm Himmel hinter Grün und Dunkel zeigend	A
wie einen unbekannten Gegenstand;	B
sich selber ruhig in der schönen Schale	X
verbreitend ohne Heimweh, Kreis aus Kreis,	C
nur manchmal träumerisch und tropfenweis	C
sich niederlassend an den Moosbehängen	D
zum letzten Spiegel, der sein Becken leis	C
von unten lächeln macht mit Übergängen.	D

Roman Fountain

Borghese

Two basins, one over the other ascending,
rising out of an ancient marble lip,
and out of the top one water gently bending
to the water waiting below, its steady drip

like speech that is gentle in its reply
while secretly showing something in its palm,
which behind green and darkness is the sky,
like an unfamiliar object that is calm

in its essence as exquisite seashells,
spreading without regret, circle from circle;
sometimes in single drops it seems to trickle

dreamily over the mossy fringes
down to the last mirror, and as it falls
the basin below smiles with tender changes.

This bears some resemblance to "Der römische Brunnen," a poem written by the Swiss poet Conrad Ferdinand Meyer in 1858, and some writers have suggested that both pieces are based on the same fountain in the Villa Borghese. In 1903–04 Rilke and Clara resided at a small studio in the Villa Strohl-Fern in Rome, which is adjacent to the Borghese gardens. Rilke mentions visiting the gardens in his letters, but does not mention the fountain. However, in his *Letters to a Young Poet,* Rilke writes from Rome to his correspondent: "Endless life-carrying water flows through the old aqueducts in the great city and dances in many places over the white, stone shells."

Das Karussell

Jardin du Luxembourg

Mit einem Dach und seinem Schatten dreht	A
sich eine kleine Weile der Bestand	B
von bunten Pferden, alle aus dem Land,	B
das lange zögert, eh es untergeht.	A
Zwar manche sind an Wagen angespannt,	C
doch alle haben Mut in ihren Mienen;	D
ein böser roter Löwe geht mit ihnen	D
und dann und wann ein weißer Elefant.	C
Sogar ein Hirsch ist da, ganz wie im Wald,	E
nur daß er einen Sattel trägt und drüber	F
ein kleines blaues Mädchen aufgeschnallt.	E
Und auf dem Löwen reitet weiß ein Junge	G
und hält sich mit der kleinen heißen Hand,	B
dieweil der Löwe Zähne zeigt und Zunge.	G
Und dann und wann ein weißer Elefant.	C
Und auf den Pferden kommen sie vorüber,	F
auch Mädchen, helle, diesem Pferdesprunge	G
fast schon entwachsen; mitten in dem Schwunge	G
schauen sie auf, irgendwohin, herüber–	F
Und dann und wann ein weißer Elefant.	C
Und das geht hin und eilt sich, daß es endet,	H
und kreist und dreht sich nur und hat kein Ziel.	I
Ein Rot, ein Grün, ein Grau vorbeigesendet,	H
ein kleines kaum begonnenes Profil–.	I

The Carousel

Jardin du Luxembourg

Under the shadow of its canopy
it revolves for just a while, this band
of painted horses, all out of that land
that dallies here then ceases to be.
Indeed, though many stand in front
of carts, they all wear valiant faces;
a fierce red lion also paces
and now and then a white elephant.

Even a stag stands, as if in a glen,
but upon his saddle we can spy
a small girl in blue, and all buckled in.

On the lion a boy in white has clung,
reining him in with a small, hot hand,
while the lion shows his teeth and tongue.

And now and then a white elephant.

And upon the horses as they pass by
some fair-haired lasses seem to swing
on the springing steeds to which they cling,
almost too old, looking far and nigh.

And now and then a white elephant.

And this goes on and hastens to the end,
turning without a purpose to portray.
A gray, a green, a red go round the bend,
a small, unfinished child's face on display.

Und manchesmal ein Lächeln, hergewendet,
ein seliges, das blendet und verschwendet
an dieses atemlose blinde Spiel...

And many a smile in which we comprehend
a bliss that seems to sparkle and to spend
itself on this blind and breathless play...

"The Carousel" contains one of the most complicated rhyme schemes in the *New Poems.* It is one of the many pieces that visit Rilke's lost land of childhood, and it was a favorite when he gave readings.

Spanische Tänzerin

Wie in der Hand ein Schwefelzündholz, weiß,   A
eh es zur Flamme kommt, nach allen Seiten   B
zuckende Zungen streckt–: beginnt im Kreis   A
naher Beschauer hastig, hell und heiß   A
ihr runder Tanz sich zuckend auszubreiten.   B

Und plötzlich ist er Flamme, ganz und gar.   C

Mit einem Blick entzündet sie ihr Haar   C
und dreht auf einmal mit gewagter Kunst   D
ihr ganzes Kleid in diese Feuersbrunst,   D
aus welcher sich, wie Schlangen die erschrecken,   E
die nackten Arme wach und klappernd strecken.   E

Und dann: als würde ihr das Feuer knapp,   F
nimmt sie es ganz zusamm und wirft es ab   F
sehr herrisch, mit hochmütiger Gebärde   G
und schaut: da liegt es rasend auf der Erde   G
und flammt noch immer und ergiebt sich nicht–.   H
Doch sieghaft, sicher und mit einem süßen   I
grüßenden Lächeln hebt sie ihr Gesicht   H
und stampft es aus mit kleinen festen Füßen.   I

Spanish Dancer

As a match in the fingers first glows white
then bursts into tongues of flame that flare,
in the ring of spectators it seems to ignite,
with blistering heat, abrupt and bright;
her spinning dance seeks to spread like fire.

And suddenly it is wholly aflame.

With a look she kindles her hair just the same,
and at once flings, with an artist's daring,
her whole dress into passionate flaring
while her bare arms flash like startled snakes,
clapping and stretching in the pose she takes.

And then, as if fire were too tight to abide,
she gathers it to her and casts it aside,
imperiously, with an arrogant turn;
as it lies on the ground, continues to burn,
flames still raging, conceding no space.
Yet triumphant and sure, as the sweet
salutation of a smile lifts her face,
she stamps it out with firm little feet.

"Spanish Dancer" was another poem that was always well received at readings.
Rilke typically quickened the pace as he went on, to add to the effect produced
by the rhyming couplets at the middle of this piece, which are supposed to evoke
the whirling dancer.

Der Turm

Tour St.-Nicolas, Furnes

Erd-Inneres. Als wäre dort, wohin	A
du blindlings steigst, erst Erdenoberfläche,	B
zu der du steigst im schrägen Bett der Bäche,	B
die langsam aus dem suchenden Gerinn	A

der Dunkelheit entsprungen sind, durch die	C
sich dein Gesicht, wie auferstehend, drängt	D
und die du plötzlich *siehst,* als fiele sie	C
aus diesem Abgrund, der dich überhängt	D

und den du, wie er riesig über dir	E
sich umstürzt in dem dämmernden Gestühle,	F
erkennst, erschreckt und fürchtend, im Gefühle:	F
o wenn er steigt, behangen wie ein Stier–:	E

Da aber nimmt dich aus der engen Endung	G
windiges Licht. Fast fliegend siehst du hier	E
die Himmel wieder, Blendung über Blendung,	G
und dort die Tiefen, wach und voll Verwendung,	G

und kleine Tage wie bei Patenier,	E
gleichzeitige, mit Stunde neben Stunde,	H
durch die die Brücken springen wie die Hunde,	H
dem hellen Wege immer auf der Spur,	I

The Tower

Tour St.-Nicolas, Furnes

Inner Earth. As if where you blindly climbed
were not even yet the planet's surface,
to which you ascend through searching darkness
slowly sprung from the sloping streambed

of that waterway–through which your face,
as if in resurrection, seems to press–
and at once you glimpse it in the space
above you, as if it fell from this abyss,

hugely looming so high above you
as it topples from its dawn-bright stool,
this thing that terrifies coming into view:
oh, if it soars, hung as it is like a bull.

But here you are snatched from the narrowing
end by a fresh light. You witness skies once more,
almost flying, dazzling over dazzling,
and there, the depths, awake and busying,

and small days as in paintings by Patenier,
showing it all at once, hour next to hour,
through which, like hounds, the bridges scour,
always on the spoor of some bright trail,

den unbeholfne Häuser manchmal nur I

verbergen, bis er ganz im Hintergrunde H

beruhigt geht durch Buschwerk und Natur. I

which the awkward houses almost conceal
from time to time, until hushed and obscure
it wanders through nature and the chaparral.

The poet visited Furnes and other places in Belgium in the summer of 1906 with his wife and daughter. Paula Becker, the talented painter who was Clara's friend before she was Rilke's, was supposed to join them there, but Rilke persuaded her in a letter not to come, telling her, "This is not what you are looking for..." Perhaps he felt guilty over his attraction to Paula and did not want to throw such an obvious ménage in Clara's face. Becker's unfinished portrait of Rilke antici- pates German Expressionism, and the poem likewise distorts reality in order to achieve an effect: it takes the point of view of someone climbing a tower. The lower stairs are full of darkness and apprehension (the abyss above and the huge bell hanging like a slaughtered bull), but as the climber mounts ever higher the vista appears through the tower windows and with it the skies, the bridges, and the bright lanes.

Der Platz

Furnes

Willkürlich von Gewesnem ausgeweitet: A
von Wut und Aufruhr, von dem Kunterbunt   B
das die Verurteilten zu Tod begleitet,   A
von Buden, von der Jahrmarktsrufer Mund,   B
und von dem Herzog der vorüberreitet   A
und von dem Hochmut von Burgund,   B

(auf allen Seiten Hintergrund):   B

ladet der Platz zum Einzug seiner Weite   C
die fernen Fenster unaufhörlich ein,   D
während sich das Gefolge und Geleite   C
der Leere langsam an den Handelsreihn   D

verteilt und ordnet. In die Giebel steigend,   E
wollen die kleinen Häuser alles sehn,   F
die Türme vor einander scheu verschweigend,   E
die immer maßlos hinter ihnen stehn.   F

The Plaza

Furnes

Randomly enlarged by past experience,
by rage and revolt, by the gaudy doings
that attend those under a death sentence,
by the shops, by the way the merchant sings
his wares, by Burgundy's arrogance
and the duke who rides past his underlings

(on all sides these background things),

the plaza invites the distant windows
to constantly enter its broad venue,
while the escorts and retinue of emptiness
slowly sort and portion themselves into

the ranks of commerce. Narrow houses that rose
high into their gables, demanding to see,
have obscured from each other's view those
towers that loom behind them so extremely.

Another of the Flemish poems that Rilke composed while visiting Belgium in
1906 with Clara and little Ruth. The family's itinerary included Ostend, Ypres,
Bruges, and Ghent. Rodin had earlier recommended visiting the cities of Flan-
ders to study their architecture, and now that the Master had unceremoniously
fired him, Rilke was following that advice. An atmosphere of darkness pervades
most of these poems; and the "narrow houses" mentioned here may portray
the bourgeoisie, who are so intent on what goes on in the public plaza that they
fail to see the powerful forces controlling their lives that "loom behind them so
extremely."

Quai du Rosaire

Brügge

Die Gassen haben einen sachten Gang A
(wie manchmal Menschen gehen im Genesen B
nachdenkend: was ist früher hier gewesen?) B
und die an Plätze kommen, warten lang A

auf eine andre, die mit einem Schritt C
über das abendklare Wasser tritt, C
darin, je mehr sich rings die Dinge mildern, D
die eingehängte Welt von Spiegelbildern D
so wirklich wird wie diese Dinge nie. E

Verging nicht diese Stadt? Nun siehst du, wie E
(nach einem unbegreiflichen Gesetz) F
sie wach und deutlich wird im Umgestellten, G
als wäre dort das Leben nicht so selten; G
dort hängen jetzt die Gärten groß und gelten, G
dort dreht sich plötzlich hinter schnell erhellten G
Fenstern der Tanz in den Estaminets. F

Und oben blieb? – Die Stille nur, ich glaube, H
und kostet langsam und von nichts gedrängt I
Beere um Beere aus der süßen Traube H
des Glockenspiels, das in den Himmeln hängt. I

Quai du Rosaire

Bruges

The alleyways have such a gentle gait
(as sometimes former shut-ins seem to ponder:
What used to be here? they might wonder)
and on reaching the plazas they often wait

for another lane, which with a stride
over the clear, twilight water seems to glide,
in which, since things around it seem to soften,
the connected world of mirror images often
becomes more real than we can ever know.

Did this city not die? Now you see how
(according to an inscrutable decree)
it wakes and sharpens as if made again,
as if life there were not an uncommon strain;
the gardens hang there, broad and germane,
and suddenly through the quickly lit pane:
the turning dance in the small café.

And above? Only silence, I suppose,
and it slowly savors berry after berry
casually from the sweet bunch of those
carillon bells hanging in the sky.

With its network of canals, Bruges is often called the Venice of the North. Small stone bridges carry the streets and alleyways of the town across the waters, in which the buildings are reflected, becoming "more real than we can ever know." This piece displays none of the darkness of some of the other Flemish poems.

Béguinage

Béguinage Sainte-Elisabeth, Brügge

I

Das hohe Tor scheint keine einzuhalten,   A
die Brücke geht gleich gerne hin und her,   B
und doch sind sicher alle in dem alten   A
offenen Ulmenhof und gehn nicht mehr   B
aus ihren Häusern, als auf jenem Streifen   C
zur Kirche hin, um besser zu begreifen   C
warum in ihnen so viel Liebe war.   D

Dort knieen sie, verdeckt mit reinem Leinen,   E
so gleich, als wäre nur das Bild der einen   E
tausendmal im Choral, der tief und klar   D
zu Spiegeln wird an den verteilten Pfeilern;   F
und ihre Stimmen gehn den immer steilern   F
Gesang hinan und werfen sich von dort,   G
wo es nicht weitergeht, vom letzten Wort,   G
den Engeln zu, die sie nicht wiedergeben.   H

Drum sind die unten, wenn sie sich erheben   H
und wenden, still. Drum reichen sie sich schweigend   I
mit einem Neigen, Zeigende zu zeigend   I
Empfangenden, geweihtes Wasser, das   J
die Stirnen kühl macht und die Munde blaß.   J

Und gehen dann, verhangen und verhalten,   K
auf jenem Streifen wieder überquer–   L
die Jungen ruhig, ungewiß die Alten   K
und eine Greisin, weilend, hinterher–   L
zu ihren Häusern, die sie schnell verschweigen   M
und die sich durch die Ulmen hin von Zeit   N

Béguinage

Béguinage Sainte-Elisabeth, Bruges

I

The lofty gate seems to refuse no one,
the bridges go just as well here or there,
and yet all are safe in the ancient run
of the courtyard, and they wander nowhere
out-of-doors, except when they might return
to the church, perhaps in order to learn
why there was so much love in them all.

Kneeling there, each in laundered linen,
each the same, as if the image of one
recurred a thousandfold in the choir stall,
deeply and clearly mirrored on the columns,
and their voices ascend steepening hymns
and hurl themselves from there to be heard
till they climb no more, from the final word
to the angels, who sing nothing in reprise.

Therefore those below, when they finally rise
to leave, are quiet. Therefore they turn about
to each other with a soft nod, and reach out
a hand, like holy water that somehow
leaves the mouth pale as it cools the brow.

And then they go, cautious and somewhat dull,
on the same pathway once again they wind,
the old uncertain, the young ones docile,
and a gray-haired crone tarrying behind,
to houses that quickly conceal them again,
which, through the elm trees from time to time,

zu Zeit ein wenig reine Einsamkeit,   N

in einer kleinen Scheibe schimmernd, zeigen.   M

II

Was aber spiegelt mit den tausend Scheiben   A

das Kirchenfenster in den Hof hinein,   B

darin sich Schweigen, Schein und Widerschein   A

vermischen, trinken, trüben, übertreiben,   A

phantastisch alternd wie ein alter Wein.   B

Dort legt sich, keiner weiß von welcher Seite,   C

Außen auf Inneres und Ewigkeit   D

auf Immer-Hingehn, Weite über Weite,   C

erblindend, finster, unbenutzt, verbleit.   D

Dort bleibt, unter dem schwankenden Dekor   E

des Sommertags, das Graue alter Winter: F

als stünde regungslos ein sanftgesinnter   F

langmütig lange Wartender dahinter   F

und eine weinend Wartende davor.   E

show bits of pure loneliness in the frame
of a small, glimmering windowpane.

II

But what, with its thousand panes, is that reflection
of chapel windows that through the courtyard shines,
in which silence, appearance, and reverberation
combine and infuse, cloud up and overrun,
fantastically aged like a blend of old wines.

There it settles, from no one knows where,
outer upon inner, and eternity
going on far and wide and forever,
blinded, glum, unused, and sealed tightly.

There remains, under the transient spell
of a summer's day, the gray old winter,
as if there stood there, stock-still and tender,
a patient man waiting behind her:
this weeping woman who waits as well.

This continues the darkness and sense of loneliness evident in most of the other
Flemish poems. The Béguinage is a group of buildings with a courtyard, in this
case used as a convent. The order took its name from Lambert le Bègue (Lam-
bert the Stutterer) a medieval priest from Liège. His order, the Beguines, estab-
lished an association of women who devoted themselves to a life of religion with-
out taking any formal vows.

Die Marien-Prozession

Gent

Aus allen Türmen stürzt sich, Fluß um Fluß,   A
hinwallendes Metall in solchen Massen   B
als sollte drunten in der Form der Gassen   B
ein blanker Tag erstehn aus Bronzeguß,   A

an dessen Rand, gehämmert und erhaben,   C
zu sehen ist der buntgebundne Zug   D
der leichten Mädchen und der neuen Knaben, C
und wie er Wellen schlug und trieb und trug, D
hinabgehalten von dem ungewissen   E
Gewicht der Fahnen und von Hindernissen   E
gehemmt, unsichtbar wie die Hand des Herrn; F

und drüben plötzlich beinah mitgerissen   E
vom Aufstieg aufgescheuchter Räucherbecken, G
die fliegend, alle sieben, wie im Schrecken   G
an ihren Silberketten zerrn.   F

Die Böschung Schauender umschließt die Schiene, H
in der das alles stockt und rauscht und rollt: I
das Kommende, das Chryselephantine,   H
aus dem sich zu Balkonen Baldachine   H
aufbäumen, schwankend im Behang von Gold. I

Und sie erkennen über all dem Weißen,   J
getragen und im spanischen Gewand,   K
das alte Standbild mit dem kleinen heißen   J
Gesichte und dem Kinde auf der Hand   K
und knieen hin, je mehr es naht und naht,   L
in seiner Krone ahnungslos veraltend   M

The Procession of the Virgin Mary

Ghent

Out of all the towers, stream upon stream
it surges, flowing metal in such quantity,
cast in the mold of the streets of this city,
as if molten bronze shone in daylight's gleam,

and wrought and embossed upon that border
can be seen the colorfully knotted train
of the young boys and lithe girls in order,
and how its waves batter and drive and strain,
delayed by the dubious, heavy sway
of the banners—many obstacles in its way,
invisible as the hand of God the Father;

and there, suddenly it seems carried astray
by the rising smoke of frightened censers,
seven of them fleeing, as if some terrors
were pulling upon their chains of silver.

Banks of onlookers flank the parade
in which everything stumbles, rushed and rolled:
the Coming One, ivory with gold inlaid,
from which canopies rise to each balustrade,
fluttering in the air with fringes of gold.

And they recognize, above the whiteness,
the ancient statue with its small, hot face,
proudly borne, swaddled in Spanish dress,
and the child, in its mother's fond embrace,
and they fall to their knees as it nears and nears,
artlessly outdated in a coronet,

und immer noch das Segnen hölzern haltend M
aus dem sich groß gebärdenden Brokat. L

Da aber wie es an den Hingeknieten N
vorüberkommt, die scheu von unten schaun, O
da scheint es seinen Trägern zu gebieten N
mit einem Hochziehn seiner Augenbraun, O
hochmütig, ungehalten und bestimmt: P
so daß sie staunen, stehn und überlegen Q
und schließlich zögernd gehn. Sie aber nimmt, P

in sich die Schritte dieses ganzen Stromes R
und geht, allein, wie auf erkannten Wegen Q
dem Glockendonnern des großoffnen Domes R
auf hundert Schultern frauenhaft entgegen. Q

the wooden-handed blessing that even yet
gestures grandly from the brocade he wears.

But then, as it passes those kneeling there,
who gaze up shyly from the street below,
it seems as if he commands those who bear
him with a sudden raising of his brow,
indignant, determined, somewhat haughty,
so that they marvel, lingering in regard,
and finally press on haltingly. But she

takes upon herself that whole processional,
alone and womanly, and moves toward
the thundering peal of the great cathedral,
borne by the hundred shoulders of her guard.

During the rule of Archduke Albert and his wife, Isabel, Spanish influence over the religious festivals of Belgium and Holland grew. The often exaggerated Spanish ceremonials stand out against the more matter-of-fact atmosphere of the Low Countries, thus the statue "swaddled in Spanish dress." Processions and pilgrimages dedicated to the Blessed Virgin became important after a plague ravaged the countryside in the seventeenth century. Rilke displays an odd juxtaposition of pronouns here: the composite statue of Virgin and Child is referred to as *it*, while the infant Christ is addressed by the masculine pronoun, and Mary, who holds the infant in her lap, is portrayed as *she*.

Die Insel

Nordsee

I

Die nächste Flut verwischt den Weg im Watt,   A
und alles wird auf allen Seiten gleich;   B
die kleine Insel draußen aber hat   A
die Augen zu; verwirrend kreist der Deich   B

um ihre Wohner, die in einen Schlaf   C
geboren werden, drin sie viele Welten   D
verwechseln, schweigend; denn sie reden selten,   D
und jeder Satz ist wie ein Epitaph   C

für etwas Angeschwemmtes, Unbekanntes,   E
das unerklärt zu ihnen kommt und bleibt.   F
Und so ist alles was ihr Blick beschreibt   F

von Kindheit an: nicht auf sie Angewandtes,   E
zu Großes, Rücksichtsloses, Hergesandtes,   E
das ihre Einsamkeit noch übertreibt.   F

II

Als läge er in einem Krater-Kreise   A
auf einem Mond: ist jeder Hof umdämmt,   B
und drin die Gärten sind auf gleiche Weise   A
gekleidet und wie Waisen gleich gekämmt   B

von jenem Sturm, der sie so rauh erzieht   C
und tagelang sie bange macht mit Toden.   D
Dann sitzt man in den Häusern drin und sieht   C
in schiefen Spiegeln was auf den Kommoden   D

The Island

North Sea

I

The next tide smears the path through the mudflat,
from every side it all appears alike;
but the small island has shut its eyes to that,
and all around stands the bewildering dike,

circling islanders who have all been born
to a sleep in which many worlds are confused,
quiet, for seldom is any speech used,
every sentence like an epitaph to mourn

something alluvial, washed up, unknown,
that comes to them unexplained and then stays.
And so it is with all described by their gaze

since childhood: not something actually *done*
to them, but things huge, ruthless, and passed on,
which greatly overstate their lonely ways.

II

As if encircled by a lunar crater,
every farm is bordered by a dam,
and the gardens also, which some creator
has clothed alike, like orphans combed the same

by storms that often school them roughly,
filling them days on end with deathly fear.
Then, shut up within the houses, one can see
in crooked mirrors what weird objects appear

Seltsames steht. Und einer von den Söhnen   E
tritt abends vor die Tür und zieht ein Tönen   E
aus der Harmonika wie Weinen weich;   F

so hörte ers in einem fremden Hafen –.   G
Und draußen formt sich eines von den Schafen   G
ganz groß, fast drohend, auf dem Außendeich.   F

III

Nah ist nur Innres; alles andre fern.   A
Und dieses Innere gedrängt und täglich   B
mit allem überfüllt und ganz unsäglich.   B
Die Insel ist wie ein zu kleiner Stern   A

welchen der Raum nicht merkt und stumm zerstört   C
in seinem unbewußten Furchtbarsein,   D
so daß er, unerhellt und überhört,   C
allein   D

damit dies alles doch ein Ende nehme   E
dunkel auf einer selbsterfundnen Bahn   F
versucht zu gehen, blindlings, nicht im Plan   F
der Wandelsterne, Sonnen und Systeme.   E

upon the dresser tops. And one of their sons
steps to the door at twilight and draws tones
from his harmonica like a soft weeping,

as he heard it played in a foreign harbor.
And outdoors one of the clouds grows larger,
sheep-shaped on the outer dike, threatening.

III

Near is just that inmost place, the rest is far.
And this place within is dense, quotidian,
crammed with everything, past comprehension.
The island is like a too-small star

which space ignores, softly annihilated
by some unconscious dreadfulness of its own,
forgotten and unilluminated,
alone

so it all takes on dark finalities
as if in its own self-realized way,
trying to go blindly, not within the sway
of the planets, suns, and galaxies.

"The Island" is the last of the Flemish poems and continues the theme of solitude and darkness that is so evident in "The Tower," "The Plaza," and "Béguinage." We should remember that Rilke had Clara and Ruth along with him for
most of this trip: loneliness may seem an odd reaction to family, but Rilke was
no family man and could write, "Near is just that inmost place, the rest is far."

Hetären-Gräber

In ihren langen Haaren liegen sie
mit braunen, tief in sich gegangenen Gesichtern.
Die Augen zu wie vor zu vieler Ferne.
Skelette, Munde, Blumen. In den Munden
die glatten Zähne wie ein Reise-Schachspiel
aus Elfenbein in Reihen aufgestellt.
Und Blumen, gelbe Perlen, schlanke Knochen,
Hände und Hemden, welkende Gewebe
über dem eingestürzten Herzen. Aber
dort unter jenen Ringen, Talismanen
und augenblauen Steinen (Lieblings-Angedenken)
steht noch die stille Krypta des Geschlechtes,
bis an die Wölbung voll mit Blumenblättern.
Und wieder gelbe Perlen, weitverrollte, –
Schalen gebrannten Tones, deren Bug
ihr eignes Bild geziert hat, grüne Scherben
von Salben-Vasen, die wie Blumen duften,
und Formen kleiner Götter: Hausaltäre,
Hetärenhimmel mit entzückten Göttern.
Gesprengte Gürtel, flache Skarabäen,
kleine Figuren riesigen Geschlechtes,
ein Mund der lacht und Tanzende und Läufer,
goldene Fibeln, kleinen Bogen ähnlich
zur Jagd auf Tier- und Vogelamulette,
und lange Nadeln, zieres Hausgeräte
und eine runde Scherbe roten Grundes,
darauf, wie eines Eingangs schwarze Aufschrift,
die straffen Beine eines Viergespannes.
Und wieder Blumen, Perlen, die verrollt sind,
die hellen Lenden einer kleinen Leier,
und zwischen Schleiern, die gleich Nebeln fallen,

Tombs of the Hetaerae

In their flowing tresses they recline,
faces bronzed, gone deep inside themselves.
The eyes are shut as if from too much distance.
Their frames and mouths and flowers. In their lips
the gleaming teeth like a traveler's chess set,
pieces ranged in rows of ivory white.
And flowers, yellow pearls, and slender bones,
hands and camisoles and wilting textures
covering the caved-in heart. However,
underneath those rings, those talismans,
those blue-eyed stones like lovers' tokens,
the quiet crypt of their gender still reclines,
its vault filled to the brim with flower petals.
And again those yellow pearls, all scattered wide,
with terra-cotta bowls, whose prow-like curve
shows their own likeness back to them, green shards
of ointment jars, fragrant as the flowers,
and images of gods on household altars,
a courtesan-heaven with captivated gods.
Loosened corsets, smoothly engraved scarabs,
small figures with enormous phalluses,
a laughing mouth and athletes and dancers,
golden brooches that seem to be small bows
used for hunting bird and animal charms,
long pins and fine domestic articles,
and a round potsherd's ruby-colored ground,
on which, like the doorway's black inscription,
stands a chariot team with tightened legs.
And again, the flowers and scattered pearls,
the luminous loins of a small Greek lyre,
and between the veils falling like haze,

wie ausgekrochen aus des Schuhes Puppe:
des Fußgelenkes leichter Schmetterling.

So liegen sie mit Dingen angefüllt,
kostbaren Dingen, Steinen, Spielzeug, Hausrat,
zerschlagnem Tand (was alles in sie abfiel),
und dunkeln wie der Grund von einem Fluß.

Flußbetten waren sie,
darüber hin in kurzen schnellen Wellen
(die weiter wollten zu dem nächsten Leben)
die Leiber vieler Jünglinge sich stürzten
und in denen der Männer Ströme rauschten.
Und manchmal brachen Knaben aus den Bergen
der Kindheit, kamen zagen Falles nieder
und spielten mit den Dingen auf dem Grunde,
bis das Gefälle ihr Gefühl ergriff:

Dann füllten sie mit flachem klaren Wasser
die ganze Breite dieses breiten Weges
und trieben Wirbel an den tiefen Stellen;
und spiegelten zum ersten Mal die Ufer
und ferne Vogelrufe –, während hoch
die Sternennächte eines süßen Landes
in Himmel wuchsen, die sich nirgends schlossen.

as if hatched from the pupae of shoes,
the ankle's pallid butterfly.

Thus they recline, replete with costly things—
gems and toys, broken baubles, furnishings,
all that was ever let go into them—
growing murky as the riverbed.

For riverbeds they were,
into which, in sudden, rushing swells
that seemed to strive for the afterlife,
the bodies of many lads pitched themselves,
and into which the men's torrents rushed.
And sometimes youthful boys broke from the alps
of childhood, and came down in anxious falls
and played with the things on the streambed
until seized by the current of their feelings:

then they filled, with clear, shallow water,
the entire breadth of this shining channel
and drove the eddies into the depths,
and mirrored for the first time the banks
and distant birdsong, while high above
the star-encrusted night of a sweet country
waxed in the heavens with no end in sight.

This belongs, with "Orpheus, Eurydice, Hermes" and "Birth of Venus," to
a suite of poems written in Rome in 1904. All of these pieces show women's
mastery of life and death—hence Rilke's grouping of them in this volume with
"Alcestis," which has a similar heroine. This Roman suite is also significant
because it contains the only unrhymed verse in the *New Poems*. The hetaerae
were women of classical Greece who served as companions to men of the upper
class. These women had specially cultivated skills, and like the geisha of Japan
they served as advisers in addition to being dancers and courtesans.

Orpheus. Eurydike. Hermes

Das war der Seelen wunderliches Bergwerk.
Wie stille Silbererze gingen sie
als Adern durch sein Dunkel. Zwischen Wurzeln
entsprang das Blut, das fortgeht zu den Menschen,
und schwer wie Porphyr sah es aus im Dunkel.
Sonst war nichts Rotes.

Felsen waren da
und wesenlose Wälder. Brücken über Leeres
und jener große graue blinde Teich,
der über seinem fernen Grunde hing
wie Regenhimmel über einer Landschaft.
Und zwischen Wiesen, sanft und voller Langmut,
erschien des einen Weges blasser Streifen,
wie eine lange Bleiche hingelegt.

Und dieses einen Weges kamen sie.

Voran der schlanke Mann im blauen Mantel,
der stumm und ungeduldig vor sich aussah.
Ohne zu kauen fraß sein Schritt den Weg
in großen Bissen; seine Hände hingen
schwer und verschlossen aus dem Fall der Falten
und wußten nicht mehr von der leichten Leier,
die in die Linke eingewachsen war
wie Rosenranken in den Ast des Ölbaums.
Und seine Sinne waren wie entzweit:
indes der Blick ihm wie ein Hund vorauslief,
umkehrte, kam und immer wieder weit
und wartend an der nächsten Wendung stand, –

Orpheus, Eurydice, Hermes

That was the fantastical mine of the soul.
Like the reticent ore of silver, like veins
through its darkness they sped. Among those roots
sprang the blood that flowed toward mankind,
appearing hard as porphyry in the darkness.
Else there was nothing red.

There were crags there
and dreamlike forests. Bridges over chasms,
and that huge, gray, and sightless pool
that hung suspended over its distant bottom
like rainclouds above a landscape.
And among the meadows, soft and patient,
appeared the faint slash of a pathway,
like a long bleaching laid out there.

And on this single path they trod.

First, the slender man in a cloak of blue,
who mutely and eagerly peered ahead.
His stride devoured the road in great bites,
without chewing; jutting out of the folds
of his garment, his heavy, fisted hands hung
and knew nothing more of his breezy lyre,
which clung to the left side of his body
like rose tendrils in the bough of an olive.
And his wits were as if divided in two:
for while his gaze ran ahead like a dog—
turned back, went on again, always onward,
and stood waiting for them at the next bend—

blieb sein Gehör wie ein Geruch zurück.
Manchmal erschien es ihm als reichte es
bis an das Gehen jener beiden andern,
die folgen sollten diesen ganzen Aufstieg.
Dann wieder wars nur seines Steigens Nachklang
und seines Mantels Wind was hinter ihm war.
Er aber sagte sich, sie kämen doch;
sagte es laut und hörte sich verhallen.
Sie kämen doch, nur wärens zwei
die furchtbar leise gingen. Dürfte er
sich einmal wenden (wäre das Zurückschaun
nicht die Zersetzung dieses ganzen Werkes,
das erst vollbracht wird), müßte er sie sehen,
die beiden Leisen, die ihm schweigend nachgehn:

Den Gott des Ganges und der weiten Botschaft,
die Reisehaube über hellen Augen,
den schlanken Stab hertragend vor dem Leibe
und flügelschlagend an den Fußgelenken;
und seiner linken Hand gegeben: *sie.*

Die So-geliebte, daß aus einer Leier
mehr Klage kam als je aus Klagefrauen;
daß eine Welt aus Klage ward, in der
alles noch einmal da war: Wald und Tal
und Weg und Ortschaft, Feld und Fluß und Tier;
und daß um diese Klage-Welt, ganz so
wie um die andre Erde, eine Sonne
und ein gestirnter stiller Himmel ging,
ein Klage-Himmel mit entstellten Sternen—:
Diese So-geliebte.

Sie aber ging an jenes Gottes Hand,
den Schritt beschränkt von langen Leichenbändern,

his hearing remained like a spoor on the trail.
Sometimes it seemed to him as if it sensed
the footfalls of those two other beings
supposed to follow this whole ascent.
Then there was just the echo of his climb
and the wind in his mantle behind him.
But he told himself they still followed,
his words trailing off as he said it aloud.
They still came behind him, but they were two
who went fearfully, softly. If only now
he could turn just once–though a backward glance
would undo the task that was now near its end–
he would have been forced to turn around
to see that hushed pair who followed him:

The god of pathways and distant messages,
his traveling hood hiding gleaming eyes,
the slender wand he bore before his body
and the fluttering wings at his ankles;
and given over to his left hand–*she.*

The So-Beloved for whom, from one lyre, came
more lament than ever from mourning women;
for whom a world came out of mourning, in which
all was once again there–wood and valley,
path and hamlet, field and flow and creature–
and around this world of lament, as if
around some other Earth, a different sun
and a starry, silent heaven went,
a heaven of mourning with misplaced stars:
this So-Beloved.

But she came along at that god's hand,
her gait confined by long winding sheets,

unsicher, sanft und ohne Ungeduld.
Sie war in sich, wie Eine hoher Hoffnung,
und dachte nicht des Mannes, der voranging,
und nicht des Weges, der ins Leben aufstieg.
Sie war in sich. Und ihr Gestorbensein
erfüllte sie wie Fülle.
Wie eine Frucht von Süßigkeit und Dunkel,
so war sie voll von ihrem großen Tode,
der also neu war, daß sie nichts begriff.

Sie war in einem neuen Mädchentum
und unberührbar; ihr Geschlecht war zu
wie eine junge Blume gegen Abend,
und ihre Hände waren der Vermählung
so sehr entwöhnt, daß selbst des leichten Gottes
unendlich leise, leitende Berührung
sie kränkte wie zu sehr Vertraulichkeit.

Sie war schon nicht mehr diese blonde Frau,
die in des Dichters Liedern manchmal anklang,
nicht mehr des breiten Bettes Duft und Eiland
und jenes Mannes Eigentum nicht mehr.

Sie war schon aufgelöst wie langes Haar
und hingegeben wie gefallner Regen
und ausgeteilt wie hundertfacher Vorrat.

Sie war schon Wurzel.

Und als plötzlich jäh
der Gott sie anhielt und mit Schmerz im Ausruf
die Worte sprach: Er hat sich umgewendet−,
begriff sie nichts und sagte leise: *Wer?*

meek, unsure, and without any eagerness.
She was within herself, like a woman expecting,
and did not think of the man who went ahead,
nor of the path that mounted up toward life.
She was within herself. And being dead
filled her like an abundance.
Like a fruit full of sweetness and darkness
she was filled with her great death, so new
to her that she could not comprehend it.

She found herself in a new maidenhood,
and untouchable; her sex was shut up
like a young bloom against the evening,
her hands had been weaned from marriage,
so much so that even that airy god's
infinitely soft and leading touch
afflicted her like too much intimacy.

She was no longer this blond-haired wife
who often rang out in the poet's song,
no more the broad marriage bed's scent
and island, and that man's chattel no more.

She had already been loosed like long hair
and given back like the fallen rain,
shared out like a hundredfold hoard.

She was already root.

And when suddenly and abruptly
the god paused with a sorrowful cry
and spoke these words: *He has turned round to look,*
she did not understand and said softly: *Who?*

Fern aber, dunkel vor dem klaren Ausgang,
stand irgend jemand, dessen Angesicht
nicht zu erkennen war. Er stand und sah,
wie auf dem Streifen eines Wiesenpfades
mit trauervollem Blick der Gott der Botschaft
sich schweigend wandte, der Gestalt zu folgen,
die schon zurückging dieses selben Weges,
den Schritt beschränkt von langen Leichenbändern,
unsicher, sanft und ohne Ungeduld.

But far away, dark before the bright hell-gate,
there posed some creature whose countenance
could not be recognized. He stood and saw
how on the thin slash of the meadow path
the messenger god with mournful aspect
turned quietly to follow the woman's figure,
already heading back the same way,
her gait confined by long winding sheets,
meek, unsure, and without any eagerness.

The impatient, somewhat naive Orpheus whom we encounter here is quite different from the mythic poet of the *Sonnets to Orpheus,* that demigod who creates the world in song. But it is Eurydice who comes across as the heroine of the poem—she has already conquered the twin worlds of life and death by her very meekness, and she is "no more the broad marriage bed's scent / and island, and that man's chattel no more."

Alkestis

Da plötzlich war der Bote unter ihnen,
hineingeworfen in das Überkochen
des Hochzeitsmahles wie ein neuer Zusatz.
Sie fühlten nicht, die Trinkenden, des Gottes
heimlichen Eintritt, welcher seine Gottheit
so an sich hielt wie einen nassen Mantel
und ihrer einer schien, der oder jener,
wie er so durchging. Aber plötzlich sah
mitten im Sprechen einer von den Gästen
den jungen Hausherrn oben an dem Tische
wie in die Höh gerissen, nicht mehr liegend,
und überall und mit dem ganzen Wesen
ein Fremdes spiegelnd, das ihn furchtbar ansprach.
Und gleich darauf, als klärte sich die Mischung,
war Stille; nur mit einem Satz am Boden
von trübem Lärm und einem Niederschlag
fallenden Lallens, schon verdorben riechend
nach dumpfem umgestandenen Gelächter.
Und da erkannten sie den schlanken Gott,
und wie er dastand, innerlich voll Sendung
und unerbittlich, –wußten sie es beinah.
Und doch, als es gesagt war, war es mehr
als alles Wissen, gar nicht zu begreifen.
Admet muß sterben. Wann? In dieser Stunde.

Der aber brach die Schale seines Schreckens
in Stücken ab und streckte seine Hände
heraus aus ihr, um mit dem Gott zu handeln.
Um Jahre, um ein einzig Jahr noch Jugend,
um Monate, um Wochen, um paar Tage,

Alcestis

Then suddenly the messenger was there
among them, tossed like some new ingredient
into the roiling broth of the wedding feast.
The drinkers felt nothing of the god's stealthy
entrance, for he held his godhood close,
like a soaking mantle that clung to him,
and seemed one of them, this one or that,
as he went through the crowd. But suddenly,
in the midst of conversation, one of the guests
saw the young lord at the head of the table,
as if wrenched upright, no longer reclining,
and every atom of his being reflected
a strange presence that addressed him dreadfully.
And in that moment, as in a clearing mixture,
was stillness; only the settlings of clouded din
on the floor, a sediment of falling prattle
already reeking with the decomposition
of the onlookers' stifled, stagnant laughter.
And then they recognized the slender god,
and how he stood there, filled with his mission
and implacable–they all but knew it.
And yet, when actually said, it was more
than all knowledge and incomprehensible.
Admetus must die. When? This very hour.

He, however, broke the shell of his fear
into shards and stretched out both his hands
before him in order to bargain with the god.
Bargaining for years, a year more of youth,
for months, for weeks, a couple of days, ah,

ach, Tage nicht, um Nächte, nur um Eine,
um Eine Nacht, um diese nur: um die.
Der Gott verneinte, und da schrie er auf
und schrie's hinaus und hielt es nicht und schrie
wie seine Mutter aufschrie beim Gebären.

Und die trat zu ihm, eine alte Frau,
und auch der Vater kam, der alte Vater,
und beide standen, alt, veraltet, ratlos,
beim Schreienden, der plötzlich, wie noch nie
so nah, sie ansah, abbrach, schluckte, sagte:
Vater,
liegt dir denn viel daran an diesem Rest,
an diesem Satz, der dich beim Schlingen hindert?
Geh, gieß ihn weg. Und du, du alte Frau,
Matrone,
was tust du denn noch hier: du hast geboren.
Und beide hielt er sie wie Opfertiere
in Einem Griff. Auf einmal ließ er los
und stieß die Alten fort, voll Einfall, strahlend
und atemholend, rufend: Kreon, Kreon!
Und nichts als das; und nichts als diesen Namen.
Aber in seinem Antlitz stand das Andere,
das er nicht sagte, namenlos erwartend,
wie ers dem jungen Freunde, dem Geliebten,
erglühend hinhielt übern wirren Tisch.
Die Alten (stand da), siehst du, sind kein Loskauf,
sie sind verbraucht und schlecht und beinah wertlos,
du aber, du, in deiner ganzen Schönheit—

Da aber sah er seinen Freund nicht mehr.
Er blieb zurück, und das, was kam, war *sie,*
ein wenig kleiner fast als er sie kannte
und leicht und traurig in dem bleichen Brautkleid.
Die andern alle sind nur ihre Gasse,

not days, but nights, only one more night,
for a single night, only this, for this.
The god denied him, and at that he cried out
and let his cry ring, and held nothing back,
and screamed as his mother had at his birth.

And she came to him then, an old woman,
and the father as well, the old patriarch,
and both stood there, ancient, timeworn, helpless,
beside the screaming one who suddenly, as if
never so near, saw them, paused, swallowed, said:
Father,
do you value so much this remainder of life,
these dregs that choke your throat like a noose?
Go and pour them away. And you, old woman,
Matron,
why are you still here—you have given birth.
And he grasped them both in a single grip
like sacrificial beasts. Then he let go
and shoved them away—full of inspiration,
beaming and breathless he cried: Creon, Creon!
And nothing else, and nothing but this one name.
But in his expression there was something else
that remained unsaid, namelessly expectant
as he offered it brightly to the young friend
who sat across the disordered table.
The old, it said, are no redemption, you see,
they are used up, unsteady, almost worthless,
you, however, you in your wholesome beauty—

But then, suddenly, he saw his friend no more.
He shrunk back, and the one who came was *she,*
perhaps a bit smaller than the woman he knew,
and slight and doleful in the pale bridal clothes.
The other guests made a path for her,

durch die sie kommt und kommt–: (gleich wird sie da sein
in seinen Armen, die sich schmerzhaft auftun).

Doch wie er wartet, spricht sie; nicht zu ihm.
Sie spricht zum Gotte, und der Gott vernimmt sie,
und alle hörens gleichsam erst im Gotte:

Ersatz kann keiner für ihn sein. Ich *bins*.
Ich bin Ersatz. Denn keiner ist zu Ende
wie ich es bin. Was bleibt mir denn von dem
was ich hier war? Das *ists* ja, daß ich sterbe.
Hat sie dirs nicht gesagt, da sie dirs auftrug,
daß jenes Lager, das da drinnen wartet,
zur Unterwelt gehört? Ich nahm ja Abschied.
Abschied über Abschied.
Kein Sterbender nimmt mehr davon. Ich ging ja,
damit das Alles, unter Dem begraben
der jetzt mein Gatte ist, zergeht, sich auflöst–.
So führ mich hin: ich sterbe ja für ihn.

Und wie der Wind auf hoher See, der umspringt,
so trat der Gott fast wie zu einer Toten
und war auf einmal weit von ihrem Gatten,
dem er, versteckt in einem kleinen Zeichen,
die hundert Leben dieser Erde zuwarf.
Der stürzte taumelnd zu den beiden hin
und griff nach ihnen wie im Traum. Sie gingen
schon auf den Eingang zu, in dem die Frauen
verweint sich drängten. Aber einmal sah
er noch des Mädchens Antlitz, das sich wandte
mit einem Lächeln, hell wie eine Hoffnung,
die beinah ein Versprechen war: erwachsen
zurückzukommen aus dem tiefen Tode
zu ihm, dem Lebenden–

and through them she came—shortly she would
be in his arms, which achingly spread toward her.

Yet as he waited she spoke, though not to him.
She spoke to the god, and the god attends her
and all hear this more or less as if within the god:

No one else can be his surrogate but I.
It is I, for no one is as finished
as I am. What remains for me from what
I once was? Only that I perish, so it must be.
Did she not mention when she sent you here
that the marriage bed, that which waits within,
is of the underworld? I have taken my leave.
Parting upon parting.
No dying one ever took more. I have gone,
so that all that is buried under him,
who is now my spouse, melts, dissolves itself.
So lead me away—I die now for him.

And like the breeze that turns the high seas,
so stepped the god, almost as to one who is dead,
and was suddenly distant from her husband,
to whom, concealed in a small offhand gesture,
the hundred life spans of this earth he tossed.
And that one launched himself at the pair,
grasping as if at a dream. They already
had stepped to the doorway, and the women
crowded there and wept. But he saw once more
the maiden's face, turning itself to him
with a smile, shining as bright as a hope
that was almost a promise, mature now,
as if newly returned from deep death
back to him, the living one.

Da schlug er jäh
die Hände vors Gesicht, wie er so kniete,
um nichts zu sehen mehr nach diesem Lächeln.

Then he abruptly slammed his hands
before his face as he knelt, that he might
not see anything more after that smile.

Probably written on Capri, this poem continues the theme of the Roman suite, and its heroine, Alcestis, is the strongest yet. Her contempt for her cowardly husband, Admetus, is barely concealed as she lays her life down for him. In the end she walks off with a god while Admetus cringes on the ground, disgraced before his people.

Geburt der Venus

An diesem Morgen nach der Nacht, die bang
vergangen war mit Rufen, Unruh, Aufruhr, –
brach alles Meer noch einmal auf und schrie.
Und als der Schrei sich langsam wieder schloß
und von der Himmel blassem Tag und Anfang
herabfiel in der stummen Fische Abgrund –:
gebar das Meer.

Von erster Sonne schimmerte der Haarschaum
der weiten Wogenscham, an deren Rand
das Mädchen aufstand, weiß, verwirrt und feucht.
So wie ein junges grünes Blatt sich rührt,
sich reckt und Eingerolltes langsam aufschlägt,
entfaltete ihr Leib sich in die Kühle
hinein und in den unberührten Frühwind.

Wie Monde stiegen klar die Kniee auf
und tauchten in der Schenkel Wolkenränder;
der Waden schmaler Schatten wich zurück,
die Füße spannten sich und wurden licht,
und die Gelenke lebten wie die Kehlen
von Trinkenden.

Und in dem Kelch des Beckens lag der Leib
wie eine junge Frucht in eines Kindes Hand.
In seines Nabels engem Becher war
das ganze Dunkel dieses hellen Lebens.
Darunter hob sich licht die kleine Welle
und floß beständig über nach den Lenden,
wo dann und wann ein stilles Rieseln war.

Birth of Venus

On this morning, after night had frightfully
flown past with shouts, turbulence, commotion,
the wide sea once more sprang open and screamed.
And as the scream slowly faded away
and again from heaven's pale dawn and day
sank into the silent abyss of the fishes,
the sea gave birth.

The foaming hair of the wide wave-womb gleamed
with the first rays of sun, and on its verge
arose the girl–white, damp, and bewildered.
As a young, green leaf stirs itself, stretches,
and slowly unfurls its involuted form,
she unfolded her body into the coolness,
into the inviolate morning breeze.

The knees rose full of light, like ascendant moons,
and merged into the cloud rims of the thighs;
the slim shadows of the calves retreated,
the feet flexed themselves and grew radiant,
and the joints quickened with life, like throats
that were drinking.

And in the shell of the pelvis lay the belly
like a young fruit in the hand of a child.
Deep in the narrow chalice of the navel
hid the only darkness of this bright life.
The slight wave heaved lightly beneath her
and steadily lapped at the beach of her loins,
where now and again came a quiet ripple.

Durchschienen aber und noch ohne Schatten,
wie ein Bestand von Birken im April,
warm, leer und unverborgen, lag die Scham.

Jetzt stand der Schultern rege Waage schon
im Gleichgewichte auf dem graden Körper,
der aus dem Becken wie ein Springbrunn aufstieg
und zögernd in den langen Armen abfiel
und rascher in dem vollen Fall des Haars.

Dann ging sehr langsam das Gesicht vorbei:
aus dem verkürzten Dunkel seiner Neigung
in klares, waagrechtes Erhobensein.
Und hinter ihm verschloß sich steil das Kinn.

Jetzt, da der Hals gestreckt war wie ein Strahl
und wie ein Blumenstiel, darin der Saft steigt,
streckten sich auch die Arme aus wie Hälse
von Schwänen, wenn sie nach dem Ufer suchen.

Dann kam in dieses Leibes dunkle Frühe
wie Morgenwind der erste Atemzug.
Im zartesten Geäst der Aderbäume
entstand ein Flüstern, und das Blut begann
zu rauschen über seinen tiefen Stellen.
Und dieser Wind wuchs an: nun warf er sich
mit allem Atem in die neuen Brüste
und füllte sie und drückte sich in sie, –
daß sie wie Segel, von der Ferne voll,
das leichte Mädchen nach dem Strande drängten.

.

But translucent and still unshadowed,
like a copse of birches in the April light,
warm, empty and evident lay the vagina.

Now the agile scale of the shoulders stood
already balanced on the well-made frame,
which rose from the pelvis like a wellspring
and hesitantly plunged into long arms,
and more swiftly into full, cascading hair.

Then the face went by very languidly:
out of the shortened shadow of its angle
into a bright, horizontal uplifting.
And then, closing itself steeply, the chin.

Now, as the neck lengthened like a sunbeam
and like a flower stem in which sap rises,
the arms also stretched themselves, like the necks
of swans when they come seeking riverbanks.

Then into this body's dark precocity blew
the morning wind like the first gasp of breath.
From the most tender branches of the vein trees
a whispering sound emerged, and the blood
began to surge through its deep locations.
And this wind swelled: now it flung itself
with all its breath into the new-made breasts
and forced itself into them, filling them
so that, like sails full of distance, it thrust
the airy maiden to the edge of the shore.

So landete die Göttin.

Hinter ihr,
die rasch dahinschritt durch die jungen Ufer,
erhoben sich den ganzen Vormittag
die Blumen und die Halme, warm, verwirrt,
wie aus Umarmung. Und sie ging und lief.

Am Mittag aber, in der schwersten Stunde,
hob sich das Meer noch einmal auf und warf
einen Delphin an jene selbe Stelle.
Tot, rot und offen.

So landed the goddess.

Behind her,
as she quickly strode over the young coastline,
sprang up all the flowers and the foliage
of the forenoon, warm and disoriented
as if from her embrace. And she walked and ran.

But at noon, in the most ponderous hour,
the sea heaved itself once more and cast up
a dolphin upon that very same place.
Dead, red, and open.

This is the last of the Roman suite of 1904 and continues its theme with the birth
of a goddess. But where Botticelli's painting of the birth of Venus gives us only
the serene magnificence of the sea-nativity, Rilke shows us the bloody afterbirth
as it is cast up on the beach.

Die Rosenschale

Zornige sahst du flackern, sahst zwei Knaben
zu einem Etwas sich zusammenballen,
das Haß war und sich auf der Erde wälzte
wie ein von Bienen überfallnes Tier;
Schauspieler, aufgetürmte Übertreiber,
rasende Pferde, die zusammenbrachen,
den Blick wegwerfend, bläkend das Gebiß
als schälte sich der Schädel aus dem Maule.

Nun aber weißt du, wie sich das vergißt:
denn vor dir steht die volle Rosenschale,
die unvergeßlich ist und angefüllt
mit jenem Äußersten von Sein und Neigen,
Hinhalten, Niemals-Gebenkönnen, Dastehn,
das unser sein mag: Äußerstes auch uns.

Lautloses Leben, Aufgehn ohne Ende,
Raum-brauchen ohne Raum von jenem Raum
zu nehmen, den die Dinge rings verringern,
fast nicht Umrissen-sein wie Ausgespartes
und lauter Inneres, viel seltsam Zartes
und Sich-bescheinendes–bis an den Rand:
ist irgend etwas uns bekannt wie dies?

Und dann wie dies: daß ein Gefühl entsteht,
weil Blütenblätter Blütenblätter rühren?
Und dies: daß eins sich aufschlägt wie ein Lid,
und drunter liegen lauter Augenlider,
geschlossene, als ob sie, zehnfach schlafend,
zu dämpfen hätten eines Innern Sehkraft.

The Bowl of Roses

You saw it flare up in anger, saw two boys
balled up together into a single thing
named Hatred, struggling in the dirt
like an animal crazed and beset by bees–
these two actors of towering excess,
like frenzied horses collapsing in the traces,
their glances flung away, their teeth bared
as if lips were peeled back from skulls.

But now you know how you have forgotten,
for before you lies the brimming bowl of roses,
so unforgettable and so replenished
with that extreme of being, of tending,
of presence, of offering and holding back,
that might be ours, our extreme as well.

Soundless existence, endlessly opening,
using space without taking up any room
since it lessens the things surrounding it,
almost without outline, as if recessed
to sheer inwardness, a strange tenderness
and self-illumination to its outer rim:
is there anything as familiar as this to us?

And then like this: that a feeling emerges
because flower petals touch flower petals?
And this: that one opens up like a lid,
and there beneath it lie only eyelids,
closed, as if they were asleep ten times over,
as if they had to absorb some inner vision.

Und dies vor allem: daß durch diese Blätter
das Licht hindurch muß. Aus den tausend Himmeln
filtern sie langsam jenen Tropfen Dunkel,
in dessen Feuerschein das wirre Bündel
der Staubgefäße sich erregt und aufbäumt.

Und die Bewegung in den Rosen, sieh:
Gebärden von so kleinem Ausschlagswinkel,
daß sie unsichtbar blieben, liefen ihre
Strahlen nicht auseinander in das Weltall.

Sieh jene weiße, die sich selig aufschlug
und dasteht in den großen offnen Blättern
wie eine Venus aufrecht in der Muschel;
und die errötende, die wie verwirrt
nach einer kühlen sich hinüberwendet,
und wie die kühle fühllos sich zurückzieht,
und wie die kalte steht, in sich gehüllt,
unter den offenen, die alles abtun.
Und *was* sie abtun, wie das leicht und schwer,
wie es ein Mantel, eine Last, ein Flügel
und eine Maske sein kann, je nach dem,
und *wie* sie's abtun: wie vor dem Geliebten.

Was können sie nicht sein: war jene gelbe,
die hohl und offen daliegt, nicht die Schale
von einer Frucht, darin dasselbe Gelb,
gesammelter, orangeröter, Saft war?
Und wars für diese schon zu viel, das Aufgehn,
weil an der Luft ihr namenloses Rosa
den bittern Nachgeschmack des Lila annahm?
Und die batistene, ist sie kein Kleid,
in dem noch zart und atemwarm das Hemd steckt,
mit dem zugleich es abgeworfen wurde

And above all this: that through these petals
the light must penetrate. Out of the thousand
heavens they slowly refine that seep of darkness
from which the glowing flame of the tangled
stamens arouses itself and rears up.

And the movement in the roses, look:
gestures of such a minute deflection
that they might remain hidden did their beams
not radiate into the universe.

Look at that white one that blessedly cracks
open and slouches with large, gaping petals
like Venus standing in the scallop shell;
and the one that blushes, as if bewildered,
turning and peering across to one who is cool,
and how the cool one draws back without feeling,
and how that cold thing stands, wrapped in itself,
among the open ones that strip off everything.
And what they take off, how light or heavy;
how it can be like a cloak, a load, a wing,
and a mask, like every one of those things;
and how they take it off–as if before a lover.

What could they not become; was that yellow one,
which lies there cupped and open, not the rind
of some fruit, within which that same yellow
was the juice, concentrated to a carmine orange?
And was fruiting too much for this one here,
when in the open air its anonymous pink
assumed the bitter aftertaste of lilac?
And that one of batiste, is it not a dress
in which the slip clings, filmy and breath-warm,
both of them cast off in the morning shadows

im Morgenschatten an dem alten Waldbad?
Und diese hier, opalnes Porzellan,
zerbrechlich, eine flache Chinatasse
und angefüllt mit kleinen hellen Faltern, –
und jene da, die nichts enthält als sich.

Und sind nicht alle so, nur sich enthaltend,
wenn Sich-enthalten heißt: die Welt da draußen
und Wind und Regen und Geduld des Frühlings
und Schuld und Unruh und vermummtes Schicksal
und Dunkelheit der abendlichen Erde
bis auf der Wolken Wandel, Flucht und Anflug,
bis auf den vagen Einfluß ferner Sterne
in eine Hand voll Innres zu verwandeln.

Nun liegt es sorglos in den offnen Rosen.

on the bank of the ancient sylvan pool?
And this one here, iridescent porcelain,
so fragile, this shallow China teacup,
and filled with small, brilliant butterflies,
and that one there, containing nothing but itself.

And are they not all so, holding just themselves,
if by self-containment we mean the changing
of the outer world—of wind and rain, the patience
of Spring, of guilt and unrest and hooded Fate
and the creeping shadow of the world's evening,
even to the approach and flight of changing clouds
and the vague influence of distant stars—
into a hand full of inwardness.

Now it lies unworried in the open roses.

Rilke, having been given a rose by Mary Gneisenau, wrote to her in September 1906: "The equilibrium that appears in a rose like that one is indescribably beautiful, a rose that has slowed down... the rhythm of its maturity until it becomes transience, evanescence, a series of slowly cadent tones." A lot of the raw material of this poem can be found in the rest of that substantial letter. But the relationship of Rilke and roses deserves a book of its own.

A mon grand Ami Auguste Rodin

Archaïscher Torso Apollos

Wir kannten nicht sein unerhörtes Haupt,   A
darin die Augenäpfel reiften. Aber   B
sein Torso glüht noch wie ein Kandelaber,   B
in dem sein Schauen, nur zurückgeschraubt,   A

sich hält und glänzt. Sonst könnte nicht der Bug   C
der Brust dich blenden, und im leisen Drehen   D
der Lenden könnte nicht ein Lächeln gehen   D
zu jener Mitte, die die Zeugung trug.   C

Sonst stünde dieser Stein entstellt und kurz   E
unter der Schultern durchsichtigem Sturz   E
und flimmerte nicht so wie Raubtierfelle;   F

und bräche nicht aus allen seinen Rändern   G
aus wie ein Stern: denn da ist keine Stelle,   F
die dich nicht sieht. Du mußt dein Leben ändern. G

Archaic Torso of Apollo

We could not ever know his wondrous head,
with eyes like apples that are ripening.
But the lamp of his torso is still glowing,
although it is turned down low, to spread

his glance, which abides and glimmers within.
Else the curve of the breast could not dazzle you,
nor, in turning, could a smile play through
those loins to the center of procreation.

Else this stone would seem stunted and defiled
and could not shimmer so, like a wild
beast's fur beneath the shoulder's sheer surface,

and it would not burst from its bounds, so rife
with light and star-like, for there is no place
that does not see you. You must change your life.

As in the first volume of *New Poems,* Rilke begins the second volume with a dedi-
cation to Apollo, god of poetry. Note that this is not the god of Nietzsche's Apol-
lonian-Dionysian distinction, but an earlier, darker Apollo whose skin is "like
a wild / beast's fur beneath the shoulder's sheer surface." Like Homer's Apollo
this god is just as prone to spread havoc as to inspire the human spirit when he
brings the life-changing moment. He serves almost the same purpose as the
Rilkean angel who must break one out of one's mold.

Kretische Artemis

Wind der Vorgebirge: war nicht ihre   A
Stirne wie ein lichter Gegenstand?   B
Glatter Gegenwind der leichten Tiere,   A
formtest du sie: ihr Gewand   B

bildend an die unbewußten Brüste   C
wie ein wechselvolles Vorgefühl?   D
Während sie, als ob sie alles wüßte,   C
auf das Fernste zu, geschürzt und kühl,   D

stürmte mit den Nymphen und den Hunden,   E
ihren Bogen probend, eingebunden   E
in den harten hohen Gurt;   F

manchmal nur aus fremden Siedelungen   G
angerufen und erzürnt bezwungen   G
von dem Schreien um Geburt.   F

Cretan Artemis

Wind of the foothills, were not her features
like some burning, luminescent thing?
Sleek headwind of the effortless creatures,
did you create her, her clothes conforming

to the bosom's unconscious contour
like some expectation of constant change?
While she, as if she were the all-knower—
cool, kilted, eyes fixed on the farthest range—

stormed beside the nymph and coursing hound,
the strong leather cinch riding high around
her waist as she tested her aim;

many a time summoned by only
the far-flung colony, then wrathfully
overpowered by the birthing scream.

The Cretan goddess, Eileithyia, was named by Homer "the goddess of birth
pangs," and by late Hellenistic times she was associated with Artemis in the
Orphic hymns—thus Cretan Artemis. However ironic, the association of the
divine huntress and patroness of virginity with childbirth is beautifully framed,
the drawn bow evoking the spreading pelvis that precedes the screams of the
laboring mother. This poem seems to play the same role as the Sapphic poems
of the first volume—an invocation to Artemis following the one to her brother,
Apollo.

Leda

Als ihn der Gott in seiner Not betrat,	A
erschrak er fast, den Schwan so schön zu finden;	B
er ließ sich ganz verwirrt in ihm verschwinden.	B
Schon aber trug ihn sein Betrug zur Tat,	A
bevor er noch des unerprobten Seins	C
Gefühle prüfte. Und die Aufgetane	D
erkannte schon den Kommenden im Schwane	D
und wußte schon: er bat um Eins,	C
das sie, verwirrt in ihrem Widerstand,	E
nicht mehr verbergen konnte. Er kam nieder	F
und halsend durch die immer schwächre Hand	E
ließ sich der Gott in die Geliebte los.	G
Dann erst empfand er glücklich sein Gefieder	F
und wurde wirklich Schwan in ihrem Schooß.	G

Leda

When the god in his need entered the swan,
almost frightened to find it so beautiful,
bewildered, he fused with the animal.
But soon enough he put on deception,

even before probing that untried being
and knowing its feelings. And the woman,
wide open, knew who was coming in the swan,
and understood that he required one thing,

which she, baffled in resisting his demand,
could no more deny him. The god alighted,
and necking his way through the slackening hand

released himself into the beloved one.
Only then in his feathers was he delighted,
and in her lap became an actual swan.

Wolfgang Leppmann, in his biography of the poet, questions if it is possible
"to extract anything new" from such a timeworn subject as Leda and the Swan.
He answers his own question affirmatively. In the throes of lust Zeus becomes a
ravishing animal, but once satisfied becomes a different kind of animal, a sort
of downy pet. Unlike in the Yeats poem of the same subject, here the god is ulti-
mately mastered by Leda and finally becomes the thing he had only pretended
to be.

Delphine

Jene Wirklichen, die ihrem Gleichen   A
überall zu wachsen und zu wohnen   B
gaben, fühlten an verwandten Zeichen   A
Gleiche in den aufgelösten Reichen,   A
die der Gott, mit triefenden Tritonen,   B
überströmt bisweilen übersteigt;   C
denn da hatte sich das Tier gezeigt: C
anders als die stumme, stumpfgemute   D
Zucht der Fische, Blut von ihrem Blute   D
und von fern dem Menschlichen geneigt.   C

Eine Schar kam, die sich überschlug,   E
froh, als fühlte sie die Fluten glänzend: F
Warme, Zugetane, deren Zug   E
wie mit Zuversicht die Fahrt bekränzend,   F
leichtgebunden um den runden Bug   E
wie um einer Vase Rumpf und Rundung,   G
selig, sorglos, sicher vor Verwundung,   G
aufgerichtet, hingerissen, rauschend   H
und im Tauchen mit den Wellen tauschend   H
die Trireme heiter weitertrug.   E

Und der Schiffer nahm den neugewährten   I
Freund in seine einsame Gefahr   J

Dolphins

Those truth seekers who allowed that ones
like them might everywhere grow and dwell,
sensed in certain signs their close relations
in the watery realms, under those inundations
which the god and his dripping Tritons swell
above sometimes, for it is in that sphere
that these sea-born creatures first appear,
different from other denizens of the flood—
the mute, dull-witted fishes—blood of their blood,
and drawn to the race of mankind from afar.

A band of them came, leaping and flipping,
as if they gladly felt the gleam of the sea:
warm ones, ardent ones, the whole pod capering
as if with confidence, crown of the journey
at the ship's rounded bow, loosely embracing
it as if circling the wine bowl's broad belly,
secure from harm, blessed and carefree,
breaching, rapturous, surging and brave,
and trading plunges with each skimming wave
they bore the trireme blithely along.

And the sailor took this new-befriended one
into his life of solitary danger

und ersann für ihn, für den Gefährten,   I
dankbar eine Welt und hielt für wahr,   J
daß er Töne liebte, Götter, Gärten   I
und das tiefe, stille Sternenjahr.   J

and thankfully devised for this companion
a world, and held as true that this sea ranger
loved music, the gods, the bliss of the garden,
and the deep and silent stellar year.

The dolphins' "circling the wine bowl's broad belly" may have been remembered from an ancient cup by Exekias in Munich, which portrays Dionysius in a ship with a grape-garlanded mast. The dolphins sport around the ship's bow "loosely embracing" it. Or the poem might have been inspired by a Samian cup in Berlin, which shows half-human dolphins: "blood of their blood, / and drawn to the race of mankind from afar." This last scene invokes an episode from Ovid in which Bacchus avenges himself on the pirates who have captured him by turning them all into dolphins.

Die Insel der Sirenen

Wenn er denen, die ihm gastlich waren,	A
spät, nach ihrem Tage noch, da sie	B
fragten nach den Fahrten und Gefahren,	A
still berichtete: er wußte nie,	B
wie sie schrecken und mit welchem jähen	C
Wort sie wenden, daß sie so wie er	D
in dem blau gestillten Inselmeer	D
die Vergoldung jener Inseln sähen,	C
deren Anblick macht, daß die Gefahr	E
umschlägt; denn nun ist sie nicht im Tosen	F
und im Wüten, wo sie immer war.	E
Lautlos kommt sie über die Matrosen,	F
welche wissen, daß es dort auf jenen	G
goldnen Inseln manchmal singt–,	H
und sich blindlings in die Ruder lehnen,	G
wie umringt	H
von der Stille, die die ganze Weite	I
in sich hat und an die Ohren weht,	J
so als wäre ihre andre Seite	I
der Gesang, dem keiner widersteht.	J

In a letter to Clara on February 22, 1907, Rilke writes from Italy about the Islands of the Sirens, which he claims to have sighted from the top of Monte Solaro. The three rocks, lying in the Gulf of Salerno, looked "as if they had once been covered in gold leaf." He reports that the sea had appeared very ancient to

The Isle of the Sirens

When among his hosts he would linger,
long past day and late into night,
who asked about the voyage and its danger,
quietly he told them, for he knew not quite

how to seize them or to use his wiles
and sudden words to sway, so that like him
they might gaze at the silent, blue sea rim
and catch the sun's abrupt gilding of those isles

that seem to rout peril once they are seen—
for now it was not in the ocean's roar,
nor in its raging, where it always has been:
silently it came upon the sailor,

who knew that there upon that very shore,
the golden island sometimes sings out,
and blindly he leaned upon his oar,
as if hemmed about

by the silence, which holds the vast expanse
and blows like a tempest upon the ears,
as if the other side of its countenance
were the song none may resist once one hears.

him, as if "Odysseus might come sailing by at any moment." The Greek Sirens,
renamed Rhinemaidens, loom large in German mythology and were the subject
of a canonical poem by Heinrich Heine, "Die Lorelei."

Klage um Antinous

Keiner begriff mir von euch den bithynischen Knaben   A
(daß ihr den Strom anfaßtet und von ihm hübt...).   B
Ich verwöhnte ihn zwar. Und dennoch: wir haben   A
ihn nur mit Schwere erfüllt und für immer getrübt.   B

Wer vermag denn zu lieben? Wer kann es? – Noch keiner.   C
Und so hab ich unendliches Weh getan –.   D
Nun ist er am Nil der stillenden Götter einer,   C
und ich weiß kaum welcher und kann ihm nicht nahn.   D

Und ihr warfet ihn noch, Wahnsinnige, bis in die Sterne,   E
damit ich euch rufe und dränge: meint ihr den?   F
Was ist er nicht einfach ein Toter. Er wäre es gerne.   E
Und vielleicht wäre ihm nichts geschehn.   F

Lament for Antinous

None of you grasped what I saw in the Bithynian lad
(or you might seize the flood and lift it away from him...).
True, I indulged him. Nevertheless, we have clad
him in heavy garments and sunk him in waters dim.

Who then is able to love? Who? There are still none.
And thus have I brought unending pain to bear.
Now he rests with the peaceful Nile gods, this one,
and I know not which and cannot ever come near.

And you madmen, you would hurl him up to some star;
is it so I might press you: is that the one you mean?
Why is he not simply dead? That would be better by far.
Perhaps then this tragedy would never have been.

This poem begins a series of three that lament the death of a lover. The grief over Antinous and Jonathan tends much closer to despair than the feelings expressed in the poem of heterosexual love that these two pieces bracket. Antinous was the lover of the emperor Hadrian, who is the presumed speaker here. It is not clear from historical records whether his death was a case of accident, suicide, or murder, but we do know that he was unpopular with the emperor's staff and that he drowned in the Nile.

Der Tod der Geliebten

Er wußte nur vom Tod was alle wissen: A
daß er uns nimmt und in das Stumme stößt.   B
Als aber sie, nicht von ihm fortgerissen,   A
nein, leis aus seinen Augen ausgelöst,   B

hinüberglitt zu unbekannten Schatten,   C
und als er fühlte, daß sie drüben nun   D
wie einen Mond ihr Mädchenlächeln hatten   C
und ihre Weise wohlzutun: D

da wurden ihm die Toten so bekannt,   E
als wäre er durch sie mit einem jeden   F
ganz nah verwandt; er ließ die andern reden   F

und glaubte nicht und nannte jenes Land   E
das gutgelegene, das immersüße—.   G
Und tastete es ab für ihre Füße.   G

The Death of the Beloved

Of death he knew only what all understand:
that it strikes us dumb and snatches us hence.
But as she, not ripped away from his hand,
no, but released so softly from his glance,

crossed to that place of unknown shadow,
and as he sensed that those on the other side
possessed the moon of her maiden smile now
and felt its ways and were gratified,

then the dead wore a familiar face,
so he felt as if related through her
to them all; he let those others chatter

but did not heed them, and named that place
a land well located, a country most sweet.
And searched its many pathways for her feet.

Much of Rilke's attitude toward death is inherent in this small poem. As he
expressed it in a letter to Claire Goll, October 22, 1923: "I think that you are first
expected to suffer death in the death of someone who is infinitely close to you...
now has come the time that you are finally able to uncover that pure secret... not
of life, but of death... since it has become available to you at the cost of some-
thing beloved, and you have become related to it as part of life."

Klage um Jonathan

Ach sind auch Könige nicht von Bestand	A
und dürfen hingehn wie gemeine Dinge,	B
obwohl ihr Druck wie der der Siegelringe	B
sich widerbildet in das weiche Land.	A
Wie aber konntest du, so angefangen	C
mit deines Herzens Initial,	D
aufhören plötzlich: Wärme meiner Wangen.	C
O daß dich einer noch einmal	D
erzeugte, wenn sein Samen in ihm glänzt.	X
Irgend ein Fremder sollte dich zerstören,	E
und der dir innig war, ist nichts dabei	F
und muß sich halten und die Botschaft hören;	E
wie wunde Tiere auf den Lagern löhren,	E
möcht ich mich legen mit Geschrei:	F
denn da und da, an meinen scheusten Orten,	G
bist du mir ausgerissen wie das Haar,	H
das in den Achselhöhlen wachst und dorten,	G
wo ich ein Spiel für Frauen war,	H
bevor du meine dort verfitzten Sinne	I
aufsträhntest wie man einen Knaul entflicht;	J
da sah ich auf und wurde deiner inne:–	I
Jetzt aber gehst du mir aus dem Gesicht.	J

Here continues the saga of David begun in volume one of these poems. After his slaying of the Philistine champion Goliath, David incurred the jealousy of King Saul, who would have had him killed. Saul's son, Jonathan, loved David and warned him of the danger. David mourned Jonathan after he was slain on

Lament for Jonathan

Ah, but not even kings are everlasting
and must pass away like things commonplace,
although their impression, like a signet ring,
leaves its image on the land's soft surface.

But how could you, whose existence started
with his heart's initial, how could you who
warmed my cheek, have suddenly departed.
Oh that someone again might father you
if only his seed should gleam within him.

That some stranger should commit this outrage,
and he who was your closest could do nothing
and had to rein himself in to hear the message;
like a wounded beast that roars from a cage
I would better calm myself with screaming:

for here and here, in those places most shy,
you are wrenched out of me like hanks of hair
that grow in the armpits, even there, where I
was but a game for the women to share,

before you took my tangled senses, spooling
them as someone untangling a knot might–
I looked up then and became your inner being,
but now you have been taken from my sight.

Mount Gilboa by the Philistines (1 Samuel 31:1–6). But David knew he himself
was to blame for his friend's death, for he had struck a deal with the Philistines
to thwart Saul, and thus: "he who was your closest could do nothing / and had
to rein himself in to hear the message."

Tröstung des Elia

Er hatte das getan und dies, den Bund A
wie jenen Altar wieder aufzubauen, B
zu dem sein weitgeschleudertes Vertrauen B
zurück als Feuer fiel von ferne, und A
hatte er dann nicht Hunderte zerhauen, B
weil sie ihm stanken mit dem Baal im Mund, A
am Bache schlachtend bis ans Abendgrauen, B

das mit dem Regengrau sich groß verband. C
Doch als ihn von der Königin der Bote D
nach solchem Werktag antrat und bedrohte, D
da lief er wie ein Irrer in das Land, C

so lange bis er unterm Ginsterstrauche E
wie weggeworfen aufbrach in Geschrei F
das in der Wüste brüllte: Gott, gebrauche E
mich länger nicht. Ich bin entzwei. F

Doch grade da kam ihn der Engel ätzen G
mit einer Speise, die er tief empfing, H
so daß er lange dann an Weideplätzen G
und Wassern immer zum Gebirge ging, H

zu dem der Herr um seinetwillen kam: I
Im Sturme nicht und nicht im Sich-Zerspalten J
der Erde, der entlang in schweren Falten J
ein leeres Feuer ging, fast wie aus Scham I
über des Ungeheuren ausgeruhtes K

The Consolation of Elijah

He had finished, everything had been done
to rebuild the covenant and that altar,
until, like some fire from afar,
his wide-scattered faith fell down upon stone,
and had he not hacked up hundreds there,
when with Baal in their mouths they fouled the air,
butchering by the stream till gray sundown,

which greatly with the gray rain was allied.
Yet as the queen's message came straightaway,
threatening him for such a bloody workday,
he fled like a madman into the countryside,

until at last among gorse and scrub he hid,
breaking into a clamor, this man cast off,
bellowing in the wastelands: God, bid
me no longer. I am broken in half.

But soon arrived the cauterizing angel,
bringing a food which he deeply received,
so that he wandered long past river and dell
as toward the distant mountains he strived,

to which, for his sake, the Lord at last came:
though not in storm, nor was the earth rent,
but along which in massive folds there went
a hollow fire, almost as if in shame
over the dormant stumbling of the Enormous

Hinstürzen zu dem angekommnen Alten,   J
der ihn im sanften Sausen seines Blutes   K
erschreckt und zugedeckt vernahm.   I

toward the old one as onward he came,
the soft racing of his blood timorous
as he listened with head covered and bent.

The queen here is Jezebel, the Phoenician princess who was the wife of King Ahab of Israel. Jezebel condemned Elijah for slaughtering the priests of Baal on Mount Carmel (1 Kings 19:1–13). Elijah's consolation comes on Mount Horeb where he has fled and where Yahweh finally speaks to him after sending a terrible wind, an earthquake, and a fire.

Saul unter den Propheten

Meinst du denn, daß man sich sinken sieht?   A
Nein, der König schien sich noch erhaben,   B
da er seinen starken Harfenknaben   B
töten wollte bis ins zehnte Glied.   A

Erst da ihn der Geist auf solchen Wegen   C
überfiel und auseinanderriß,   D
sah er sich im Innern ohne Segen,   C
und sein Blut ging in der Finsternis   D
abergläubig dem Gericht entgegen.   C

Wenn sein Mund jetzt troff und prophezeite,   E
war es nur, damit der Flüchtling weit   F
flüchten könne. So war dieses zweite   E
Mal. Doch einst: er hatte prophezeit   F

fast als Kind, als ob ihm jede Ader   G
mündete in einen Mund aus Erz;   H
Alle schritten, doch er schritt gerader.   G
Alle schrieen, doch ihm schrie das Herz.   H

Und nun war er nichts als dieser Haufen   I
umgestürzter Würden, Last auf Last;   J

Saul among the Prophets

Do you suppose one sees his own decline?
No, the king thought himself still great, and had
ordered the death of his mighty harp lad
even unto the tenth member of his line.

Not till the ghost of the road that he went
had fallen on him and ripped him apart
did he look within, finding no sacrament,
and his blood wandered in a dark heart
superstitiously toward judgment.

If his mouth now oozed and prophesied
it was only that the fugitive might flee
from him and for a second time might hide.
Yet once he had the gift of prophecy

almost like a child's, as if his every vein
flowed like a mouth with precious ore;
all strode, but his stride held a straighter line;
all cried out, but he cried from his heart's core.

And now he was nothing but this pile
of overturned grandeur, heap upon heap,

und sein Mund war wie der Mund der Traufen, I

der die Güsse, die zusammenlaufen, I

fallen läßt, eh er sie faßt. J

and his mouth was like that of a gargoyle
which lets the gushing waters merge and spill
but never can hold on to a single drop.

The story of David and Saul is the subject of fully four poems in the two volumes of *New Poems.* Perhaps it is no coincidence that David's relationship to King Saul parallels, in a sense, Rilke's to Rodin. At first David is a prodigy who is mentored by Saul. Later Saul turns on his young protégé and this results not in David's downfall but in his ascendance. But as we see in the poem "Abishag," David cannot escape Saul's fate of decline—for it is the fate of all mortals. The incident in the above poem occurs when the assassins that Saul has sent after David encounter a group of prophets who are singing and playing musical instruments, and these killers are distracted from their mission (1 Samuel 19:18–24).

Samuels Erscheinung vor Saul

Da schrie die Frau zu Endor auf: Ich sehe–   A
Der König packte sie am Arme: Wen?   B
Und da die Starrende beschrieb, noch ehe,   A
da war ihm schon, er hätte selbst gesehn: B

Den, dessen Stimme ihn noch einmal traf: C
Was störst du mich? Ich habe Schlaf.   C
Willst du, weil dir die Himmel fluchen,   D
und weil der Herr sich vor dir schloß und schwieg,   E
in meinem Mund nach einem Siege suchen?   D
Soll ich dir meine Zähne einzeln sagen?   F
Ich habe nichts als sie… Es schwand. Da schrie   X
das Weib, die Hände vors Gesicht geschlagen,   F
als ob sie's sehen müßte: Unterlieg–   E

Und er, der in der Zeit, die ihm gelang,   G
das Volk wie ein Feldzeichen überragte,   H
fiel hin, bevor er noch zu klagen wagte: H
so sicher war sein Untergang.   G

Die aber, die ihn wider Willen schlug,   I
hoffte, daß er sich faßte und vergäße;   J
und als sie hörte, daß er nie mehr äße,   J
ging sie hinaus und schlachtete und buk   I

und brachte ihn dazu, daß er sich setzte;   K
er saß wie einer, der zu viel vergißt: L

Samuel's Visitation of Saul

Here the woman of Endor cried out: I see...
The King caught her by the arm. Whom? he inquired.
And even before the seer described it, he
was certain, and had seen what had transpired:

that one whose voice struck once more from the deep.
Why do you trouble me? it asked. I sleep.
Would you seek victory in my mouth because
the heavens curse you, and has the Lord's splendor
left you—is that what you seek in these jaws?
Should I count my teeth for you, one by one?
I have nothing else... all gone. And the woman,
her hands pounding her face when she was done,
as if she'd been forced to see, screamed: Surrender!

And he who in his days of victory
rose above the folk like a battle pennant,
collapsed, even before he had dared lament:
so sure he was of ruin and ignominy.

But she, who had struck him against her will,
hoped he would master himself and forget;
and when she heard he had eaten nothing yet,
went about and slaughtered and cooked a meal

and brought him to the table and bade him sit;
he sat like one who, save for one last thing,

alles was war, bis auf das Eine, Letzte.   K
Dann aß er wie ein Knecht zu Abend ißt.   L

forgets too much—almost all within his wit.
Then he ate like a workman at day's ending.

Here Saul has reached the end of his life's road. In the face of a vast Philistine army at Mount Gilboa, Saul consults the witch of Endor, compelling her to summon up the spirit of the prophet Samuel, even though Saul, as king, has declared witchcraft a capital crime. Samuel's ghost has no comfort for the king —Saul realizes that he is about to face his death. And in the face of death, Saul finally surrenders to it and sits down to a last meal (1 Samuel 28:4-25). This surrender to death's secrets is expressed in a letter from Rilke to Reinhold von Walter, June 4, 1921: "There is no task as important as to learn, every day, how to die, but our knowledge of death is never enhanced by renunciation of life; only the ripe fruit of the present moment, grasped and eaten, will spread its ineluctable taste in us."

Ein Prophet

Ausgedehnt von riesigen Gesichten,   A
hell vom Feuerschein aus dem Verlauf   B
der Gerichte, die ihn nie vernichten,–   A
sind die Augen, schauend unter dichten   A
Brauen. Und in seinem Innern richten   A
sich schon wieder Worte auf,   B

nicht die seinen (denn was wären seine   C
und wie schonend wären sie vertan)   D
andre, harte: Eisenstücke, Steine,   C
die er schmelzen muß wie ein Vulkan,   D

um sie in dem Ausbruch seines Mundes   E
auszuwerfen, welcher flucht und flucht;   F
während seine Stirne, wie des Hundes   E
Stirne, *das* zu tragen sucht,   F

was der Herr von seiner Stirne nimmt: G
Dieser, Dieser, den sie alle fänden,   H
folgten sie den großen Zeigehänden,   H
die Ihn weisen wie Er ist: ergrimmt.   G

A Prophet

Greatly enlarged by enormous foresight,
alight from the fire-shine of a long chain
of judgments, which never deny or spite:
it is thus we see his eyes, burning bright
from under bushy brows. And now, in the light
of inner being, words stand in ranks again,

not his words—for what are his alone,
and how gently they would all be lost—
but harder ones, those of iron and stone
he must melt down like a volcano first,

so that in the eruptions of his tongue,
they are flung out as it curses and curses;
while his brow like that of a dog is hung,
seeking to bear only those verses

which the Lord plucks from his forehead:
This One, This One, whom anyone might find
if only they followed the great pointing hand
that shows Him the way He is: infuriated.

"This One" whom the prophet strives to see and to voice is, for Rilke, a kind of
center around which human existence revolves. As he writes to Ilse Blumenthal-
Weiss in 1921: "And man, dwelling at the most distant periphery of this circle,
belongs to this powerful center even if he happens to turn his face to it just once,
perhaps while he is dying."

Jeremia

Einmal war ich weich wie früher Weizen,   A
doch, du Rasender, du hast vermocht,   B
mir das hingehaltne Herz zu reizen,   A
daß es jetzt wie eines Löwen kocht.   B

Welchen Mund hast du mir zugemutet,   C
damals, da ich fast ein Knabe war: D
eine Wunde wurde er: nun blutet   C
aus ihm Unglücksjahr um Unglücksjahr.   D

Täglich tönte ich von neuen Nöten,   E
die du, Unersättlicher, ersannst,   F
und sie konnten mir den Mund nicht töten;   E
sieh du zu, wie du ihn stillen kannst,   F

wenn, die wir zerstoßen und zerstören,   G
erst verloren sind und fernverlaufen   H
und vergangen sind in der Gefahr: I
denn dann will ich in den Trümmerhaufen   H
endlich meine Stimme wiederhören,   G
die von Anfang an ein Heulen war.   I

Jeremiah

Once I was tender as new-sprouted wheat,
yet you have been able, you raging one,
to provoke my proffered heart's beat
till it boils like the heart of a lion.

What a mouth you recruited to your needs,
back when I was just a boy, long before
it grew to be a wound, and now it bleeds
through tragic year after tragic year.

I ring out with new miseries every day,
contrived by you who are never sated,
but the words of my mouth they could not slay;
how will you still what you have created

once those ones whom we hammered and tore
apart at length are scattered in fear,
lost in peril and gone from the earth:
because then among the ruins I would hear,
at long last, my own voice once more,
which has been a howling since my birth.

The many biblical subjects in Rilke's *New Poems* can be perhaps explained by
quoting from *Letters to a Young Poet,* letter 2: "Out of all my books, there are
only a few I find indispensable, and two of them are with me always, wherever
I am... the Bible, and the books of the great Danish poet Jens Peter Jacobsen."
The Jeremiah of this piece is the reluctant prophet who is not at all happy with
being God's mouthpiece and who wishes he had never been chosen—nonethe-
less he performs his duty, his plight not unlike that of the poet who sees art as a
hard taskmaster.

Eine Sibylle

Einst, vor Zeiten, nannte man sie alt.   A
Doch sie blieb und kam dieselbe Straße   B
täglich. Und man änderte die Maße,   B
und man zählte sie wie einen Wald   A

nach Jahrhunderten. Sie aber stand   C
jeden Abend auf derselben Stelle,   D
schwarz wie eine alte Citadelle   D
hoch und hohl und ausgebrannt;   C

von den Worten, die sich unbewacht   E
wider ihren Willen in ihr mehrten,   F
immerfort umschrieen und umflogen,   G
während die schon wieder heimgekehrten   F
dunkel unter ihren Augenbogen   G
saßen, fertig für die Nacht.   E

A Sibyl

Once they named her ancient in ages past,
yet she remained and strode the same street daily.
And then they decided to change the tally
and reckoned her age like a forest,

in terms of centuries. But she stood just so,
each evening in the same familiar place,
black as the walls of an ancient fortress
that rose, towering, gutted and hollow;

as words seemed to flow in unhindered flight—
steadily against her will they increased—
evermore screaming and circling now,
while those which had just come home to roost
perched beneath the arches of her brow,
shadowed and ready for the night.

The Prophet, the Sibyl, the Alchemist, the Stranger, and the Saint all become
analogues of the poet in the second volume of *New Poems.* The Sibyl above
seems subject to violent fits of prophecy, but it is a violence of the spirit, not
physical violence. Rilke wrote to Erich Katzenstein in 1922: "Violence is a crude
tool and one that cannot be rehearsed. That is why the spirit falls short of it,
since it does not recognize acts of [physical] violence, for violence of the spirit
is a victory of insuperable tenderness."

Absaloms Abfall

Sie hoben sie mit Geblitz: A
der Sturm aus den Hörnern schwellte B
seidene, breitgewellte B
Fahnen. Der herrlich Erhellte B
nahm im hochoffenen Zelte, B
das jauchzendes Volk umstellte, B
zehn Frauen in Besitz, A

die (gewohnt an des alternden Fürsten C
sparsame Nacht und Tat) D
unter seinem Dürsten C
wogten wie Sommersaat. D

Dann trat er heraus zum Rate, E
wie vermindert um nichts, F
und jeder, der ihm nahte, E
erblindete seines Lichts. F

So zog er auch den Heeren G
voran wie ein Stern dem Jahr; H
über allen Speeren G
wehte sein warmes Haar, H
das der Helm nicht faßte, I
und das er manchmal haßte, I
weil es schwerer war H
als seine reichsten Kleider. X

Der König hatte geboten, J
daß man den Schönen schone. K
Doch man sah ihn ohne K

Absalom's Downfall

They raised their flags to a sky rent
by horns of storm and lightning—
silken flags, widely swelling.
The splendid son of the king,
whom shouting hordes were circling,
took ten women as an offering
into the heat of his roofless tent,

and these (used to the old king's fleet
and almost frugal deeds of night)
undulated like summer wheat
beneath the prince's appetite.

Then he strode to meet his council,
and not at all weary he appeared,
and the light from him blinded all,
every single one who neared.

Thus like a star that brings the year,
so it was that he drew his army;
over each and every spear
his warm braids of hair waved freely—
those his helmet could not enclose—
and often it was he hated those
because they were more weighty
than even his richest clothes.

The king himself had commanded
that they spare the splendid one.
Still, when seen, his helmet undone,

Helm an den bedrohten   J
Orten die ärgsten Knoten   J
zu roten Stücken von Toten   J
auseinanderhaun.   L
Dann wußte lange keiner   M
von ihm, bis plötzlich einer   M
schrie: Er hängt dort hinten   N
an den Terebinthen   N
mit hochgezogenen Braun.   L

Das war genug des Winks.   O
Joab, wie ein Jäger,   P
erspähte das Haar–: ein schräger   P
gedrehter Ast: da hings.   O
Er durchrannte den schlanken Kläger,   P
und seine Waffenträger   P
durchbohrten ihn rechts und links.   O

he stood at the place of greatest dread,
hacking into great hunks of red
the direst knots, while the dead
lay all around him in a heap.
And then for a while he was gone,
till suddenly from the mouth of one
a scream emerged: He hangs back there
from the terebinth tree, his hair
is tangled and his brow drawn up.

That was the word they hoped to hear.
Like a hunter Joab came on:
he spied the hair beneath the span
of a twisted branch—it clung there.
Through the slim claimant he ran
his spear and his comrades pierced the man
right and left as he hung in the air.

Absalom, King David's third son, meets his fate at the Battle of Ephraim
Wood (2 Samuel 18:1–18). Although David had asked that his rebellious son be
spared, Joab ignored him and was later condemned to death by Solomon for this
betrayal, in fulfillment of David's dying request.

Esther

Die Dienerinnen kämmten sieben Tage   A
die Asche ihres Grams und ihrer Plage   A
Neige und Niederschlag aus ihrem Haar,   B
und trugen es und sonnten es im Freien   C
und speisten es mit reinen Spezereien   C
noch diesen Tag und den: dann aber war   B

die Zeit gekommen, da sie, ungeboten,   D
zu keiner Frist, wie eine von den Toten   D
den drohend offenen Palast betrat,   E
um gleich, gelegt auf ihre Kammerfrauen,   F
am Ende ihres Weges *Den* zu schauen,   F
an dem man stirbt, wenn man ihm naht.   E

Er glänzte so, daß sie die Kronrubine   G
aufflammen fühlte, die sie an sich trug;   H
sie füllte sich ganz rasch mit seiner Miene   G
wie ein Gefäß und war schon voll genug   H

und floß schon über von des Königs Macht,   I
bevor sie noch den dritten Saal durchschritt,   J
der sie mit seiner Wände Malachit   J
grün überlief. Sie hatte nicht gedacht,   I

so langen Gang zu tun mit allen Steinen,   K
die schwerer wurden von des Königs Scheinen   K
und kalt von ihrer Angst. Sie ging und ging–   L

Esther

For seven days her maids had combed the ash
of her grief, as well as the whole cache
of woeful recollections, from her hair,
and had borne it and bathed it in sunshine,
sustained it and nurtured it with fine
spices day after day; but then and there

the time had come when, uninvited,
with no more respite than the dead,
she finally entered the palace door,
draped upon her women, to see Him—
that one at whose bidding and whim
one dies if one ever dare come near.

He shone so that she felt his brilliance
in the rubies she wore, which seemed aflame;
like a jar she was filled up with his presence,
and quickly she was full to the brim,

before she had reached the third chamber's end
she overflowed with the great king's might,
and it seemed that the walls of malachite
flooded her in green. She did not intend

this long walk with her every gemstone
growing heavier as the king shone,
growing cold with fear. She kept walking.

Und als sie endlich, fast von nahe, ihn,   M
aufruhend auf dem Thron von Turmalin,   M
sich türmen sah, so wirklich wie ein Ding: L

empfing die rechte von den Dienerinnen   N
die Schwindende und hielt sie zu dem Sitze.   O
Er rührte sie mit seines Szepters Spitze: O
...und sie begriff es ohne Sinne, innen.   N

And as she at last approached that one
sitting high on the tourmaline throne,
looming above her like an actual thing,

she was caught by her near-at-hand women,
who bore their fainting mistress to a chair.
He touched her with the tip of his scepter;
and without thought she conceived it within.

Esther was the Jewish wife of the Persian king Ahasuerus. When Haman, one of
the king's underlings, hatched a plot to destroy all the Jews within the bound-
aries of the Persian Empire, Esther went to appeal to King Ahasuerus, although
she broke the law by coming into the king's presence without his summons and
could have been killed for this breach (Esther 5:1–3). Her bravery saved the Jews
from Haman's plot, and Haman the Agagite was hanged on the very gallows
he had meant for Mordecai, Esther's cousin and a leader of the Persian Jews.
Ahasuerus (who may have been the historical Xerxes II) shows Esther that he
accepts her visit by touching her with his scepter. And the "it" that Esther con-
ceives at that moment is, presumably, the plan to save the Jews of Persia from
Haman's plot.

Der aussätzige König

Da trat auf seiner Stirn der Aussatz aus   A
und stand auf einmal unter seiner Krone   B
als wär er König über allen Graus,   A
der in die Andern fuhr, die fassungsohne   B

hinstarrten nach dem furchtbaren Vollzug   C
an jenem, welcher, schmal wie ein Verschnürter,   D
erwartete, daß einer nach ihm schlug;   C
doch noch war keiner Manns genug: C
als machte ihn nur immer unberührter   D
die neue Würde, die sich übertrug.   C

The Leper King

Then leprosy broke out on his forehead
and suddenly appeared beneath his crown,
as if he were king of all that dread
he drew from all of them, all who had grown

uneasy gaping at what dreadfully grew
on this monarch slim as a man bound up tight,
who now expected some treacherous coup,
although there were none quite man enough, who
was made more untouchable by his plight:
that new grandeur that showed itself now.

The Leper King of the poem is perhaps Baldwin ɪᴠ of Jerusalem who, despite his infirmity, was able to maintain his crown until he succumbed to his disease in 1185 ᴄ.ᴇ. Some writers suggest that it might also be King Uzziah of Judah, who was afflicted with the disease by God for sacrilege. But Uzziah was deposed in favor of his son once the disease manifested. In Rilke's poem it is the disease itself that protects the king from being deposed, and this perhaps reflects a belief that it is the poet's disease—the solitude that grows out of estrangement from the normal relationships of society—that sustains him.

Legende von den drei Lebendigen und den drei Toten

Drei Herren hatten mit Falken gebeizt	A
und freuten sich auf das Gelag.	B
Da nahm sie der Greis in Beschlag	B
und führte. Die Reiter hielten gespreizt	A
vor dem dreifachen Sarkophag,	B
der ihnen dreimal entgegenstank,	X
in den Mund, in die Nase, ins Sehn;	C
und sie wußten es gleich: da lagen lang	D
drei Tote mitten im Untergang	D
und ließen sich gräßlich gehn.	C
Und sie hatten nur noch ihr Jägergehör	E
reinlich hinter dem Sturmbandlör;	E
doch da zischte der Alte sein:	F
–Sie gingen nicht durch das Nadelöhr	E
und gehen niemals–hinein.	F
Nun blieb ihnen noch ihr klares Getast,	G
das stark war vom Jagen und heiß;	H
doch das hatte ein Frost von hinten gefaßt	G
und trieb ihm Eis in den Schweiß.	H

Legend of the Three Living and the Three Dead

Three noblemen sported at falconry,
anticipating the coming feast.
The old man met them there in the mist,
leading them on till they stopped suddenly
before the coffins spread out there—three—

which in their faces three times stank:
in the mouth, in the eye, and in the nose,
and they knew at once that three corpses lay,
rank and lingering long in decay,
and each had begun to decompose.

And their hearing was all they had to go by,
that sense on which hunters have to rely,
as the old man hissed in a voice so shrill:
These couldn't pass through the needle's eye,
he said, and now they never will.

Now all that they had left was their sense of touch,
refined from hunting, still hot and precise;
but a frost had crept up and seized upon each
and had frozen their very sweat to ice.

The legend of the three living and the three dead, which first appeared in the thirteenth century, could have been seen by Rilke in Berlin in the illuminated manuscript called *The Hours of Berlin of Mary of Burgundy* and is almost identical to one in *The Hours of Joanna of Castile*. It was also depicted on the walls of many churches in Europe, where it served as a kind of memento mori. The subject often constituted half of a diptych, paired with the prancing skeletons of the danse macabre, which is the subject of another poem in this volume.

Der König von Münster

Der König war geschoren;	A
nun ging ihm die Krone zu weit	B
und bog ein wenig die Ohren,	A
in die von Zeit zu Zeit	B
gehässiges Gelärme	C
aus Hungermäulern fand.	D
Er saß, von wegen der Wärme,	C
auf seiner rechten Hand,	D
mürrisch und schwergesäßig.	E
Er fühlte sich nicht mehr echt:	F
der Herr in ihm war mäßig,	E
und der Beischlaf war schlecht.	F

The King of Münster

The king's hair had been shorn;
now the crown was too big for him
and bent the ears which had borne
it, which from time to time

caught the spiteful alarm
the mouths of the hungry spawned.
He sat, as if to keep it warm,
upon his own right hand,

heavy-bottomed and glum.
He felt no longer noble;
the Lord was small within him,
and the cohabitation was dreadful.

The king referred to here is Jan Bockelson, a tailor, one of the leaders of the Ana-
baptist revolt of 1534. Bockelson made himself into a proletarian king, known
to history as John of Leiden, and proceeded to install polygamy and communal
sharing of goods in the city of Münster. He took sixteen wives, one of whom he
had beheaded. He and his followers were deposed by a Catholic counterrevolu-
tion and were executed in 1536. Their bodies were displayed in cages hung from
the steeple of Saint Lambert's Church, and the cages hang there to this day as a
reminder to would-be heretics.

Toten-Tanz

Sie brauchen kein Tanz-Orchester;   A
sie hören in sich ein Geheule   B
als wären sie Eulennester.   A
Ihr Ängsten näßt wie eine Beule,   B
und der Vorgeruch ihrer Fäule   B
ist noch ihr bester Geruch.   C

Sie fassen den Tänzer fester,   A
den rippenbetreßten Tänzer,   D
den Galan, den ächten Ergänzer   D
zu einem ganzen Paar.   X
Und er lockert der Ordensschwester   A
über dem Haar das Tuch;   C
sie tanzen ja unter Gleichen.   E
Und er zieht der wachslichtbleichen   E
leise die Lesezeichen   E
aus ihrem Stunden-Buch.   C

Bald wird ihnen allen zu heiß,   F
sie sind zu reich gekleidet;   G
beißender Schweiß verleidet   G
ihnen Stirne und Steiß   F
und Schauben und Hauben und Steine;   H
sie wünschen, sie wären nackt   I
wie ein Kind, ein Verrückter und Eine: H
die tanzen noch immer im Takt.   I

In German-speaking countries the danse macabre portrayed here is known as the *Totentanz*. The earliest depiction of this grisly scene was in a fresco in the cemetery of the Church of the Holy Innocents in Paris, which was destroyed in 1669, though a woodcut copy by Guyot Marchant still exists. Rilke might have

Danse Macabre

They need no orchestra to dance;
as if each nested like an owl
to some inner howl they prance.
Their fear weeps like a lanced boil,
and just a whiff of their foul smell
is the best of what they reckon.

They grip more tightly and commence
with the laced-up-in-his-rib-cage dancer,
the squire, the forbidding partner,
complement of a perfect pair.
And he undoes with nonchalance
the silken headband of the nun,
for they dance among their equals there.
And quietly he pulls the marker
from its place in the book of prayer
of this pale-as-candle-wax one.

Soon they are grown too hot and damp,
much too richly swathed in clothes;
and how the caustic sweat then flows,
estranging them from brow and rump,
from cloak and hood and precious stone,
till they wish they were naked in the heat
as an infant, a madman, or one
of those still dancing to the heartbeat.

been familiar with versions by Hans Holbein the Younger and Pieter Brueghel
the Elder. And he probably had heard a musical interpretation, part of the sec-
ond movement of Mahler's Symphony no. 4, which debuted in 1901.

Das Jüngste Gericht

So erschrocken, wie sie nie erschraken,   A
ohne Ordnung, oft durchlocht und locker,   B
hocken sie in dem geborstnen Ocker   B
ihres Ackers, nicht von ihren Laken   A

abzubringen, die sie liebgewannen.   C
Aber Engel kommen an, um Öle   D
einzuträufeln in die trocknen Pfannen   C
und um jedem in die Achselhöhle   D

das zu legen, was er in dem Lärme   E
damals seines Lebens nicht entweihte;   F
denn dort hat es noch ein wenig Wärme,   E

daß es nicht des Herren Hand erkälte   G
oben, wenn er es aus jeder Seite   F
leise greift, zu fühlen, ob es gälte.   G

The Last Judgment

Frightened as ever, this disordered crowd,
all of them loosely jointed, full of holes,
they cower in bursting furrows, these souls
who are so reluctant to leave the shroud

that from custom they have grown to love.
But angels arrive and begin to pour
oil into the dried-out joints from above,
and in each one's armpits they must store

whatever is unprofaned and pure
that from the riot of their lives abides,
because there is still some warmth left there,

so as not to chill the hand of the Lord, who,
reaching down, grabs them gently on both sides,
to see if the grace left within them will do.

Young Malte, who is Rilke's alter ego, makes a curious comment regarding the
Last Judgment in *The Notebooks of Malte Laurids Brigge*. He mentions the
strange controversy stirred up by Pope John XXII concerning the Beatific Vision.
That pontiff first maintained that the souls of even the righteous do not see God
until the Last Judgment, and remain in the dark until then. Eventually John
relented on this point of dogma; however, Rilke seems to privilege that very
belief in this poem.

Die Versuchung

Nein, es half nicht, daß er sich die scharfen   A
Stacheln einhieb in das geile Fleisch;   B
alle seine trächtigen Sinne warfen   A
unter kreißendem Gekreisch   B

Frühgeburten: schiefe, hingeschielte   C
kriechende und fliegende Gesichte,   D
Nichte, deren nur auf ihn erpichte   D
Bosheit sich verband und mit ihm spielte.   C

Und schon hatten seine Sinne Enkel;   E
denn das Pack war fruchtbar in der Nacht   F
und in immer bunterem Gesprenkel   E
hingehudelt und verhundertfacht.   F
Aus dem Ganzen ward ein Trank gemacht: F
seine Hände griffen lauter Henkel,   E
und der Schatten schob sich auf wie Schenkel   E
warm und zu Umarmungen erwacht–.   F

Und da schrie er nach dem Engel, schrie: G
Und der Engel kam in seinem Schein   H
und war da: und jagte sie   G
wieder in den Heiligen hinein,   H

daß er mit Geteufel und Getier   I
in sich weiterringe wie seit Jahren   J

The Temptation

No, it did not help that he shoved sharp spikes
into his lustful flesh, and all his pregnant
senses flung, amidst the labored shrieks
of premature births, those twisted and bent,

those creeping, flying, leered-at visions,
vast legions of these nothing-nieces,
who joined him eagerly in vices,
sporting with him in apparitions.

And his wits had grandchildren already,
for fruitful in the night was this brood,
this teeming and painted potpourri,
badly made and hundreds in multitude.
Out of all of it a drink was brewed;
he grasped the garish handles tightly
and the shadows separated slightly
like warm thighs waking to be wooed.

And then he called out, for the angel he called,
and in all his glory the angel came,
and all those visions it compelled–
back into the saint the angel drove them,

so that when beasts and demons were sent
he might strive as he had for many a year

und sich Gott, den lange noch nicht klaren,

J

innen aus dem Jäsen destillier.

I

to distill God, that one who is not yet clear,
out of the vat of that inner ferment.

Malte Laurids Brigge remarks that Paris "is a huge city, full of weird tempta-
tions." Rilke also must have felt this about the city that alternately attracted and
repelled him. In Rilke's case the angel that emerged to chase these visions away
was his work. Rodin had taught him that an artist's work takes precedence over
distractions and temptations. Ironically, Rodin was at that phase in his life when
such distractions were increasingly making demands on his energies. Rilke was
more successful, especially in the prolific years of 1904–1908, in resisting temp-
tation and distilling art out of its ferment.

Der Alchimist

Seltsam verlächelnd schob der Laborant   A
den Kolben fort, der halbberuhigt rauchte.   B
Er wußte jetzt, was er noch brauchte,   B
damit der sehr erlauchte Gegenstand   A

da drin entstände. Zeiten brauchte er,   C
Jahrtausende für sich und diese Birne   D
in der es brodelte; im Hirn Gestirne   D
und im Bewußtsein mindestens das Meer.   C

Das Ungeheuere, das er gewollt,   E
er ließ es los in dieser Nacht. Es kehrte   F
zurück zu Gott und in sein altes Maß;   G

er aber, lallend wie ein Trunkenbold,   E
lag über dem Geheimfach und begehrte   F
den Brocken Gold, den er besaß.   G

The Alchemist

Strangely smiling the lab assistant
pushed back the half-bubbling, smoking flask.
He knew at last what was needed for the task
by which he would gain the desired element.

He knew it would take a millennium,
ages were needed for this pear-shaped glass,
the stars in his brain; in his consciousness
he needed the sea at minimum.

The enormity that he himself had willed
he let go of that very night. It was swept
back to its ancient measure, back to God;

but, prattling like a drunkard then, he sprawled
over the strongbox and the treasure it kept,
wanting that gold hunk he already had.

This poem seems to proceed from comments made in *The Notebooks of Malte Laurids Brigge,* as do the last two poems, leading us to believe that they were all composed while Rilke was also working on that short novel. Malte muses that one to whom God has given the will toward quiet and objectless work has found the Philosopher's Stone ("the desired element" in the poem) and was therefore compelled to create the gold of his fate out of the lead lump of patience. The Alchemist in the poem above misses this opportunity, desiring only "that gold hunk he already had."

Der Reliquienschrein

Draussen wartete auf alle Ringe	A
und auf jedes Kettenglied	B
Schicksal, das nicht ohne sie geschieht.	B
Drinnen waren sie nur Dinge, Dinge	A
die er schmiedete; denn vor dem Schmied	B
war sogar die Krone, die er bog,	C
nur ein Ding, ein zitterndes und eines,	D
das er finster wie im Zorn erzog	C
zu dem Tragen eines reinen Steines.	D
Seine Augen wurden immer kälter	E
von dem kalten täglichen Getränk;	F
aber als der herrliche Behälter	E
(goldgetrieben, köstlich, vielkarätig)	G
fertig vor ihm stand, das Weihgeschenk,	F
daß darin ein kleines Handgelenk	F
fürder wohne, weiß und wundertätig:	G
blieb er ohne Ende auf den Knien,	H
hingeworfen, weinend, nichtmehr wagend,	I
seine Seele niederschlagend	I
vor dem ruhigen Rubin,	H
der ihn zu gewahren schien	H
und ihn, plötzlich um sein Dasein fragend,	I
ansah wie aus Dynastien.	H

The Reliquary

Waiting out there for all of the rings,
waiting for every link of those chains,
was Fate, for without them nothing happens.
Within themselves they were just things, things
he had forged, since before the smith fashions
the crown and bends it to his desire,
it is only a quivering thing, and one
that he parents darkly, as if in anger,
to become the setting of a pure stone.

The eyes in his head grew ever more cold
every day before the cold libation;
but even as the noble vessel of gold
(embossed, many-karated, and exquisite)
stood completed before him – this creation,
soon some tiny wrist-bone's habitation,
where it might dwell, wonder-working and white –

he remained steadily on bended knees,
set back, sobbing, no longer adventurous,
his soul beaten down and tremulous
before one of the placid rubies
that seemed to know him and to suddenly seize
him with a questioning of his purpose,
gazing at him as if from dynasties.

Like the reliquary that Rilke shows us here the thing-poem is something solid,
something crafted laboriously, link by link, something the poet "parents darkly"
until it holds the pure stone of his art. As he writes to Lou Andreas-Salomé on
August 8, 1903: "Only things speak to me, Rodin's things, the things on the
Gothic cathedrals, the things of the ancients."

Das Gold

Denk es wäre nicht: es hätte müssen   A
endlich in den Bergen sich gebären   B
und sich niederschlagen in den Flüssen   A
aus dem Wollen, aus dem Gären   B

ihres Willens; aus der Zwang-Idee,   C
daß ein Erz ist über allen Erzen.   D
Weithin warfen sie aus ihren Herzen   D
immer wieder Meroë   C

an den Rand der Lande, in den Äther,   E
über das Erfahrene hinaus;   F
und die Söhne brachten manchmal später   E
das Verheißene der Väter,   E
abgehärtet und verhehrt, nachhaus;   F

wo es anwuchs eine Zeit, um dann   G
fortzugehn von den an ihm Geschwächten,   H
die es niemals liebgewann.   G
Nur (so sagt man) in den letzten Nächten   H
steht es auf und sieht sie an.   G

Gold

Suppose it did not exist—it would still
have been born in the mountain's erosion
and from the very dregs of its own will,
in the rivers, out of the fermentation

of *their* wills, out of the necessity
that one ore must exceed all the rest.
Widely out of their hearts they cast
yet more cities of Meroë

on the coasts of the land, into the ether,
even beyond the world known to men;
and afterward each son would gather
and bring this promised thing to his father,
the hardened and venerated specimen;

where for a time it seemed to increase,
to abandon those weakened by its sway,
those it had never shown its grace.
Only in their last nights (or so they say)
does it rise and stare them in the face.

The last stanza of this verse reveals Rilke's constant worries about money. As
someone to whom gold "had never shown its grace," Rilke became even more
anxious over his financial state after marrying Clara Westhoff in 1901 and con-
ceiving a child with her. In 1902 the poet lost a small stipend he had from his
family, and his worries grew even more acute. Writing that year to a potential
benefactor, Frau Julie Weinmann, he related that he had always borne his pov-
erty well, "But this winter, for the first time, it stood before me like a ghost, for
months, and I lost myself and all my most cherished aspirations and all the light
of my heart." Meroë ('mer-ō-ē) was an ancient city of a Nubian kingdom on the
upper Nile that was known for its gold-smelting industry.

Der Stylit

Völker schlugen über ihm zusammen,   A
die er küren durfte und verdammen;   A
und erratend, daß er sich verlor,   B
klomm er aus dem Volksgeruch mit klammen   A
Händen einen Säulenschaft empor,   B

der noch immer stieg und nichts mehr hob,   C
und begann, allein auf seiner Fläche,   D
ganz von vorne seine eigne Schwäche   D
zu vergleichen mit des Herren Lob;   C

und da war kein Ende: er verglich;   E
und der Andre wurde immer größer.   F
Und die Hirten, Ackerbauer, Flößer   F
sahn ihn klein und außer sich   E

immer mit dem ganzen Himmel reden,   G
eingeregnet manchmal, manchmal licht;   H
und sein Heulen stürzte sich auf jeden,   G
so als heulte er ihm ins Gesicht.   H
Doch er sah seit Jahren nicht,   H

wie der Menge Drängen und Verlauf   I
unten unaufhörlich sich ergänzte,   J
und das Blanke an den Fürsten glänzte   J
lange nicht so hoch hinauf.   I

Aber wenn er oben, fast verdammt   K
und von ihrem Widerstand zerschunden,   L
einsam mit verzweifeltem Geschreie   M

The Stylite

The nations brawled together over him,
over those he might elect or might condemn;
and guessing he had lost himself somewhere,
he forsook the stench of the people to climb,
with dampened hands, the column rising there,

ever higher, though it held no other things.
Alone at its top in contemplation,
with praise for the Lord and all his creation
he began to compare his own shortcomings;

and there was no end to it—he compared,
and the difference grew ever greater.
And the shepherd, the boatman, and the farmer
saw him small and feverish as they stared,

always speaking with the whole of heaven,
obscured by rain sometimes, sometimes a trace
of brightness; and his howls plunged down upon
them all, as if he howled into each one's face.
Yet he did not see through the years in that place

how the crowds below had surged and lurched
as he gazed on the ceaselessly growing throng,
and the aura of princes had for long
gleamed ever dimmer from where he perched.

But when from above, almost damned, and cut
to pieces by the mob's hostile sounds,
alone, and with desperate screams so loud,

schüttelte die täglichen Dämonen: N

fielen langsam auf die erste Reihe M

schwer und ungeschickt aus seinen Wunden L

große Würmer in die offnen Kronen N

und vermehrten sich im Samt. K

he shook off the daily visions of demons:
slowly, on the very first row of the crowd,
heavily and awkwardly from his wounds,
immense worms fell upon their bare crowns,
and these propagated in the velvet.

Rilke's life of artistic asceticism is evident, in many poems in the second volume of this work, by his focus on the early desert saints of the Church. Among the works so oriented are "A Prophet," "The Temptation," "The Egyptian Mary," "From the Life of a Saint," and of course, this one. The pillar saint in this piece bears a relation to Rilke's beggars, lepers, and lunatics, which is underscored in a poem from the first volume, "The Portal," where the poet emphasizes that Christ appears in the guise "of the mad man, the blind, and the ignoble."

Die Ägyptische Maria

Seit sie damals, bettheiß, als die Hure   A
übern Jordan floh und, wie ein Grab   B
gebend, stark und unvermischt das pure   A
Herz der Ewigkeit zu trinken gab,   B

wuchs ihr frühes Hingegebensein   C
unaufhaltsam an zu solcher Größe,   D
daß sie endlich, wie die ewige Blöße   D
Aller, aus vergilbtem Elfenbein   C

dalag in der dürren Haare Schelfe.   E
Und ein Löwe kreiste; und ein Alter   F
rief ihn winkend an, daß er ihm helfe: E

(und so gruben sie zu zwein.)   G

Und der Alte neigte sie hinein.   G
Und der Löwe, wie ein Wappenhalter,   F
saß dabei und hielt den Stein.   G

The Egyptian Mary

Since the time she had fled, bed-hot,
like a whore over Jordan, soft as a grave,
strong and undiluted, her pure heart
to the thirst of Eternity she gave,

her early sacrifice relentlessly grew
finally to such an enormous scale
that like the eternal bareness of all,
like aging ivory that yellows in hue,

she lay there, her brittle hair like a husk.
And a lion circled; and an old man
beckoned, crying out for help with his task

(and so the two of them dug together).

And into the hole the old man bent her.
And like a shield bearer the lion
sat hard by and held the stone marker.

In his formidable book on poetic myth, *The White Goddess,* Robert Graves connects Saint Mary of Egypt with Mary Gypsy, a British mythic figure who corresponds to the continental *Maria Stellis*. Both are manifestations of Aphrodite, as would be appropriate to the reformed prostitute we meet in this poem. According to Mary's vita, the old man depicted here is Saint Zosimas of Palestine, who came upon her lifeless body in the desert and buried her with the help of a lion he met wandering there.

Kreuzigung

Längst geübt, zum kahlen Galgenplatze	A
irgend ein Gesindel hinzudrängen,	B
ließen sich die schweren Knechte hängen,	B
dann und wann nur eine große Fratze	A
kehrend nach den abgetanen Drein.	C
Aber oben war das schlechte Henkern	D
rasch getan; und nach dem Fertigsein	C
ließen sich die freien Männer schlenkern.	D
Bis der eine (fleckig wie ein Selcher)	E
sagte: Hauptmann, dieser hat geschrien.	F
Und der Hauptmann sah vom Pferde: Welcher?	E
und es war ihm selbst, er hätte ihn	F
den Elia rufen hören. Alle	G
waren zuzuschauen voller Lust,	H
und sie hielten, daß er nicht verfalle,	G
gierig ihm die ganze Essiggalle	G
an sein schwindendes Gehust.	H
Denn sie hofften noch ein ganzes Spiel	I
und vielleicht den kommenden Elia.	J
Aber hinten ferne schrie Maria,	J
und er selber brüllte und verfiel.	I

Crucifixion

Long experienced in shoving some vermin
toward the bleak location of the cross,
the lumbering death-workers still hung close,
sweeping keen grimaces now and then

over toward the done-for trinity.
But above them the foul execution
concluded, and there in its vicinity
the idle ones dangled when it was done.

Until one (bloodied as a butcher) began:
Centurion, one of them now cries out.
And the mounted centurion asked: Which one?
And he himself heard the man, so he thought,

calling for Elijah. The company
gazing on this were eager enough,
and so that he might not die too quickly
offered the vinegar sponge directly,
held aloft to the man's dwindling cough.

For they hoped to see the whole play perhaps,
and maybe even Elijah's coming.
But behind them they heard Mary's screaming
as her son cried out his final collapse.

This is one of a series of pieces in the two volumes of *New Poems* that takes its subject from the New Testament. Others are "The Departure of the Prodigal Son," "The Olive Orchard," "Pietà," "The Resurrected," and "Magnificat." The Roman soldiers here, not fluent in the local language, think they hear Jesus crying out for Elijah when actually he is appealing to God: *Eloi, Eloi, lama sabachthani?*

Der Auferstandene

Er vermochte niemals bis zuletzt   A
ihr zu weigern oder abzuneinen,   B
daß sie ihrer Liebe sich berühme;   C
und sie sank ans Kreuz in dem Kostüme   C
eines Schmerzes, welches ganz besetzt   A
war mit ihrer Liebe größten Steinen.   B

Aber da sie dann, um ihn zu salben,   D
an das Grab kam, Tränen im Gesicht,   E
war er auferstanden ihrethalben,   D
daß er seliger ihr sage: Nicht–   E

Sie begriff es erst in ihrer Höhle,   F
wie er ihr, gestärkt durch seinen Tod,   G
endlich das Erleichternde der Öle   F
und des Rührens Vorgefühl verbot,   G

um aus ihr die Liebende zu formen   H
die sich nicht mehr zum Geliebten neigt,   I
weil sie, hingerissen von enormen   H
Stürmen, seine Stimme übersteigt.   I

The Resurrected

He was never able, until his last breath,
to deny her anything she would have
so that her love might grow in renown,
and in sorrow's costume she sank down
before the cross at his moment of death,
her pain set with the greatest gems of her love.

But when at last she approached his tomb
with a tearful face in order to anoint
him, he rose for the sake of her whom
he addressed blissfully, saying: Don't.

Back in her hovel she grasped what he meant,
how, braced by his death, he forbade that grace,
the alleviation of the ointment
and the anticipation of embrace,

in order to shape from her loving arms
one no longer to the beloved bound,
for enraptured by enormous storms,
she has risen beyond his voice's sound.

Rilke writes to Countess Mary Gneisenau on September 11, 1906: "That is why loneliness, which so often multiplies their sorrows beyond number, is so appropriate to the situation of women: because only in loneliness is such a transfiguration possible; this being submerged yet unimplicated in the suffered wrong, this inability to ever become commonplace, this integrity, is this too dearly paid for by all that women have endured? Who can pity women yet observe how they grow beyond all abuse and pettiness, how they are a thing untouched?" The woman in the poem is undoubtedly Mary Magdalene, and this could be considered a companion piece to "Pietà."

Magnificat

Sie kam den Hang herauf, schon schwer, fast ohne   A
an Trost zu glauben, Hoffnung oder Rat;   B
doch da die hohe tragende Matrone   A
ihr ernst und stolz entgegentrat   B

und alles wußte ohne ihr Vertrauen,   C
da war sie plötzlich an ihr ausgeruht;   D
vorsichtig hielten sich die vollen Frauen,   C
bis daß die junge sprach: Mir ist zumut,   D

als wär ich, Liebe, von nun an für immer.   E
Gott schüttet in der Reichen Eitelkeit   F
fast ohne hinzusehen ihren Schimmer;   E
doch sorgsam sucht er sich ein Frauenzimmer   E
und füllt sie an mit seiner fernsten Zeit.   F

Daß er mich fand. Bedenk nur; und Befehle   G
um meinetwillen gab von Stern zu Stern–.   H

Verherrliche und hebe, meine Seele,   G
so hoch du kannst: den HERRN.   H

Magnificat

She came up the hillside, heavily, like one
unconvinced of solace, hope, or counsel,
but when the tall, child-heavy matron,
grave and proud, greeted her and knew it all,

without a word having been spoken,
in that presence she was suddenly calm;
carefully they embraced, the pregnant women,
until the man-child spoke: I feel that I am,

and will exist, Love, now until forever.
God indulges the rich folk's vanity
with hardly a glance at their glitter;
yet carefully seeks out a womb to stir
and fills a woman full of eternity.

That he should find me, just think, and even
for me from star to star he sent his word.

Exalt, my soul, and raise up to heaven,
as high as ever you can, the LORD.

This is the closest Rilke gets to Christian prayer, of which he writes to Mimi
Romanelli, January 5, 1910: "Prayer is a beam proceeding from existence that
has been suddenly set ablaze; it is an infinite purposeless direction; it is a violent
correspondence to our aspirations that travels the universe without ever arriv-
ing at a destination." The poem concerns the visitation of the Virgin Mary to
Saint Elizabeth, who, though an old woman, was pregnant with John the Baptist.

Adam

Staunend steht er an der Kathedrale   A
steilem Aufstieg, nah der Fensterrose,   B
wie erschreckt von der Apotheose,   B
welche wuchs und ihn mit einem Male   A

niederstellte über die und die.   C
Und er ragt und freut sich seiner Dauer   D
schlicht entschlossen; als der Ackerbauer   D
der begann, und der nicht wußte, wie   C

aus dem fertig-vollen Garten Eden   E
einen Ausweg in die neue Erde   F
finden. Gott war schwer zu überreden;   E

und er drohte ihm, statt zu gewähren,   G
immer wieder, daß er sterben werde.   F
Doch der Mensch bestand: sie wird gebären.   G

Adam

Astounded on the cathedral's steep rise
he stands, near the rose window's location,
as if frightened by the transformation
which took place and to his surprise

set him down here, far above you and you.
And there he looms, rejoicing in endurance,
artlessly resolute in the plowman's stance –
he who started out and then did not know

how to find a path from Eden's glade,
full and fruitful, into the newly made earth.
God was difficult for him to persuade,

and, instead of conceding, threatened,
on and on, that he would die in the end.
Yet mankind survived: she will give birth.

The cathedral facade whereupon Adam stands astounded is no doubt that of
Notre Dame de Paris. At the center of the facade, near the gallery of the Virgin,
stands a rose window measuring almost ten meters in diameter, which was cre-
ated ca. 1225. It forms a halo above a statue of the Virgin and Child, which stands
between two angels. To the right and left of it are freestanding statues of Adam
and Eve, which are supposed to remind the faithful of original sin.

Eva

Einfach steht sie an der Kathedrale   A
großem Aufstieg, nah der Fensterrose,   B
mit dem Apfel in der Apfelpose,   B
schuldlos-schuldig ein für alle Male   A

an dem Wachsenden, das sie gebar,   C
seit sie aus dem Kreis der Ewigkeiten   D
liebend fortging, um sich durchzustreiten   D
durch die Erde, wie ein junges Jahr.   C

Ach, sie hätte gern in jenem Land   E
noch ein wenig weilen mögen, achtend   F
auf der Tiere Eintracht und Verstand.   E

Doch da sie den Mann entschlossen fand,   E
ging sie mit ihm, nach dem Tode trachtend;   F
und sie hatte Gott noch kaum gekannt.   E

Eve

Artlessly she stands atop the cathedral,
near the huge window shaped like a rose,
with the apple in hand, in the apple pose,
guiltlessly guilty through time, responsible

for the growing, to which she gave birth
since she ventured forth from the circle
of eternity, in order to struggle
her way like an infant year through the earth.

Ah, she would gladly have stayed in that land,
biding her time a bit longer, minding
what the peaceful animals understand.

Yet since the man's mind was already made,
she went with him, seeking death, and finding
that she had barely gotten to know God.

The statues of Adam and Eve on the facade of Notre Dame de Paris were rebuilt by Viollet-le-Duc in the nineteenth century. Rilke often visited the cathedrals of Paris and its vicinity with the Master, Rodin, who pointed out various architectural and artistic features to the young poet. He mentions the two statues to Clara in a letter dated August 31, 1902, and also writes how Rodin was shepherding him around the city.

Irre im Garten

Dijon

Noch schließt die aufgegebene Kartause	A
sich um den Hof, als würde etwas heil.	B
Auch die sie jetzt bewohnen, haben Pause	A
und nehmen nicht am Leben draußen teil.	B

Was irgend kommen konnte, das verlief.	C
Nun gehn sie gerne mit bekannten Wegen,	D
und trennen sich und kommen sich entgegen,	D
als ob sie kreisten, willig, primitiv.	C

Zwar manche pflegen dort die Frühlingsbeete,	E
demütig, dürftig, hingekniet;	F
aber sie haben, wenn es keiner sieht,	F
eine verheimlichte, verdrehte	E

Gebärde für das zarte frühe Gras,	G
ein prüfendes, verschüchtertes Liebkosen:	H
denn das ist freundlich, und das Rot der Rosen	H
wird vielleicht drohend sein und Übermaß	G

und wird vielleicht schon wieder übersteigen,	I
was ihre Seele wiederkennt und weiß.	J
Dies aber läßt sich noch verschweigen:	I
wie gut das Gras ist und wie leis.	J

The "abandoned charterhouse" mentioned here is the Chartreuse de Champ-mol, which Rilke visited in April 1903. The place has an interesting history, of which Rilke may or may not have been aware. It now contains an archaeological museum with a collection of Roman stone monuments, the archives of the town,

The Insane in the Garden

Dijon

The abandoned charterhouse seems to enclose
the courtyard as if it would keep it secure.
And the inmates who take their rest there, those
have no life outside its enclosure.

What happens in that place has always been.
Now gladly on familiar lanes they gather
and break into groups and come together,
as if in some primitive, willing routine.

Indeed many attend flower beds there,
humble and meager and genuflecting,
but they have, when no one is inspecting
them, a surreptitious, contorted gesture,

a sign that stands for the tender Spring grass,
a probing but careful, caressing pose,
for it is friendly, and the red of the rose
is ominous and almost seems to harass

them, pushing them too far beyond that
which their souls recognize and understand.
But this they still keep as their secret:
how good the grass is, how soft to the hand.

and the principal museum, which houses, besides valuable paintings and other
works of art, the tombs of Philip the Bold and John the Fearless, dukes of Bur-
gundy. These were inherited from the Chartreuse, which was built by Philip the
Bold as a mausoleum and afterward replaced by the asylum.

Die Irren

Und sie schweigen, weil die Scheidewände   A
weggenommen sind aus ihrem Sinn,   B
und die Stunden, da man sie verstände,   A
heben an und gehen hin.   B

Nächtens oft, wenn sie ans Fenster treten: C
plötzlich ist es alles gut.   D
Ihre Hände liegen im Konkreten,   C
und das Herz ist hoch und könnte beten,   C
und die Augen schauen ausgeruht   D

auf den unverhofften, oftentstellten   E
Garten im beruhigten Geviert,   F
der im Widerschein der fremden Welten   E
weiterwächst und niemals sich verliert.   F

The Insane

And they hold their tongues, for now quite gone
are the walls of their minds' compartments,
and time, as one understands it, ticks on
as the hours increase and advance.

Often by night, when they step to the casement,
suddenly everything seems to be right.
Their hands touch the solid and evident,
and their hearts are soaring while they are bent
in prayer, and the rested eyes receive the light

of the unexpected, often ruinous
garden in the courtyard's tranquil gulf,
which in the reflection of those curious
worlds grows on and never loses itself.

Rilke had a particular identification with the sick and the insane, as we can see
in this piece. In a long letter to Lou Andreas-Salomé dated July 18, 1903, Rilke
says, "All those folk who are in some transitional phase, men and women, pro-
ceeding from madness to cure, perhaps into delirium; all of them having some-
thing eternally beautiful in their faces, with love, joy, knowledge, like a light that
burns woefully, waveringly, yet which might become bright again if someone
would just watch over it and help it…. But there is no one to help."

Gebet für die Irren und Sträflinge

Ihr, von denen das Sein	A
leise sein großes Gesicht	B
wegwandte: ein	A
vielleicht Seiender spricht	B
draußen in der Freiheit	C
langsam bei Nacht ein Gebet:	D
Daß euch die Zeit vergeht,	D
denn ihr habt Zeit.	C
Wenn es euch jetzt gedenkt,	E
greift euch zärtlich durchs Haar:	F
alles ist weggeschenkt,	E
alles, was war.	F
Oh, daß ihr stille bliebt,	G
wenn euch das Herz verjährt;	H
daß keine Mutter erfährt,	H
daß es das gibt.	G
Oben hob sich der Mond,	I
wo sich die Zweige entzwein,	J
und, wie von euch bewohnt,	I
bleibt er allein.	J

In the letter to Lou Andreas-Salomé of July 1903, Rilke describes his helplessness before the sight of all the sick, insane, and downtrodden people he meets in the streets of Paris: "Oh, Lou, I have tortured myself for days on end. For I apprehend these people, and although I had avoided them in a great arc, they held no secrets back from me.... I often had to assure myself that I was not one of them....

Prayer for the Lunatic and the Convict

You, away from whom Being
softly turns its great vision,
one perhaps among the living
utters this benediction

slowly in the night, this rhyme
where the fields of freedom lie:
Because time passes you by,
this is the reason you have time.

When you think it over now,
fondly it touches your hair;
everything fades somehow,
everything that was there.

Oh, that you are still tongueless
when cast out by your heart,
no mother to heal your hurt,
that that's just the way it is.

Above you the moon is swelling
where branching twigs have grown,
and, as if it were your dwelling,
it remains there, alone.

And yet, as I noticed my clothes growing more threadbare, week upon week, and
saw how shabby and worn they were, I was shocked and felt that I would soon
belong among the hopelessly lost should some passerby see me and number me,
even half-consciously, one of them." Rilke's fear of joining the homeless multi-
tude is evident in the line, "one *perhaps* among the living" (emphasis mine).

Aus dem Leben eines Heiligen

Er kannte Ängste, deren Eingang schon   A
wie Sterben war und nicht zu überstehen.   B
Sein Herz erlernte, langsam durchzugehen;   B
er zog es groß wie einen Sohn.   A

Und namenlose Nöte kannte er,   C
finster und ohne Morgen wie Verschläge;   D
und seine Seele gab er folgsam her,   C
da sie erwachsen war, auf daß sie läge   D

bei ihrem Bräutigam und Herrn; und blieb   E
allein zurück an einem solchen Orte,   F
wo das Alleinsein alles übertrieb,   E
und wohnte weit und wollte niemals Worte.   F

Aber dafür, nach Zeit und Zeit, erfuhr   G
er auch das Glück, sich in die eignen Hände,   H
damit er eine Zärtlichkeit empfände,   H
zu legen wie die ganze Kreatur.   G

From the Life of a Saint

Many fears he knew, whose doors already shone
like death, like something he could not bear.
But his heart had learned to slowly enter there,
and he nurtured this as if it were a son.

And he knew a nameless adversity,
dark and dawnless as a prisoner's cell;
and he gave up his soul compliantly
when it matured, in order that it dwell

beside its lord and bridegroom, remaining
behind in just that sort of circumstance
where loneliness overstates everything,
forsaking words, living in the distance.

But because of this, time and time again,
in his own hands he came to know happiness,
and in that knowledge he sensed a tenderness
lying there like the whole of creation.

The second volume of *New Poems* contains a loose group of pieces that seem to
be self-portraits of the artist—this one in particular portrays the poet as an aes-
thetic seeker akin to one of the hermit-saints of the early Church. Other poems
in this volume which seem to be self-portraits include "The Alchemist," "The
Reliquary," "The Adventurer," "The Stranger," and "The Reader."

Die Bettler

Du wußtest nicht, was den Haufen   A
ausmacht. Ein Fremder fand   B
Bettler darin. Sie verkaufen   A
das Hohle aus ihrer Hand.   B

Sie zeigen dem Hergereisten   C
ihren Mund voll Mist,   D
und er darf (er kann es sich leisten)   C
sehn, wie ihr Aussatz frißt.   D

Es zergeht in ihren zerrührten   E
Augen sein fremdes Gesicht;   F
und sie freuen sich des Verführten   E
und speien, wenn er spricht.   F

The Beggars

That heap you saw, you could not tell
what it might be. A stranger found
some beggars there. They sell
the hollow of their hand.

They show this one who's traveled here
their mouths all filled up with manure;
if he can stand it he might stare
as leprosy devours each sore.

His stranger's face soon melts away
within their agitated eyes,
and now, rejoicing in their quarry,
they spit when they hear his voice.

Malte Laurids Brigge writes in his notebooks how he habitually meets two beggars on the boulevard Saint-Michel or the rue Racine "who stare at me and know it. They know that I, in fact, belong to them, that I am only playing a role in a comedy. They do not want to spoil my walk so they only leer at me a bit and wink their eyes.... Occasionally I shiver a bit and give them a couple of sous.... It is certainly the time of Carnival." Mikhail Bakhtin, the Russian philosopher and critic, posited the "carnivalesque" as one of the chronotopes of the European novel, and the world described in *New Poems* sometimes seems to skew toward the carnivalesque—that feeling that the order of the universe has been turned on its head.

Fremde Familie

So wie der Staub, der irgendwie beginnt   A
und nirgends ist, zu unerklärtem Zwecke   B
an einem leeren Morgen in der Ecke,   B
in die man sieht, ganz rasch zu Grau gerinnt,   A

so bildeten sie sich, wer weiß aus was,   C
im letzten Augenblick vor deinen Schritten   D
und waren etwas Ungewisses mitten   D
im nassen Niederschlag der Gasse, das   C

nach dir verlangte. Oder nicht nach dir.   E
Denn eine Stimme, wie vom vorigen Jahr,   F
sang dich zwar an und blieb doch ein Geweine;   G
und eine Hand, die wie geliehen war,   F
kam zwar hervor und nahm doch nicht die deine.   G
Wer kommt denn noch? Wen meinen diese vier?   E

Foreign Family

As the dust that settles every day
appears from nowhere for some strange reason
during an empty morning in which one
stares at the corner where it gathers gray,

so they composed themselves, from who knows what,
in the blink of an eye, before your stride,
and became like things unknown that abide
in the damp dregs of the alley, things that

yearned for you. Or not for you at all.
Since a voice, as if from years ago,
sang out for you, then remained like tears;
and a hand, like something one might borrow,
indeed reached for you but did not take yours.
Who comes? Whom do these four think they recall?

Like his alter ego, Malte, Rilke treasured solitude and was often upset when confronted by people he did not recognize but who seemed to know him. Malte writes in his notebooks: "Who are these people? What do they want from me? Do they wait for me here? Where do they know me from?"

Leichenwäsche

Sie hatten sich an ihn gewöhnt. Doch als   A
die Küchenlampe kam und unruhig brannte   B
im dunkeln Luftzug, war der Unbekannte   B
ganz unbekannt. Sie wuschen seinen Hals,   A

und da sie nichts von seinem Schicksal wußten,   C
so logen sie ein anderes zusamm,   D
fortwährend waschend. Eine mußte husten   C
und ließ solang den schweren Essigschwamm   D

auf dem Gesicht. Da gab es eine Pause   E
auch für die zweite. Aus der harten Bürste   F
klopften die Tropfen; während seine grause   E
gekrampfte Hand dem ganzen Hause   E
beweisen wollte, daß ihn nicht mehr dürste.   F

Und er bewies. Sie nahmen wie betreten   G
eiliger jetzt mit einem kurzen Huster   H
die Arbeit auf, so daß an den Tapeten   G
ihr krummer Schatten in dem stummen Muster H

sich wand und wälzte wie in einem Netze,   I
bis daß die Waschenden zu Ende kamen.   J
Die Nacht im vorhanglosen Fensterrahmen   J
war rücksichtslos. Und einer ohne Namen   J
lag bar und reinlich da und gab Gesetze.   I

Malte Laurids Brigge speaks about seeing a body whose hair "looked as if it
had been combed by corpse-washing women, stiff as the hair of a stuffed and
mounted animal. I observed it all with great attention, and was struck by the
fact that this was also the place appointed to me, for I reckoned that finally this

Washing the Corpse

They had been used to him. But as the wick
of the kitchen lamp flared, and its flame shone
fitfully in the dim draft, wholly unknown
was the Unknown One. They scrubbed his neck,

and since they knew nothing of his case,
they lied between themselves about his life,
constantly washing. The one had to cough
and propped the vinegar-sponge on his face.

The other washer paused a while as well.
Out of her stiff brush, charged with water,
the droplets slowly dropped; while his hand fell
gruesome and contorted, and seemed to tell
the whole house that it thirsted no longer.

And he affirmed it. And now they began,
with a curt cough, working hastily at last,
as if ashamed, so their shadows were cast
upon the wallpaper's unspeaking span,

squirming over the wall as they bent,
as if caught in a net, till the washing came
to an end. Night in the drapeless window frame
was ruthless. And one lay there without a name,
naked, spotless, and rendering judgment.

is where I would end up. Yes, Fate walks a marvelous path." We are judged by the
dead simply because they force us to confront death, and therefore to account
for our lives.

Eine von den Alten

Paris

Abends manchmal (weißt du, wie das tut?)   A
wenn sie plötzlich stehn und rückwärts nicken   B
und ein Lächeln, wie aus lauter Flicken,   B
zeigen unter ihrem halben Hut.   A

Neben ihnen ist dann ein Gebäude,   C
endlos, und sie locken dich entlang   D
mit dem Rätsel ihrer Räude,   C
mit dem Hut, dem Umhang und dem Gang.   D

Mit der Hand, die hinten unterm Kragen   E
heimlich wartet und verlangt nach dir: F
wie um deine Hände einzuschlagen   E
in ein aufgehobenes Papier.   F

One of the Old Ones

Paris

Evenings sometimes (you know how it is?)
when they rise and give a backward nod while
from under their half-moon hats they smile—
a smile as odd as loud-colored patches.

Next to them stands the endless facade
of the buildings, and they lure you on,
with the hat, the cape, with the way they plod,
with the riddle of their mangy skin.

With the hand that lingers below the lapel
and secretly longs for you like a lover,
as if to wrap your hand in a parcel
made up of pieces of scrounged-up paper.

Older women were often drawn to Rilke, and he to them. Perhaps the poet was
constantly seeking a mother to replace Phia, who was too self-absorbed to give
him a mother's love. And so his life was full of surrogate mothers: Lou Andreas-
Salomé, Ellen Key, and even his first fiancée, Valerie von David-Rhônfeld. This
piece suggests that there was at least some ambivalence on Rilke's part.

Der Blinde

Paris

Sieh, er geht und unterbricht die Stadt,	A
die nicht ist auf seiner dunkeln Stelle,	B
wie ein dunkler Sprung durch eine helle	B
Tasse geht. Und wie auf einem Blatt	A
ist auf ihm der Widerschein der Dinge	C
aufgemalt; er nimmt ihn nicht hinein.	D
Nur sein Fühlen rührt sich, so als finge	C
es die Welt in kleinen Wellen ein:	D
eine Stille, einen Widerstand–,	E
und dann scheint er wartend wen zu wählen:	F
hingegeben hebt er seine Hand,	E
festlich fast, wie um sich zu vermählen.	F

The Blind Man

Paris

Watch how his walking disrupts the city,
which does not exist at his dim location,
as if a dark crack had traced its striation
through a light-colored cup. As if he

were a blank page and these reflections
were painted on him, he can't absorb any.
Stirring inside him are only emotions,
which trap the world in waves so tiny:

stillness and a kind of resistance stand
there as he hesitates to choose someone; abandoned, he raises up
his hand
as if to wed himself, almost solemn.

Malte Laurids Brigge encounters a blind man who sells newspapers in the Jardin du Luxembourg, "shuffling back and forth the whole evening long." The man reminds him of ivory carvings of the fallen Christ, which he has seen around Paris. Young Malte muses that he is a coward next to this unfortunate soul, who seems to embrace his fate and live life without hesitation or regret.

Eine Welke

Leicht, wie nach ihrem Tode   A
trägt sie die Handschuh, das Tuch.   B
Ein Duft aus ihrer Kommode   A
verdrängte den lieben Geruch,   B

an dem sie sich früher erkannte.   C
Jetzt fragte sie lange nicht, wer   D
sie sei (: eine ferne Verwandte),   C
und geht in Gedanken umher   D

und sorgt für ein ängstliches Zimmer,   E
das sie ordnet und schont,   F
weil es vielleicht noch immer   E
dasselbe Mädchen bewohnt.   F

The Wilted One

Lightly she wears the gloves and shawl
as if she were already dead,
the scent from her dresser has all
but dispossessed the beloved

smell of herself from earlier on.
Now she has long stopped questioning
who she is–a distant relation?
And deep in thought she is fretting

as she wanders the fussy room
that she tidies and keeps with care,
for perhaps she might still assume
the same young girl lives there.

In a letter to Clara dated June 26, 1906, Rilke wrote of waiting on a train platform while he closely observed his friend and correspondent Ellen Key, the Swedish feminist. "I comprehend now," he writes, "how this old maid was only one of many who lay up memories… of one thing: of that kind of love which… had already been so enthusiastically taken up by their hearts that the experience of it no longer needed to come at all." Key was fifty-seven at the time, and would die only a few months before Rilke, in 1926.

Abendmahl

Ewiges will zu uns. Wer hat die Wahl   A
und trennt die großen und geringen Kräfte?   B
Erkennst du durch das Dämmern der Geschäfte   B
im klaren Hinterraum das Abendmahl: A

wie sie sichs halten und wie sie sichs reichen   C
und in der Handlung schlicht und schwer beruhn.   D
Aus ihren Händen heben sich die Zeichen;   C
sie wissen nicht, daß sie sie tun   D

und immer neu mit irgendwelchen Worten   E
einsetzen, was man trinkt und was man teilt.   F
Denn da ist keiner, der nicht allerorten   E
heimlich von hinnen geht, indem er weilt.   F

Und sitzt nicht immer einer unter ihnen,   G
der seine Eltern, die ihm ängstlich dienen,   G
wegschenkt an ihre abgetane Zeit?   H
(Sie zu verkaufen, ist ihm schon zu weit.)   H

The Last Supper

The Eternal seeks us. But between greater
and lesser powers who can discriminate?
Do you see through the dimming shops, late
in the bright hinter-room, the last supper:

how they linger and pass the serving things,
and depend on this heavy and simple rite.
From their open hands many a sign springs,
yet they cannot see what they have wrought,

and no matter their words, invariably
they point to what one would drink or share.
For there is none who is not secretly,
even while remaining, absent from there.

And isn't there always one whose parents cater
to him timidly, who sends them away later
though he can see how old and used up they are?
(To sell them, he thinks, would be going too far.)

This portrait of a mundane family dinner reflects Rilke's dissatisfaction with
conventional family life, with people who sit around a common table but are
"secretly... absent from there." Concerning such a family Rilke wrote to Clara
in October 1907: "I have noticed that, when observed from the street, it always
reminds one of the Last Supper—so huge and solemn throughout the darkened
room." The title of this piece is often translated as simply "Evening Meal."
But Germans seldom use the term that way and refer to supper as *Abendbrot*,
Abendessen, Nachtmahl, or *Nachtessen. Abendmahl,* on the other hand, almost
always refers to the Last Supper or the Lord's Supper, and the betrayal in the
last stanza, one that parallels the betrayal by Judas, would make no sense with-
out this translation.

Die Brandstätte

Gemieden von dem Frühherbstmorgen, der   A
mißtrauisch war, lag hinter den versengten   B
Hauslinden, die das Heidehaus beengten,   B
ein Neues, Leeres. Eine Stelle mehr,   A

auf welcher Kinder, von Gott weiß woher,   A
einander zuschrien und nach Fetzen haschten.   C
Doch alle wurden stille, sooft er,   A
der Sohn von hier, aus heißen, halbveraschten   C

Gebälken Kessel und verbogne Tröge   D
an einem langen Gabelaste zog,–   E
um dann mit einem Blick als ob er löge   D
die andern anzusehn, die er bewog   E

zu glauben, was an dieser Stelle stand.   F
Denn seit es nicht mehr war, schien es ihm so   G
seltsam: phantastischer als Pharao.   G
Und er war anders. Wie aus fernem Land.   F

The Scene of the Fire

Shunned by the wary autumn-morning light,
somewhere behind the singed linden boughs
that crowded around the moorland house,
lay a newness, an emptiness. One more site

where children, from only God knows where,
screamed to each other, snatching at trash.
Yet all hushed when the boy who had lived there
dug among the hot embers and ash

pulling out kettles and pails warped by fire
with the long, forked branch of a tree;
and then, with the dubious look of a liar,
he fixed the others, to persuade them to see

the thing that had stood there just recently.
For since it was gone, it seemed to him so
peculiar and strange, fantastic as Pharaoh.
And he was changed. As if from some far country.

In *The Notebooks of Malte Laurids Brigge,* Malte writes about an imaginary fire:
"I suppose that in the course of great fires such an incident of extreme tension
must often occur: the streams of water fall back, the firefighters scramble up
their ladders, no one moves. Silently a fire-blackened cornice leans overhead,
and a high wall, with flames rising behind it, tips forward, soundlessly. Every-
one there stands and waits for the horrible crash, with shoulders raised and faces
lined above their eyes."

Die Gruppe

Paris

Als pflückte einer rasch zu einem Strauß: A
ordnet der Zufall hastig die Gesichter,   B
lockert sie auf und drückt sie wieder dichter,   B
ergreift zwei ferne, läßt ein nahes aus,   A

tauscht das mit dem, blast irgendeines frisch,   C
wirft einen Hund, wie Kraut, aus dem Gemisch   C
und zieht, was niedrig schaut, wie durch verworrne D
Stiele und Blätter, an dem Kopf nach vorne   D

und bindet es ganz klein am Rande ein;   E
und streckt sich wieder, ändert und verstellt   F
und hat nur eben Zeit, zum Augenschein   E

zurückzuspringen mitten auf die Matte,   G
auf der im nächsten Augenblick der glatte   G
Gewichteschwinger seine Schwere schwellt.   F

The Group

Paris

As if one quickly gathered a bouquet
Chance hurriedly arranges the faces,
loosens them and then tightly presses,
grabs two strays, throws a near one away,

swaps some out, blows off pollen and seed,
tosses a dog out of the bunch like a weed,
and pulls one up tall—through twisted stems and leaves—
that seems too short and mean where it now cleaves,

and tight at the stems it binds them together,
and stretches itself, changed and skewed again,
and has only just enough time to appear

to leap back into the center of the shot where,
in the next moment, sweating and bare,
the weight lifter stands and swells with the strain.

A lot of the elements in this poem, including the figure of the weight lifter,
the flowers and their pollen, the group of people made up like a bouquet, are
reprised in the fifth Duino Elegy. Like that poem, this one describes the antics
of a troupe of street performers led by Père Rollin, who were also the probable
subject of Picasso's *La Famille des saltimbanques* (1905). Their performance
might have been seen by Rilke at the Cirque Medrano in Montmartre, where
Picasso viewed them.

Schlangen-Beschwörung

Wenn auf dem Markt, sich wiegend, der Beschwörer A
die Kürbisflöte pfeift, die reizt und lullt, B
so kann es sein, daß er sich einen Hörer A
herüberlockt, der ganz aus dem Tumult B

der Buden eintritt in den Kreis der Pfeife, C
die will und will und will und die erreicht, D
daß das Reptil in seinem Korb sich steife C
und die das steife schmeichlerisch erweicht, D

abwechselnd immer schwindelnder und blinder E
mit dem, was schreckt und streckt, und dem, was löst−; F
und dann genügt ein Blick: so hat der Inder E
dir eine Fremde eingeflößt, F

in der du stirbst. Es ist als überstürze G
glühender Himmel dich. Es geht ein Sprung H
durch dein Gesicht. Es legen sich Gewürze G
auf deine nordische Erinnerung, H

die dir nichts hilft. Dich feien keine Kräfte, I
die Sonne gärt, das Fieber fällt und trifft; J
von böser Freude steilen sich die Schäfte, I
und in den Schlangen glänzt das Gift. J

Snake Charming

When the swaying charmer in the market square
pipes upon the teasing gourd-flute, he soothes
and sometimes lures a listener there,
who from the din and tumult of the booths

enters into the circle of the pipe,
which insists and insists with its tune,
till the reptile assumes a stiffer shape
that the charming flatterer softens soon

with swaying, blindly climbing derring-do
that frightens and lengthens; and after this
a mere glance suffices, and the Hindu
infuses you with foreignness,

in which you die. It's as if a glowing sky
had overtaken you. A fault runs through
your broken face. Your Nordic memory
fills with spices that are no help to you.

There is no power that can cure you then,
fever fells you, and the sun ferments,
from baleful joy the pillars steepen,
and poison glistens within the serpents.

In 1908 Clara Rilke sent her husband the speeches of Gautama Buddha as translated by Karl Neumann, an expert on Indian languages and culture. Rilke could not read it, writing back to her that with the book's first words he was convulsed with a shudder of recognition. He went on at length to state how he must defend his own work from all rivals for his attention. Similar fears of exotic influence are perhaps expressed in the poem above.

Schwarze Katze

Ein Gespenst ist noch wie eine Stelle,   A
dran dein Blick mit einem Klange stößt;   B
aber da, an diesem schwarzen Felle   A
wird dein stärkstes Schauen aufgelöst: B

wie ein Tobender, wenn er in vollster   C
Raserei ins Schwarze stampft,   D
jählings am benehmenden Gepolster   C
einer Zelle aufhört und verdampft.   D

Alle Blicke, die sie jemals trafen,   E
scheint sie also an sich zu verhehlen,   F
um darüber drohend und verdrossen   G
zuzuschauern und damit zu schlafen.   E
Doch auf einmal kehrt sie, wie geweckt,   H
ihr Gesicht und mitten in das deine: I
und da triffst du deinen Blick im geelen   F
Amber ihrer runden Augensteine   I
unerwartet wieder: eingeschlossen   G
wie ein ausgestorbenes Insekt.   H

Black Cat

If anything, a ghost is like some place
upon which your glance loudly trips and falls;
but here in this black pelt, within this space
your most intense gaze fades—it recalls

how a demon-inspired, maniacal rage
stomps into inscrutable darkness where,
stopped abruptly by the confining edge
of a padded cell, it dissolves in the air.

All the gazes that have ever touched her
she seems to conceal underneath her skin,
querulously looming above them where
she can watch them, lulling them to slumber.
Then she turns her features, which connect
her waking glance abruptly with your own;
and you encounter your own gaze within
the amber lump of each round eye-stone,
once again unforeseen, embedded there
like the fossil of an extinct insect.

The fur of the black cat, in which the gaze of the observer vanishes, serves as a
metaphor for the way we find ourselves in our observations of the world. As Rilke
wrote to Clara in 1907: "To observe something is such a marvelous thing—some-
thing of which we yet know little. When we observe we are turned wholly toward
the outside by this activity. But just when we are most turned outward something
occurs within us that has desired the unobserved moment, and while it unfolds
within us, whole and curiously anonymous, its significance takes place *without
us*, and shapes itself in the form of a strong, persuasive name, indeed, the only
possible name." And so, although the gaze is lost in the black fur, we discover
our own eyes in the eyes of the cat.

Vor-Ostern

Neapel

Morgen wird in diesen tiefgekerbten   A
Gassen, die sich durch getürmtes Wohnen   B
unten dunkel nach dem Hafen drängen,   C
hell das Gold der Prozessionen rollen;   D
statt der Fetzen werden die ererbten   A
Bettbezüge, welche wehen wollen,   D
von den immer höheren Balkonen   B
(wie in Fließendem gespiegelt) hängen.   C

Aber heute hämmert an den Klopfern   E
jeden Augenblick ein voll Bepackter,   F
und sie schleppen immer neue Käufe;   G
dennoch stehen strotzend noch die Stände.   H
An der Ecke zeigt ein aufgehackter   F
Ochse seine frischen Innenwände,   H
und in Fähnchen enden alle Läufe.   G
Und ein Vorrat wie von tausend Opfern   E

drängt auf Bänken, hängt sich rings um Pflöcke,   I
zwängt sich, wölbt sich, wälzt sich aus dem Dämmer   J
aller Türen, und vor dem Gegähne   K
der Melonen strecken sich die Brote.   L
Voller Gier und Handlung ist das Tote;   L
doch viel stiller sind die jungen Hähne   K
und die abgehängten Ziegenböcke   I
und am allerleisesten die Lämmer,   J

die die Knaben um die Schultern nehmen   M
und die willig von den Schritten nicken;   N
während in der Mauer der verglasten   O

Easter Eve

Naples

Tomorrow, past each piled-up dwelling,
through these deeply indented alleyways
that surge darkly down to the harbor,
the gold of the procession will brightly roll;
instead of rags and tatters, swelling
heirloom linens, which long to open whole
to the breeze, will hang from lofty balconies
as if mirrored in the flowing water.

But today each loaded-down peddler pounds
with the steady clocking of every beat,
dragging new merchandise in his bags
past the kiosks that are well supplied.
On the corner the ox hangs by its feet,
split apart to show the fresh tripe inside,
its pendant hooves arrayed with tiny flags.
And as if from a thousand altars, mounds

of meat cover tables, joints hang from the pegs,
pressing, arching, wallowing in the jambs
of twilight doors; and before the widely
gaping melons the loaves stretch themselves.
Full of greed and action, death stocks these shelves;
yet much stiller are the young poultry
and the goat carcass hanging by its legs,
and most mild are the tender, young lambs,

which the young lads bear on their shoulders,
and which nod consentingly to their gait;
while within the glass-sided enclosure

spanischen Madonna die Agraffe P

und das Silber in den Diademen M

von dem Lichter-Vorgefühl beglänzter Q

schimmert. Aber drüber in dem Fenster Q

zeigt sich blickverschwenderisch ein Affe P

und führt rasch in einer angemaßten O

Haltung Gesten aus, die sich nicht schicken. N

of the Spanish Madonna, the brooch she wears
with the silver coronet shimmers,
anticipating daylight's advent.
But high above in the window casement
a gaze-wasting monkey suddenly appears,
and with a most impertinent posture
makes quick gestures that are inappropriate.

This is one of the most elaborate rhyme schemes in *New Poems*—with rhymes
separated by as many as six lines. The Spanish Madonna seems to bear some
relation to "The Procession of the Virgin Mary" from the first volume of these
poems. The "gaze-wasting monkey" at the end is perhaps one of the first depic-
tions of masturbation in a German poem, and it owes much to Baudelaire's *Les
Fleurs du mal,* as does the image of the ox carcass.

Der Balkon

Neapel

Von der Enge, oben, des Balkones   X
angeordnet wie von einem Maler   A
und gebunden wie zu einem Strauß   B
alternder Gesichter und ovaler,   A
klar im Abend, sehn sie idealer,   A
rührender und wie für immer aus.   B

Diese aneinander angelehnten   C
Schwestern, die, als ob sie sich von weit   D
ohne Aussicht nacheinander sehnten,   C
lehnen, Einsamkeit an Einsamkeit;   D

und der Bruder mit dem feierlichen   E
Schweigen, zugeschlossen, voll Geschick,   F
doch von einem sanften Augenblick   F
mit der Mutter unbemerkt verglichen;   E

und dazwischen, abgelebt und länglich,   G
längst mit keinem mehr verwandt,   H
einer Greisin Maske, unzugänglich,   G
wie im Fallen von der einen Hand   H

aufgehalten, während eine zweite   I
welkere, als ob sie weitergleite,   I
unten vor den Kleidern hängt zur Seite   I

von dem Kinder-Angesicht,   J
das das Letzte ist, versucht, verblichen,   K

The Balcony

Naples

Above in the corner of the balcony,
as if they were posed with a painter's skill,
gathered together like a bouquet,
made up of aging faces, each oval
seen by evening's light seems more ideal,
more poignant, as if in a timeless way.

These sisters lean against each other,
as if hopeless, in a distant mood,
as if they longed for one another
they lean, solitude on solitude;

and the brother with his ritual silence,
shut up inside himself, full of fate,
yet compared with the mother, his opposite,
in a gentle and unnoticed glance;

and in between them, gaunt and miserable,
long since related to none of them at all,
a crone's mask that seems impenetrable,
as if caught by a hand in midfall,

while another gaunt hand seems to abide
as if it would float away on some tide,
hanging down from her clothing beside

the face of a child, the last one met,
which like something attempted seems to fade,

von den Stäben wieder durchgestrichen K
wie noch unbestimmbar, wie noch nicht. J

crossed out by the bars of the balustrade,
as if indefinable, as if not yet.

In this piece we clearly see Rilke's painterly way of looking at a subject. It is a poem that contains elements of and serves as a link between other poems in these two volumes. The metaphor of a group of people being made up like a bouquet of flowers also occurs in "The Group." The sour atmosphere of the family portrayed links it with "The Last Supper." And the child who is "indefinable, as if not yet" echoes the sentiments of "The Child."

Auswanderer-Schif

Neapel

Denk: daß einer heiß und glühend flüchte,	A
und die Sieger wären hinterher,	B
und auf einmal machte der	B
Flüchtende kurz, unerwartet, kehr	B
gegen Hunderte–: so sehr	B
warf sich das Erglühende der Früchte	A
immer wieder an das blaue Meer:	B
als das langsame Orangen-Boot	C
sie vorübertrug bis an das große	D
graue Schiff, zu dem, von Stoß zu Stoße,	D
andre Boote Fische hoben, Brot,–	C
während es, voll Hohn, in seinem Schooße	D
Kohlen aufnahm, offen wie der Tod.	C

Emigrant Ship

Naples

Imagine someone fled, hot and glowing,
and the victors were not far behind,
and suddenly this one fleeing blind
unexpectedly stopped short to find
himself confronting hundreds combined—
thus the fruit-colored gleam was flung
again and again where the blue sea reclined;

and as the orange-boat stole slowly by,
bearing them to the great gray ship, other craft,
from wave to wave, loaded the big boat aft
and forward with its fish and bread supply
while it scornfully took coal into the cleft
of its lap, which lay open as death might lie.

When Rilke was composing these poems, around the beginning of the twentieth century, Naples was the primary embarkation point for Italian emigrants, most of whom were from the impoverished south of the country. Many of them would have been bound for North or South America, and the poet would have glimpsed the motley craft, such as the orange boat mentioned here, that ferried the emigrants to larger oceangoing ships anchored out in the bay. Rilke was staying at the Hotel Hassler in Naples during November and December 1906.

Landschaft

Wie zuletzt, in einem Augenblick   A
aufgehäuft aus Hängen, Häusern, Stücken   B
alter Himmel und zerbrochnen Brücken,   B
und von drüben her, wie vom Geschick,   A
von dem Sonnenuntergang getroffen,   C
angeschuldigt, aufgerissen, offen–   C
ginge dort die Ortschaft tragisch aus: D

fiele nicht auf einmal in das Wunde,   E
drin zerfließend, aus der nächsten Stunde   E
jener Tropfen kühlen Blaus,   D
der die Nacht schon in den Abend mischt,   F
so daß das von ferne Angefachte   X
sachte, wie erlöst, erlischt.   F

Ruhig sind die Tore und die Bogen,   G
durchsichtige Wolken wogen   G
über blassen Häuserreihn   H
die schon Dunkel in sich eingesogen;   G
aber plötzlich ist vom Mond ein Schein   H
durchgeglitten, licht, als hätte ein   H
Erzengel irgendwo sein Schwert gezogen.   G

Landscape

How at last in a single moment,
heaped up from houses and broken bridges,
from hills and bits of old sky at its edges,
from things past, as if destiny-sent,
struck by the setting sun's expiring flare,
incriminated, ripped open and bare;
the village would be tragically snuffed out

if at once into the wound there didn't fall,
within the hour, dissolving into it all,
that drop of cooling blue, that last rout
of day that already mixes the night
with evening; so that what has been lit
from afar dies gently, redeemed by twilight.

The gates and arcades rest in concord,
clouds sweep by in a diaphanous horde
over rows of houses fraught with paleness
that are already taking darkness aboard;
but suddenly from the moon a brightness
shines through, brilliantly, as if one no less
than an archangel had unsheathed his sword.

Referring to Paul Cézanne, Rilke writes Clara on October 9, 1907: "In the case of landscapes... he still made the thing his own by means of complicated detours. Beginning with the darkest hue... extending color upon color, he gradually reached another contrasting element of the picture, from which he then proceeded, in a similar way, from some new center." Compare that to the way Rilke constructs this poem.

Römische Campagna

Aus der vollgestellten Stadt, die lieber	A
schliefe, träumend von den hohen Thermen,	B
geht der grade Gräberweg ins Fieber;	A
und die Fenster in den letzten Fermen	B
sehn ihm nach mit einem bösen Blick.	C
Und er hat sie immer im Genick,	C
wenn er hingeht, rechts und links zerstörend,	D
bis er draußen atemlos beschwörend	D
seine Leere zu den Himmeln hebt,	E
hastig um sich schauend, ob ihn keine	F
Fenster treffen. Während er den weiten	G
Aquädukten zuwinkt herzuschreiten,	G
geben ihm die Himmel für die seine	F
ihre Leere, die ihn überlebt.	E

Rilke was an avid admirer of the Danish writer Jens Peter Jacobsen; in fact he said that he kept only the works of this writer and the Bible with him at all times. This poem evokes a passage from Jacobsen's short story "There Should Have Been Roses," translated from the Danish by Anna Grabow:

> And now the houses hide him, they hide everything on that side. They hide one another and the road and the city, but on the other side there is still a distant view. There the road swings in an indolent, slow curve down toward the river, down toward the mournful bridge. And behind this lies the immense Campania.

Roman Campagna

Out of the crowded city that would rather
sleep, dreaming of the elegant *thermae,*
the road of tombs heads straight into fever;
and the last windows that it passes by

focus the evil eye upon its back.
And it always has them at its neck
as it rolls by, shaking them left and right
till past the walls, attesting in breathless flight,

it lifts its emptiness up to the skies,
hastily glancing about itself to see
that there are no windows. While it summons

the distant aqueducts to it, the heavens
seem to trade their emptiness freely
for its own, and will outlast it likewise.

> The gray and the green of such large plains…. It is as if the weariness
> of many tedious miles rose out of them and settled with a heavy weight
> upon one, and made one feel lonely and forsaken, and filled one with
> desires and yearning.

The "road of tombs" is, of course, the Appian Way, which is lined with ancient
Roman graves as it heads south into Campania. And the "elegant *thermae*" are
likely the Baths of Caracalla, which are the last great ruins this ancient road
passes before it leaves the walls of Rome.

Lied vom Meer

Capri, Piccola Marina

Uraltes Wehn vom Meer,	A
Meerwind bei Nacht:	B
du kommst zu keinem her;	A
wenn einer wacht,	B
so muß er sehn, wie er	A
dich übersteht:	C
uraltes Wehn vom Meer,	A
welches weht	C
nur wie für Ur-Gestein,	D
lauter Raum	E
reißend von weit herein...	D
O wie fühlt dich ein	D
treibender Feigenbaum	E
oben im Mondschein.	D

Song out of the Sea

Capri, Piccola Marina

Ancient breeze of the sea,
sea wind in the night,
 you come seeking nobody;
if one wakes before light
he is bound to see how he
may finally weather you;
 ancient breeze of the sea,
blowing anew
merely as if for ancient stone,
blatant space
coming from some place unknown.
 Oh how the sprouts full-blown
on the fig tree embrace
you by the light of the moon.

One of many poems written at the Villa Discopoli on Capri. Rilke first read this piece to his hostess, Baroness von Nordeck zur Rabenau, and her guests on the evening of January 6, 1907. "Ancient stone" evokes the limestone *rocca viva* of the island. The *treibender Feigenbaum,* or sprouting fig tree, probably is a reference to fruiting, not flowering sprouts, since the fig flowers internally. Or it might refer to the *Fichi d'india* (fig of the Indies), the imported Mexican cactus pear that has naturalized on Capri and many another island in the Mediterranean and that does, in fact, flower.

Nächtliche Fahrt

Sankt Petersburg

Damals als wir mit den glatten Trabern   A
(schwarzen, aus dem Orloff'schen Gestüt)–,   B
während hinter hohen Kandelabern   A
Stadtnachtfronten lagen, angefrüht,   B
stumm und keiner Stunde mehr gemäß–,   C
fuhren, nein: vergingen oder flogen   D
und um lastende Paläste bogen   D
in das Wehn der Newa-Quais,   C

hingerissen durch das wache Nachten,   E
das nicht Himmel und nicht Erde hat,–   F
als das Drängende von unbewachten   E
Gärten gärend aus dem Ljetnij-Ssad   F
aufstieg, während seine Steinfiguren   G
schwindend mit ohnmächtigen Konturen   G
hinter uns vergingen, wie wir fuhren–:   G

damals hörte diese Stadt   F
auf zu sein. Auf einmal gab sie zu,   H
daß sie niemals war, um nichts als Ruh   H
flehend; wie ein Irrer, dem das Wirrn   I
plötzlich sich entwirrt, das ihn verriet,   J
und der einen jahrelangen kranken   K
gar nicht zu verwandelnden Gedanken,   K
den er nie mehr denken muß: Granit–   J

.

Night Journey

Saint Petersburg

At that time, behind the silken team
(the black trotters, foals of the Orlov stud),
while beyond the streetlight's lofty beam
shone the night facades of the city arrayed
in the coming morning, soundless, unallied
with any hour, we were driving, no, fading
or flying, as past the last palaces we swung
into the wind of the Neva dockside,

enraptured through the watchful nighttime,
where no trace of heaven or earth had spread,
as the surge of the unguarded gardens came
fermenting up out of the Letny Sad
while its bank-side escort of marble figures,
diminishing with its helpless contours,
vanished behind as we traveled its course:

at that time this city had
ceased to be. It granted never having been,
pleading only for peace, like a madman
all of a sudden waking to find
the betraying chaos untangled a bit,
who afterward is never again fraught
with diseased, unending, unchanging thought,
which he need nevermore suffer: granite –

aus dem leeren schwankenden Gehirn   I
fallen fühlt, bis man ihn nicht mehr sieht.   J

falling from the empty, wavering mind,
until one can no longer even see it.

It seems likely that this poem was written on Capri at the Villa Discopoli. Maksim Gorky was one of the expatriates that Rilke met there, and the Russian evidently brought back memories of Rilke's visit to Saint Petersburg with Lou Andreas-Salomé in 1900. Rilke writes to Karl von der Heydt: "We were able to understand each other first in Russian.... Later I spoke German and Madame Gorky translated." Some elements from Gorky's play *Children of the Sun* seem to echo in the poem. The oblivion of the city and its "bank-side escort of marble figures, / diminishing with its helpless contours" reflects the lack of awareness in the intellectual elites portrayed in the drama.

Papageien-Park

Jardin des Plantes, Paris

Unter türkischen Linden, die blühen, an Rasenrändern,	A
in leise von ihrem Heimweh geschaukelten Ständern	A
atmen die Ara und wissen von ihren Ländern,	A
die sich, auch wenn sie nicht hinsehn, nicht verändern.	A
Fremd im beschäftigten Grünen wie eine Parade,	B
zieren sie sich und fühlen sich selber zu schade,	B
und mit den kostbaren Schnäbeln aus Jaspis und Jade	B
kauen sie Graues, verschleudern es, finden es fade.	B
Unten klauben die duffen Tauben, was sie nicht mögen,	C
während sich oben die höhnischen Vögel verbeugen	D
zwischen den beiden fast leeren vergeudeten Trögen.	C
Aber dann wiegen sie wieder und schläfern und äugen,	D
spielen mit dunkelen Zungen, die gerne lögen,	C
zerstreut an den Fußfesselringen. Warten auf Zeugen.	D

Parrot Park

Jardin des Plantes, Paris

Under the Turkish lindens blooming on the grassy strand,
hushed by homesickness, each on its own swaying stand,
the parrots breathe and ponder, thinking of their distant land,
which has not changed for these who cannot see it firsthand.

On this bustling strip of green they seem strange as a parade,
putting on a coyness in which self-pity is portrayed,
and with sumptuous beaks that recall jasper and jade
they try gray morsels, find them tasteless, let them cascade

where drab-colored turtledoves pick up the throwaways
while above the sneering parrots bow with scornfulness
between the two neglected, almost empty feeder trays.

But then they drowse and sway again, showing tongues of darkness
that would gladly savor lies below eyes that seem to gaze,
distraught and pecking at their foot chains, waiting for a witness.

The Jardin des Plantes in Paris sits on the Seine where the quai Saint-Bernard
meets the place Valhubert, and Rilke was fond of walking the grounds and view-
ing the animals in the menagerie. The parrots might have been located on the
allée Buffon, as they appear to be of the species *Ara,* among which are num-
bered *Ara ambiguus* or Buffon's Macaw, a large, bright green bird. Georges-Louis
Leclerc, Comte de Buffon, was the French naturalist for whom both the parrot
and the park road were named.

Die Parke

I

Unaufhaltsam heben sich die Parke	A
aus dem sanft zerfallenden Vergehn;	B
überhäuft mit Himmeln, überstarke	A
Überlieferte, die überstehn,	B
um sich auf den klaren Rasenplänen	C
auszubreiten und zurückzuziehn,	D
immer mit demselben souveränen	C
Aufwand, wie beschützt durch ihn,	D
und den unerschöpflichen Erlös	E
königlicher Größe noch vermehrend,	F
aus sich steigend, in sich wiederkehrend:	F
huldvoll, prunkend, purpurn und pompös.	E

The Parks

I

Relentlessly the parks swell up among
the heaps of soft and moldering rot,
overwhelmed with sky, with overly strong
birthrights, prevailing so they might,

along these discrete networks of grass,
finally propagate and then retreat,
always with the selfsame, sovereign mass
of luxury, as if they were guarded by it;

and their never-ending revenues thus
seem endless as the grandeur of a king,
rising from themselves, in themselves recurring–
gracious, flaunting, purple and pompous.

II

Leise von den Alleen   A
ergriffen, rechts und links,   B
folgend dem Weitergehen   A
irgend eines Winks,   B

trittst du mit einem Male   C
in das Beisammensein   D
einer schattigen Wasserschale   C
mit vier Bänken aus Stein;   D

in eine abgetrennte   E
Zeit, die allein vergeht.   F
Auf feuchte Postamente,   E
auf denen nichts mehr steht,   F

hebst du einen tiefen   G
erwartenden Atemzug;   H
während das silberne Triefen   G
von dem dunkeln Bug   H

dich schon zu den Seinen   I
zählt und weiterspricht.   J
Und du fühlst dich unter Steinen   I
die hören, und rührst dich nicht.   J

Softly seized by the promenades
at the left- and rightmost sides,
as if following someone's nods
to go on with urgent strides,

you come within a moment's pace
to a fountain, a dappled one,
entering the gathering place
with four seats made of stone

as a single, severed minute falls,
and all alone it ends.
At damp and weathered pedestals
whereupon nothing stands,

sinking deep in expectation
you feel a sighing swell
while the silvery libation
slips from the shadowed shell

that already counts you as its own,
and now it speaks anew.
And you feel as if all this stone
hears, but does not move you.

III

Den Teichen und den eingerahmten Weihern   A
verheimlicht man noch immer das Verhör   B
der Könige. Sie warten unter Schleiern,   A
und jeden Augenblick kann Monseigneur   B

vorüberkommen; und dann wollen sie   C
des Königs Laune oder Trauer mildern   D
und von den Marmorrändern wieder die   C
Teppiche mit alten Spiegelbildern   D

hinunterhängen, wie um einen Platz: E
auf grünem Grund, mit Silber, Rosa, Grau,   F
gewährtem Weiß und leicht gerührtem Blau   F
und einem Könige und einer Frau   F
und Blumen in dem wellenden Besatz.   E

III

The bordered ponds and ornamental pools
forever obscure the king's arraignment
as they wait beneath their misted veils,
for My Lord might stroll by at any moment,

and then these waters would appear to hedge
the royal sadness, or perhaps its temper,
and once again at the marble's very edge
carpets of ancient reflections linger,

hanging down as if around a square:
green ground, with rose, gray, and silver hues,
genuine white and lightly emoting blues,
and a king and a woman seem to muse
over flowers in the swelling beds there.

IV

Und Natur, erlaucht und als verletze   A
sie nur unentschloßnes Ungefähr,   B
nahm von diesen Königen Gesetze,   A
selber selig, um den Tapis-vert   B

ihrer Bäume Traum und Übertreibung   C
aufzutürmen aus gebauschtem Grün   D
und die Abende nach der Beschreibung   C
von Verliebten in die Avenün   D

einzumalen mit dem weichen Pinsel,   E
der ein firnisklares aufgelöstes   F
Lächeln glänzend zu enthalten schien: G

der Natur ein liebes, nicht ihr größtes,   F
aber eines, das sie selbst verliehn,   G
um auf rosenvoller Liebes-Insel   E
es zu einem größern aufzuziehn.   G

IV

And illustrious Nature, as if hurt
only by the aimlessly approximate,
took the laws of these kings to heart,
blessedly, as if to accumulate

a green carpet of exaggerations
and tree-dreams from its verdant billows,
taking evenings from the narrations
of lovers' trysts among the avenues,

painted with supple brush in hand,
which seems in its gleaming stroke to cast
a transitory, clear-lacquered smile,

which Nature loves, not yet her greatest,
but one that she herself might will,
as if, on some rose-filled love-island,
to raise it up to something greater still.

V

Götter von Alleen und Altanen,   A
niemals ganzgeglaubte Götter, die   B
altern in den gradbeschnittnen Bahnen,   A
höchstens angelächelte Dianen   A
wenn die königliche Venerie   B

wie ein Wind die hohen Morgen teilend   C
aufbrach, übereilt und übereilend–;   C
höchstens angelächelte, doch nie   B

angeflehte Götter. Elegante   D
Pseudonyme, unter denen man   E
sich verbarg und blühte oder brannte,–   D
leichtgeneigte, lächelnd angewandte   D
Götter, die noch manchmal dann und wann   E

das gewähren, was sie einst gewährten,   F
wenn das Blühen der entzückten Gärten   F
ihnen ihre kalte Haltung nimmt;   G
wenn sie ganz von ersten Schatten beben   H
und Versprechen um Versprechen geben,   H
alle unbegrenzt und unbestimmt.   G

V

Gods of the promenades and balconies,
never-fully-believed-in gods who age
in the neatly manicured pathways,
at their best like smiled-upon effigies
of Diana when the royal entourage,

like a wind dividing lofty tomorrows,
broke forth, rash and rushing, at best those
smiled-upon gods whom we might engage

but whom we never beseech. Elegant
pseudonyms among whose multitude one
hid oneself to bloom or burn, nonchalant
gods of the most practical covenant,
those who nevertheless now and again

may yet grant that which they once granted when
the heady blossoms of the charmed garden
relieved them of their cold bearing and pride,
when they quake with the first shadows and this
seems to give out promise upon promise,
all of them boundless and unspecified.

VI

Fühlst du, wie keiner von allen   A
Wegen steht und stockt;   B
von gelassenen Treppen fallen,   A
durch ein Nichts von Neigung   X
leise weitergelockt,   B
über alle Terrassen   C
die Wege, zwischen den Massen   C
verlangsamt und gelenkt,   D
bis zu den weiten Teichen,   E
wo sie (wie einem Gleichen)   E
der reiche Park verschenkt   D

an den reichen Raum: den Einen,   F
der mit Scheinen und Widerscheinen   F
seinen Besitz durchdringt,   G
aus dem er von allen Seiten   X
Weiten mit sich bringt,   G
wenn er aus schließenden Weihern   H
zu wolkigen Abendfeiern   H
sich in die Himmel schwingt.   G

VI

Do you sense how none among all
these paths could stop or stagnate:
from serene stairways they fall,
over the barely rising grade,
easily progressing straight
over all the terraces
along the way, between masses
that channel them, slowing their pace,
right up to the distant pools
where the opulent park fills
(like an equal) sumptuous space,

instilling it with that union
which with light and its reflection
infuses all of its possessions,
that which from every side
opens wide with expansions
when from the concluding lakes
to the clouded twilight feasts it breaks,
resonating to the heavens.

VII

Aber Schalen sind, drin der Najaden   A
Spiegelbilder, die sie nicht mehr baden,   A
wie ertrunken liegen, sehr verzerrt;   B
die Alleen sind durch Balustraden   A
in der Ferne wie versperrt.   B

Immer geht ein feuchter Blätterfall   C
durch die Luft hinunter wie auf Stufen,   D
jeder Vogelruf ist wie verrufen,   D
wie vergiftet jede Nachtigall.   C

Selbst der Frühling ist da nicht mehr gebend,   E
diese Büsche glauben nicht an ihn;   F
ungern duftet trübe, überlebend   E
abgestandener Jasmin   F

alt und mit Zerfallendem vermischt.   G
Mit dir weiter rückt ein Bündel Mücken,   H
so als würde hinter deinem Rücken   H
alles gleich vernichtet und verwischt.   G

VII

But there are fountains where Naiad
reflections no longer seem to wade,
lying there as if drowned and faded,
and those pathways seen through the balustrade
in the distance, which seem barricaded.

The damp leaves fall in a shimmering veil
downward through the air as if in swells,
and every birdcall infamously trills,
as if poisoned by the nightingale.

Even Spring is no longer generous,
the bushes no longer believe in its spell;
begrudgingly the barely prosperous
jasmine issues a cloying smell,

one that is old and rot-permeated.
Then moving with you a swarm of midges
hovers behind you and at your edges,
till everything there is blurred and negated.

In a letter to Clara on October 3, 1907, Rilke writes of Van Gogh and his render-
ing of parks: "And so he sees everything as a poor man would; one need only to
compare his parks. These also he states so quietly and simply, as if for the poor,
so they might understand it…. He takes no sides, not even the side of the parks,
and his love for it all proceeds toward the nameless and thus has become hidden
by him. He doesn't show it, he possesses it." This seems to be a different quality
from the one Rilke is aiming for in this extended piece. Rilke's parks are empty,
lonely places. As William H. Gass wrote of him: "Rilke's strategy for the defeat
of time was to turn it into space," and in the seven sections that constitute this
poem, Rilke turned his hours on the grounds of Versailles into spaces in which
eternity echoes.

Bildnis

Dass von dem verzichtenden Gesichte   X
keiner ihrer großen Schmerzen fiele,   A
trägt sie langsam durch die Trauerspiele   A
ihrer Züge schönen welken Strauß,   B
wild gebunden und schon beinah lose;   C
manchmal fällt, wie eine Tuberose,   C
ein verlornes Lächeln müd heraus.   B

Und sie geht gelassen drüber hin,   D
müde, mit den schönen blinden Händen,   E
welche wissen, daß sie es nicht fänden, –   E

und sie sagt Erdichtetes, darin   D
Schicksal schwankt, gewolltes, irgendeines, F
und sie giebt ihm ihrer Seele Sinn,   D
daß es ausbricht wie ein Ungemeines: F
wie das Schreien eines Steines –   F

und sie läßt, mit hochgehobnem Kinn,   D
alle diese Worte wieder fallen,   G
ohne bleibend; denn nicht eins von allen G
ist der wehen Wirklichkeit gemäß,   H
ihrem einzigen Eigentum,   I
das sie, wie ein fußloses Gefäß,   H

Portrait

She wears her face of resignation
so that none of her sorrows are on display,
and as she slowly bears this faded bouquet
through tragic plays, her wildly gathered pose
already seems to be unraveling;
sometimes a falling smile seems to spring
from her, lost and weary, like a tuberose.

And tired and indifferent she passes by,
with blind and lovely hands that understand
that there is something they might never find,

and she says fictitious things that fly
in the face of fate, willful things, anything,
with meanings her soul seeks to justify,
that erupt and flow from her like something
extraordinary, like a stone's screaming,

and she allows, with her chin flung high,
all these words to fall again, headlong,
without lingering, for not one among
them is worth a reality so sorrowful:
her single possession, that she therefore
must hold, like some sort of footless vessel,

halten muß, hoch über ihren Ruhm
und den Gang der Abende hinaus.

raising it high over her own splendor
as over the road of evening she goes.

A very common extended metaphor in *New Poems* is one in which Rilke compares the features of a person or the attributes of a group of people to a bouquet and its composition. Along with this poem the device is also used in "Tombs of the Hetaerae," "The Group," and "The Balcony." Something in this portrait seems to suggest that its subject might be Ellen Key, the Swedish feminist writer who was Rilke's friend. She was often mistaken (according to Rilke) in her critical evaluation of the poet's work ("she says fictitious things... willful things"). And Rilke is often less than generous in his comments on her appearance, her face's "faded bouquet," as when he describes her as an old maid in a letter to his wife, Clara. The poet's ambivalent relationship with her was probably due to his reliance on her for money, which Key, a very frugal though well-off woman, dispensed in meager amounts.

Venezianischer Morgen

Richard Beer-Hofmann zugeeignet

Fürstlich verwöhnte Fenster sehen immer,   A
was manchesmal uns zu bemühn geruht: B
die Stadt, die immer wieder, wo ein Schimmer   A
von Himmel trifft auf ein Gefühl von Flut,   B

sich bildet ohne irgendwann zu sein.   C
Ein jeder Morgen muß ihr die Opale   D
erst zeigen, die sie gestern trug, und Reihn   C
von Spiegelbildern ziehn aus dem Kanale   D
und sie erinnern an die andern Male: D
dann giebt sie sich erst zu und fällt sich ein   C

wie eine Nymphe, die den Zeus empfing.   E
Das Ohrgehäng erklingt an ihrem Ohre;   F
sie aber hebt San Giorgio Maggiore   F
und lächelt lässig in das schöne Ding.   E

Venetian Morning

for Richard Beer-Hofmann

Windows of opulence forever gaze
upon what to us often seems troubling:
the city, wherein the shimmering skies
collide with a sense of water flooding,

forever takes shape without existing.
Each dawn she must first display the opals
that she wore yesterday, those hanging
like rows of reflections in the canals,
invoking other times that she recalls;
she first concedes and then, welcoming

Zeus like a nymph, down she comes tumbling.
The earrings at her ears tinkle and sway,
but she raises up San Giorgio Maggiore
and smiles casually into that fair thing.

The mysterious and mythic figure looming large over the Venetian landscape
here, who "raises up San Giorgio Maggiore," may have been inspired by Mimi
Romanelli, with whom Rilke fell in love during his 1907 visit to that city. At the
time he wrote her that he was "happy that I gave myself up without reserve to
your beauty, like a bird surrendering itself to space." He corresponded with
Mimi, a brilliant pianist who was also admired by the poet Gabriele D'Annunzio,
for many years afterward. Richard Beer-Hofmann, Rilke's friend to whom this
piece is dedicated, was a poet in his own right.

Spätherbst in Venedig

Nun treibt die Stadt schon nicht mehr wie ein Köder, A
der alle aufgetauchten Tage fängt. B
Die gläsernen Paläste klingen spröder A
an deinen Blick. Und aus den Gärten hängt B

der Sommer wie ein Haufen Marionetten C
kopfüber, müde, umgebracht. D
Aber vom Grund aus alten Waldskeletten C
steigt Willen auf: als sollte über Nacht D

der General des Meeres die Galeeren E
verdoppeln in dem wachen Arsenal, F
um schon die nächste Morgenluft zu teeren E

mit einer Flotte, welche ruderschlagend G
sich drängt und jäh, mit allen Flaggen tagend, G
den großen Wind hat, strahlend und fatal. F

Late Autumn in Venice

Now the city drifts no longer like a lure
that catches all the breaching tomorrows.
The glassy palaces ring harshly before
your eyes. And among the garden rows

summer hangs head-over-heels and oppressed,
done for, like marionettes in a heap.
But from each skeleton of the forest,
from each sunken pile, the will rises from sleep:

as if overnight the marshal of the seas
had to double the galleys in the arsenal
in order to tar the next morning's breeze

with a fleet, which, with oars surging,
thrusts itself suddenly, all flags converging,
and catches the great wind, beaming and fatal.

Rilke loved Venice, and had visited the city in 1897 and 1903 before returning in 1907, while he was composing the works that would make up *New Poems.* Upon leaving he was saddened, and recalled that as he took a water taxi to the train station on a winter's morning the gondolier's call upon approaching the juncture of another canal "echoed unanswered as if in the face of death."

San Marco

Venedig

In diesem Innern, das wie ausgehöhlt	A
sich wölbt und wendet in den goldnen Smalten,	B
rundkantig, glatt, mit Köstlichkeit geölt,	A
ward dieses Staates Dunkelheit gehalten	B
und heimlich aufgehäuft, als Gleichgewicht	C
des Lichtes, das in allen seinen Dingen	D
sich so vermehrte, daß sie fast vergingen –.	D
Und plötzlich zweifelst du: vergehn sie nicht?	C
und drängst zurück die harte Galerie,	E
die, wie ein Gang im Bergwerk, nah am Glanz	F
der Wölbung hängt; und du erkennst die heile	G
Helle des Ausblicks: aber irgendwie	E
wehmütig messend ihre müde Weile	G
am nahen Überstehn des Viergespanns	F

San Marco

Venice

This inner space, hollowed out and tiled,
arches and turns with gilded cobalt,
round-edged, glazed, expensively oiled:
the darkness of the state was stored in this vault,

secretly collected, like a counterweight
to the light, that in its every way
increases till it almost seems to decay.
And at once you muse: isn't this its fate?

And you turn from the severe gallery,
that mine shaft tracing a vein of ore
through the vaulted radiance, and you spy

the vista's hale brightness, in some way
measuring its own weary tenure by
the approaching shape of the coach and four.

In the autumn of 1907 Rilke wrote his wife, Clara, from Venice: "*This* Venice
seems to me almost difficult to admire and has to be learned over and over again
from the outset. Its marble stands there, ashen, gray in the grayness, light as the
ashen rim of a log that has just now been aglow."

Ein Doge

Fremde Gesandte sahen, wie sie geizten   A
mit ihm und allem was er tat;   B
während sie ihn zu seiner Größe reizten,   A
umstellten sie das goldene Dogat   B

mit Spähern und Beschränkern immer mehr,   C
bange, daß nicht die Macht sie überfällt,   D
die sie in ihm (so wie man Löwen hält)   D
vorsichtig nährten. Aber er,   C

im Schutze seiner halbverhängten Sinne,   E
ward dessen nicht gewahr und hielt nicht inne,   E
größer zu werden. Was die Signorie   F

in seinem Innern zu bezwingen glaubte,   G
bezwang er selbst. In seinem greisen Haupte   G
war es besiegt. Sein Antlitz zeigte wie.   F

A Doge

The foreign ambassadors saw the way
they resented him and all his business,
even while spurring him to greatness they
circumscribed the Doge's golden office

ever more with constraints and with spies,
fearful lest the might they nourished in him
(the way men keep lions) should fall upon them.
But he, in the shelter and disguise

of his close-held intellect, was unaware
and would not regress, so that everywhere
he kept on growing greater. So that now

what the Council sought to overcome
he himself overcame. In his graying dome
it was conquered. His face showed how.

Perhaps this piece is a portrait of Rodin, as the Buddha poems are all portraits of
the great sculptor. Read this way, one of the foreign ambassadors would be Rilke
himself, and the council, no doubt, would be the critical establishment of Paris.
As Rilke says of Rodin in a letter to Clara on September 2, 1902: "That forehead,
the relationship it bears to his nose.... The character of stone is in that brow and
that nose." But it is just as likely the poem was inspired by some painting Rilke
had observed. The actual Doge of Venice endured the checks and balances of a
Council of Ten, which could either approve or veto his measures.

Die Laute

Ich bin die Laute. Willst du meinen Leib   A
beschreiben, seine schön gewölbten Streifen: B
sprich so, als sprächest du von einer reifen   B
gewölbten Feige. Übertreib   A

das Dunkel, das du in mir siehst. Es war   C
Tullias Dunkelheit. In ihrer Scham   D
war nicht so viel, und ihr erhelltes Haar   C
war wie ein heller Saal. Zuweilen nahm   D

sie etwas Klang von meiner Oberfläche   E
in ihr Gesicht und sang zu mir.   F
Dann spannte ich mich gegen ihre Schwäche,   E
und endlich war mein Inneres in ihr.   F

The Lute

I am the Lute. If you would portray
my body, its splendid, arching stripe,
tell it so: as if a bursting-ripe
fig were your subject. Overplay

the darkness you see in me. It was fair
Tullia's dark quality. But in the nook
of her private place there was less, and her hair
was like a chamber of light. At times she took

some tones from my sounding surface
into her face, and she sang me an air.
Then I stretched myself against her softness,
and at last my essence was within her.

This seems to be the last of the Venetian suite of poems that starts with "Vene-
tian Morning." The Tullia mentioned here is Tullia d'Aragona, a Venetian cour-
tesan who was the lover of the Renaissance poet Bernardo Tasso. Her father was
probably Cardinal Luigi d'Aragona, by whom she was educated. This poem also
serves as a companion piece to "The Courtesan," a verse from volume one. Both
poems are in the first-person singular, present tense, which occurs only rarely
in *New Poems.*

Der Abenteuerer

I

Wenn er unter jene, welche *waren*
trat: der Plötzliche, der *schien,*
war ein Glanz wie von Gefahren
in dem ausgesparten Raum um ihn,

den er lächelnd überschritt, um einer
Herzogin den Fächer aufzuheben:
diesen warmen Fächer, den er eben
wollte fallen sehen. Und wenn keiner

mit ihm eintrat in die Fensternische
(wo die Parke gleich ins Träumerische
stiegen, wenn er nur nach ihnen wies),
ging er lässig an die Kartentische
und gewann. Und unterließ

nicht, die Blicke alle zu behalten,
die ihn zweifelnd oder zärtlich trafen,
und auch die in Spiegel fielen, galten.
Er beschloß, auch heute nicht zu schlafen,

wie die letzte lange Nacht, und bog
einen Blick mit seinem rücksichtslosen
welcher war: als hätte er von Rosen
Kinder, die man irgendwo erzog.

The Adventurer

Walking among those who merely *existed,*
the Sudden One suddenly *shone,*
and an aura of danger persisted
and from the space around him had grown;

that space he crossed with a smile to see
whether a duchess may raise up her fan,
that warm fan, desiring nothing more than
its falling. And if none of the party

joined him beneath the window gable
(where the parks achieved a dreamlike spell
merely from his act of pointing there)
he went casually to the card table
and won. And not once did he forbear

to gather all the glances that intersected
his stare, some of them tender, some doubtful,
even those in the mirror he collected.
He decided not to sleep today as well,

as he had not slept last night, and his own
reckless vision inflected his glance,
which seemed as if it had borne children once
from roses someone somewhere had grown.

II

In den Tagen – (nein, es waren keine),   A
da die Flut sein unterstes Verlies   B
ihm bestritt, als wär es nicht das seine,   A
und ihn, steigend, an die Steine   A
der daran gewöhnten Wölbung stieß,   B

fiel ihm plötzlich einer von den Namen   C
wieder ein, die er vor Zeiten trug.   D
Und er wußte wieder: Leben kamen,   C
wenn er lockte; wie im Flug   D

kamen sie: noch warme Leben Toter,   E
die er, ungeduldiger, bedrohter,   E
weiterlebte mitten drin;   F
oder die nicht ausgelebten Leben,   G
und er wußte sie hinaufzuheben,   G
und sie hatten wieder Sinn.   F

Oft war keine Stelle an ihm sicher,   H
und er zitterte: Ich bin – – –   F
doch im nächsten Augenblicke glich er   H
dem Geliebten einer Königin.   F

Immer wieder war ein Sein zu haben: I
die Geschicke angefangner Knaben,   I
die, als hätte man sie nicht gewagt,   J
abgebrochen waren, abgesagt,   J
nahm er auf und riß sie in sich hin;   F
denn er mußte einmal nur die Gruft   K
solcher Aufgegebener durchschreiten,   L

II

In those days (but no, there were none)
in which the climbing tide had confronted
him, flowing into his lowest dungeon,
which was no longer his and overrun,
raising him to the stone vault as it mounted,

one of the names from some former time,
one he had once borne, came suddenly to light.
And again he understood: lives came to him
as he lured them forth, as if in flight

the still-warm lives of the dead came winging,
and each of those he kept on living,
impatient, threatened at first—
even those lives that had not been lived out—
and he understood how to turn them about,
until they were meaningful at last.

Often around him no place was secure
and he shuddered, insisting: I exist—
then suddenly he would wear the allure
of the beloved one of a queen's tryst.

An existence was always there to be had:
the fortunes of many a barely grown lad—
all dismantled, revoked, and undone,
as if one dared not gamble even one—
he took up and carried away in his fist,
for he had only once to wander there,
through the tomb of such lost personalities,

und die Düfte ihrer Möglichkeiten
lagen wieder in der Luft.

and the perfumes of their possibilities
once more lay evident in the open air.

Rilke uses the adventurer here as a rather extreme model for the artist. In a letter
to Clara he expounds this theory: "Works of art are always the end products of
having been in danger, of having explored to the very end of experience, to where
one can go no further. The further one ventures the more personal and unique,
the more one's own the experience becomes, and the artwork, finally, becomes
the essential, irrepressible, perhaps definitive expression of that uniqueness."

Falken-Beize

Kaiser sein heißt unverwandelt vieles	A
überstehen bei geheimer Tat:	B
wenn der Kanzler nachts den Turm betrat,	B
fand er *ihn,* des hohen Federspieles	A
kühnen fürstlichen Traktat	B
in den eingeneigten Schreiber sagen;	C
denn er hatte im entlegnen Saale	D
selber nächtelang und viele Male	D
das noch ungewohnte Tier getragen,	C
wenn es fremd war, neu und aufgebräut.	E
Und er hatte dann sich nie gescheut,	E
Pläne, welche in ihm aufgesprungen,	F
oder zärtlicher Erinnerungen	F
tieftiefinneres Geläut	E
zu verachten, um des bangen jungen	F
Falken willen, dessen Blut und Sorgen	G
zu begreifen er sich nicht erließ.	H
Dafür war er auch wie mitgehoben,	I
wenn der Vogel, den die Herren loben,	I
glänzend von der Hand geworfen, oben	I
in dem mitgefühlten Frühlingsmorgen	G
wie ein Engel auf den Reiher stieß.	H

The emperor referred to here is most probably Frederick II, often called *stupor mundi,* the wonder of the world. Frederick's *De arte venandi cum avibus,* one of the most renowned books on the art of falconry, is a meticulous and comprehensive work dealing not only with falcons but also with the taxonomy, anatomy,

Falconry

To be emperor is but to endure
unchanged through some secret achievement:
when each evening the chancellor went
up into the tower, he met his lord there,
dictating the princely, bold, and eminent

falconry treatise to the hunched-over scribe;
for his lord had paced an outlying chamber
through many nights, bearing that creature
still unmastered, in order to probe

this thing so new, so strange and unknown.
And he never hesitated to postpone
the plans that uncoiled within him or sprang
from each fond reminiscence that rang
deep inside him, disdaining their tone
for the benefit of that trembling young

falcon, never once giving up seeking
to understand its blood and affliction.
And so he likewise seemed almost to soar
when the nobly lauded bird, once more
launched brightly from the hand into the air
of a sympathetic Spring morning,
dove like an angel down on the heron.

and habits of many birds that are the falcon's prey. Rilke may have been inspired
by the illustrations in a copy of the book from the Vatican, or from some private
library.

Corrida

In memoriam Montez, 1830

Seit er, klein beinah, aus dem Toril   A
ausbrach, aufgescheuchten Augs und Ohrs,   B
und den Eigensinn des Picadors   B
und die Bänderhaken wie im Spiel   A

hinnahm, ist die stürmische Gestalt   C
angewachsen – sieh: zu welcher Masse,   D
aufgehäuft aus altem schwarzen Hasse,   D
und das Haupt zu einer Faust geballt,   C

nicht mehr spielend gegen irgendwen,   E
nein: die blutigen Nackenhaken hissend   F
hinter den gefällten Hörnern, wissend   F
und von Ewigkeit her gegen Den,   E

der in Gold und mauver Rosaseide   G
plötzlich umkehrt und, wie einen Schwarm   H
Bienen und als ob ers eben leide,   G
den Bestürzten unter seinem Arm   H

durchläßt, – während seine Blicke heiß   I
sich noch einmal heben, leichtgelenkt,   J
und als schlüge draußen jener Kreis   I
sich aus ihrem Glanz und Dunkel nieder   K
und aus jedem Schlagen seiner Lider,   K

ehe er gleichmütig, ungehässig,   L
an sich selbst gelehnt, gelassen, lässig   L

Corrida

in memoriam Montez, 1830

After it burst from the gate in the ring,
almost small, aroused in the eyes and ears,
and took the picadors' beribboned spears,
enduring that obstinate piercing

as if done in play, this shape like a tempest
suddenly swelled to such a mass and weight,
heaped up out of a black and ancient hate,
its head balled up as if it were a fist,

no longer sporting against just anyone,
no: hoisting the bloody neck-barbs behind
its low-pitched horns, finally its mind
focused on the timeless foe, who alone

in the silken gold and mauve of his jacket
suddenly turns as if facing a bee swarm,
spins as if he merely endured it,
and allows the confused one under his arm,

while once more lifting his torrid glance,
uncontested he presses forward,
as though this arena might condense
from what the darkness and light comprise,
from out of the very blaze of his eyes,

before he serenely and without malice,
leaning upon his own casual bliss,

in die wiederhergerollte große M

Woge über dem verlornen Stoße M

seinen Degen beinah sanft versenkt. J

into that huge and rolling wave of dust,
over his opponent's wasted thrust,
almost softly sinks his killing sword.

Francisco Montez Reina, the Spanish matador to whom this piece is dedicated, pioneered new techniques in bullfighting and introduced the *traje de luz,* the "suit of light" that matadors wear to this day. Paquiro, as he was called, was the most prominent figure in bullfighting until he retired in 1848. Rilke had never seen a bullfight, as he admits in a letter to Clara on September 29, 1907: "But how much one actually has all of it within one the more one shuts one's eyes tight. I felt that again when I wrote the corrida, which I had never seen: how I knew and had seen it all!"

Don Juans Kindheit

In seiner Schlankheit war, schon fast entscheidend,   A
der Bogen, der an Frauen nicht zerbricht;   B
und manchmal, seine Stirne nicht mehr meidend,   A
ging eine Neigung durch sein Angesicht   B

zu einer die vorüberkam, zu einer   C
die ihm ein fremdes altes Bild verschloß: D
er lächelte. Er war nicht mehr der Weiner,   C
der sich ins Dunkel trug und sich vergoß.   D

Und während ein ganz neues Selbstvertrauen   E
ihn öfter tröstete und fast verzog,   F
ertrug er ernst den ganzen Blick der Frauen,   E
der ihn bewunderte und ihn bewog.   F

Don Juan's Childhood

In his slenderness was the very bow,
near fully drawn, that no woman could break,
and sometimes, no longer shunning his brow,
an inclination of his face seemed to take

to someone passing by, whose manner
sealed a peculiar and ancient sign –
he smiled. He was no longer the whiner,
slinking off into darkness to pine.

And while a whole new self-possession
had consoled and almost spoiled him lately,
he earnestly bore the full gaze of women,
and they adored him and moved him greatly.

Rilke wrote in his diary in 1902: "Every period of history is full of a smoldering desire for those great individuals who are different: for they have always carried the future within themselves. But when any individuality emerges in a child it is treated scornfully, condescendingly, or even with derision, which is even more painful to the child."

Don Juans Auswahl

Und der Engel trat ihn an: Bereite   A
dich mir ganz. Und da ist mein Gebot.   B
Denn daß einer jene überschreite,   A
die die Süßesten an ihrer Seite   A
bitter machen, tut mir not.   B
Zwar auch du kannst wenig besser lieben,   C
(unterbrich mich nicht: du irrst),   D
doch du glühest, und es steht geschrieben,   C
daß du viele führen wirst   D
zu der Einsamkeit, die diesen   E
tiefen Eingang hat. Laß ein   F
die, die ich dir zugewiesen,   E
daß sie wachsend Heloïsen   E
überstehn und überschrein.   F

Don Juan's Selection

And thus the angel commanded: Prepare
for me completely. And here is my decree.
For insomuch as anyone should dare
to transform that sweetest fare
to bitterness, they afflict me.
Yet you are no better at love than any
(do not interrupt me, you are mistaken)
but you smolder and thus will drive many
to solitude it is written,
and solitude is the site
of this deep doorway. Take those
to yourself whom I invite
that in surviving they might
surpass the tears of Heloise.

The two Don Juan poems in this volume speak to Rilke's privileging of the physi-
cal. As he writes in *Letters to a Young Poet:* "Even spiritual creativity springs
forth from the physical, is one substance identical with it, and is only a more ten-
der, more rapturous, ever-enduring repetition of physical joy."

Sankt Georg

Und sie hatte ihn die ganze Nacht   A
angerufen, hingekniet, die schwache   B
wache Jungfrau: Siehe, dieser Drache,   B
und ich weiß es nicht, warum er wacht.   A

Und da brach er aus dem Morgengraun   C
auf dem Falben, strahlend Helm und Haubert,   D
und er sah sie, traurig und verzaubert   D
aus dem Knieen aufwärtsschaun   C

zu dem Glanze, der er war.   E
Und er sprengte glänzend längs der Länder   F
abwärts mit erhobnem Doppelhänder   F
in die offene Gefahr,   E

viel zu furchtbar, aber doch erfleht.   G
Und sie kniete knieender, die Hände   H
fester faltend, daß er sie bestände;   H
denn sie wußte nicht, daß Der besteht,   G

den ihr Herz, ihr reines und bereites,   I
aus dem Licht des göttlichen Geleites   I
niederreißt. Zuseiten seines Streites   I
stand, wie Türme stehen, ihr Gebet.   G

There are two earlier, uncollected poems by Rilke on Saint George, both of them
preliminary sketches of this final version. Rilke wrote to Franz Kappus in 1904:
"Perhaps all the dragons in our lives are princesses who are just waiting to see
us act with beauty and courage. Perhaps everything that frightens us is, in its

Saint George

And as she knelt there her strident cry
rang out through the night. Behold this dragon,
cried the frail yet vigilant virgin,
he wakes now, although I know not why.

At that he burst from the gray morning mist,
on a gray stallion with helmet and shield,
and caught sight of that spellbound one, who kneeled
helplessly there and greatly oppressed,

glancing upward at his coming splendor.
And brilliantly he sprang forth the length
and breadth of nations, with high-held strength,
bearing the two-handed blade into danger

that was much too fearful yet assured.
And she knelt more humbly, hands together,
praying that somehow he would save her,
for she knew not whether he endured,

he whom her heart, fully prepared and fine,
snatches down from the light of the divine
guardians. And beside his battle line
her prayer rose as a tower soars skyward.

deepest essence, something helpless that wants our love." This piece, which may
portray Raphael's Saint George from the Louvre or Vittore Carpaccio's, which
Rilke might have seen in Venice, captures the saint's rescue of the maiden.

Dame auf einem Balkon

Plötzlich tritt sie, in den Wind gehüllt,   A
licht in Lichtes, wie herausgegriffen,   B
wahrend jetzt die Stube wie geschliffen   B
hinter ihr die Türe füllt   A

dunkel wie der Grund einer Kamee,   C
die ein Schimmern durchläßt durch die Ränder;   D
und du meinst der Abend war nicht, ehe   C
sie heraustrat, um auf das Geländer   D

noch ein wenig von sich fortzulegen,   E
noch die Hände, – um ganz leicht zu sein: F
wie dem Himmel von den Häuserreihn   F
hingereicht, von allem zu bewegen.   E

Lady on a Balcony

Suddenly she appears, swaddled in the wind,
singled out, stepping brightly into light,
while even now, as if it were cut to fit,
the parlor fills the entranceway behind

her, dark as a cameo's incised ground
where a gleam around the edges has played;
and you supposed evening not yet crowned
until she stepped outside and displayed

just a bit of herself at the railing,
just her hands, completely casually,
handed over as the heavens might be
by the terraces, moved by everything.

The progression of this poem and its changing focus, from the lady on the balcony, down to a hard gem-sized thing, then out into the infinite heavens, shows the way Rilke can condense an experience yet keep it ultimately indefinable. It is his unmatchable power of observation that cuts the stone and shines its light into the sky. On March 9, 1899, he wrote Elena Woronina: "For us, seeing is the most genuine possibility of acquiring something. If only God had made our hands like our eyes—so willing to grasp, so willing to let go of all things—then we could truly acquire riches. We do not acquire riches by letting something languish and wither in our hands, but only by letting all of it pass through their compass as if through the celebratory gate of homecoming."

Begegnung in der Kastanien-Allee

Ihm ward des Eingangs grüne Dunkelheit   A
kühl wie ein Seidenmantel umgegeben,   B
den er noch nahm und ordnete: als eben   B
am andern transparenten Ende, weit,   A

aus grüner Sonne, wie aus grünen Scheiben,   C
weiß eine einzelne Gestalt   D
aufleuchtete, um lange fern zu bleiben   C
und schließlich, von dem Lichterniedertreiben   C
bei jedem Schritte überwallt,   D

ein helles Wechseln auf sich herzutragen,   E
das scheu im Blond nach hinten lief.   F
Aber auf einmal war der Schatten tief,   F
und nahe Augen lagen aufgeschlagen   E

in einem neuen deutlichen Gesicht,   G
das wie in einem Bildnis verweilte   H
in dem Moment, da man sich wieder teilte: H
erst war es immer, und dann war es nicht.   G

Encounter in the Avenue of Chestnuts

The verdant darkness of the avenue
enclosed him, cool as a silken jacket,
as if he had just donned and buttoned it,
when there at its end, in distant view,

from green sunlight, as if from panes of green,
a lone, white shape was illuminated;
for a long time from a distance it was seen,
till at last the downward-driven sheen
of light welled over, at each step awaited,

pulsating brilliantly as it came on
and shyly bleached to blonder tones behind.
But swiftly the shadows seemed deeply defined,
and eyes approached that seemed struck open

in a face newly and distinctly wrought,
which lingered like an image in the moment
as farther and farther away from it one went:
first it was forever, and then it was not.

From a letter to Clara we learn that when Rilke returned to Paris early in June
1907, he boarded at the Hôtel du Quai Voltaire. His room was right over that of
Paula Modersohn-Becker. Paula was a friend of both Rilke and Clara, a painter
whose work anticipated Expressionism and who would die after giving birth to
a daughter the following November. Rilke described an avenue of chestnut trees
leading to a convent that his window overlooked. This is the view that would
greet him during his next few months in Paris.

Die Schwestern

Sieh, wie sie dieselben Möglichkeiten   A
anders an sich tragen und verstehn,   B
so als sähe man verschiedne Zeiten   A
durch zwei gleiche Zimmer gehn.   B

Jede meint die andere zu stützen,   C
während sie doch müde an ihr ruht;   D
und sie können nicht einander nützen,   C
denn sie legen Blut auf Blut,   D

wenn sie sich wie früher sanft berühren   E
und versuchen, die Allee entlang   F
sich geführt zu fühlen und zu führen: E
Ach, sie haben nicht denselben Gang.   F

The Sisters

See how they take on and comprehend
these same possibilities differently,
as one might see the time of day blend
the light in similar rooms distinctly.

Each supposes she supports her sister
while she rests upon her in her weary mood,
and they cannot depend on one another,
for you cannot lean blood upon blood;

when they touch softly, as when they were younger,
and on tree-shaded lanes they circulate,
as one leads or is led by the other,
alas, they do not walk with the same gait.

In 1922 Rilke wrote the following diary entry: "Nothing locks people into error as much as the constant repetition of error—and how many ultimately tied to each other in a frozen fate could have won for themselves, by means of a few small separations, that rhythm through which the mystifying movement of their hearts would have tirelessly endured in the deep closeness of their inner world space."

Übung am Klavier

Der Sommer summt. Der Nachmittag macht müde;	A
sie atmete verwirrt ihr frisches Kleid	B
und legte in die triftige Etüde	A
die Ungeduld nach einer Wirklichkeit,	B
die kommen konnte: morgen, heute abend–,	C
die vielleicht da war, die man nur verbarg;	D
und vor den Fenstern, hoch und alles habend,	C
empfand sie plötzlich den verwöhnten Park.	D
Da brach sie ab; schaute hinaus, verschränkte	E
die Hände; wünschte sich ein langes Buch–	F
und schob auf einmal den Jasmingeruch	F
erzürnt zurück. Sie fand, daß er sie kränkte.	E

Piano Practice

The summer hums. The midday wearies;
distracted, she breathes the freshness of her dress
and adds to her well-played piano studies
the quick impatience of a certain realness

that might arrive tomorrow or this evening,
that might already be there, hidden and dark;
and through the windows, tall and all-containing,
she suddenly saw the trimmed and pampered park.

At that she stopped playing, peering over the sill,
folded hands yearning for a leisurely novel,
then in quick anger she thrust the jasmine's smell
away from her. She found that it made her ill.

The pianist in the above poem may well be modeled on Mimi Romanelli, the sister of Pietro Romanelli, an art dealer Rilke knew from Paris. Rilke had experienced a flirtation and possible affair with her in Venice, but feared he would distract her from music (she was a brilliant pianist). Worried also that she might interfere with his solitary poet's life, he wrote her in August 1908, citing Sappho, Eleanora Duse, Gaspara Stampa, and other women who had sacrificed the distractions of love for their art.

Die Liebende

Das ist mein Fenster. Eben   A
bin ich so sanft erwacht.   B
Ich dachte, ich würde schweben.   A
Bis wohin reicht mein Leben,   A
und wo beginnt die Nacht?   B

Ich könnte meinen, alles   C
wäre noch Ich ringsum;   D
durchsichtig wie eines Kristalles   C
Tiefe, verdunkelt, stumm.   D

Ich könnte auch noch die Sterne   E
fassen in mir; so groß   F
scheint mir mein Herz; so gerne   E
ließ es ihn wieder los   F

den ich vielleicht zu lieben,   G
vielleicht zu halten begann.   H
Fremd, wie niebeschrieben   G
sieht mich mein Schicksal an.   H

Was bin ich unter diese   I
Unendlichkeit gelegt,   J
duftend wie eine Wiese,   I
hin und her bewegt,   J

rufend zugleich und bange,   K
daß einer den Ruf vernimmt,   L

The Woman in Love

That is my window beckoning.
Waking now in such gentle light,
I supposed I might be floating.
Toward what is my life reaching,
and where begins the night?

I might suppose that all
of it still surrounded me,
clear as the depths of a crystal,
unspeaking and shadowy.

I feel I could even contain
the stars within me, so mighty
does my heart seem, once again
it has willingly set him free

whom perhaps I began to love,
perhaps began to embrace.
Strangely, a thing never dreamed of,
my fate stares into my face.

Why am I laid out below
such endless repetition,
fragrant as a sweet meadow,
yet wind-shifted hither and yon,

calling out, yet ever in fear
that someone might hear my call,

und zum Untergange   K
in einem Andern bestimmt.   L

destined to find in another
lover yet another downfall.

In 1904 Rilke wrote to his brother-in-law, Friedrich Westhoff: "It is my experience time and time again that there is scarcely anything as difficult as loving someone. It is work, day labor, truly a constant task: God only knows, there is no other way of saying it. Young people are not prepared for the great task of love. Our society has tried to make this complicated and acute relation into something light and effortless, it has spread the illusion that anyone is capable of love. But that is not the case. To love is difficult."

Das Rosen-Innere

Wo ist zu diesem Innen	A
ein Außen? Auf welches Weh	B
legt man solches Linnen?	A
Welche Himmel spiegeln sich drinnen	A
in dem Binnensee	B
dieser offenen Rosen,	C
dieser sorglosen, sieh:	D
wie sie lose im Losen	C
liegen, als könnte nie	D
eine zitternde Hand sie verschütten.	X
Sie können sich selber kaum	E
halten; viele ließen	F
sich überfüllen und fließen	F
über von Innenraum	E
in die Tage, die immer	G
voller und voller sich schließen,	F
bis der ganze Sommer ein Zimmer	G
wird, ein Zimmer in einem Traum.	E

Interior of a Rose

Where does there exist an outside
for this inside? For what wound's sake
is such a linen bandage tied?
What heaven's reflection is spied
on the mirrored surface of the lake
of these open roses, perfected
in these blissful blooms; and see
how they lie loosely collected,
as if a trembling hand could hardly
spill them or overturn them.
They can barely even contain
themselves; among them many
let themselves overflow any
interior space, and they rain
into days, closing continually,
fuller and fuller they gleam,
until all of summer seems to be
a room, a room in a dream.

In September 1906 Rilke wrote to Countess Mary Gneisenau from the Villa Discopoli on Capri concerning a rose she had sent him: "There is a deep restfulness in it; it lies at the very bottom of its name, rose, there where the word grows dim, rose, and everything that it holds of movement, of remembrance, of memories ebbing and flowing, of quickly ascending longings, flows away from it, over it, and touches it no more."

Damen-Bildnis aus den Achtziger-Jahren

Wartend stand sie an den schwergerafften   A
dunklen Atlasdraperien,   B
die ein Aufwand falscher Leidenschaften   A
über ihr zu ballen schien;   B

seit den noch so nahen Mädchenjahren   C
wie mit einer anderen vertauscht: D
müde unter den getürmten Haaren,   C
in den Rüschen-Roben unerfahren   C
und von allen Falten wie belauscht   D

bei dem Heimweh und dem schwachen Planen,   E
wie das Leben weiter werden soll: F
anders, wirklicher, wie in Romanen,   E
hingerissen und verhängnisvoll, –   F

daß man etwas erst in die Schatullen   G
legen dürfte, um sich im Geruch   H
von Erinnerungen einzulullen;   G
daß man endlich in dem Tagebuch   H

einen Anfang fände, der nicht schon   I
unterm Schreiben sinnlos wird und Lüge,   J
und ein Blatt von einer Rose trüge   J
in dem schweren leeren Medaillon,   I

welches liegt auf jedem Atemzug.   K
Daß man einmal durch das Fenster winkte;   L

Portrait of a Lady from the Eighties

She lingered before the dark background
of the luxurious Berber drapes,
the counterfeit passion so tightly bound
above her in closely gathered shapes;

since her maiden years, just recently,
she remained as if in another's place—
weary beneath the hair's heaped canopy,
callow in her robe of ruffled finery,
as if watched over by its embrace,

homesick and making all her feeble
plans of a life that should be much more—
different, genuine, like in a novel,
full of calamity and full of rapture,

so that one might lay it all away
in a jewel case, that it might then bring
the lulling perfume of memory,
that one might at last find a beginning

in one's diary that has not already,
in writing it, grown mindless and deceitful,
and it might hold a single rose petal
within a locket heavy and empty,

weighing upon her every inhalation.
So that once she waved this hand so slight

diese schlanke Hand, die neuberingte,

hätte dran für Monate genug.

with its new rings through the window's light,
which act would do for many months' duration.

In a letter to Clara of June 1907, Rilke writes of a visit "to the Bagatelle place [Château de Bagatelle in the Bois de Boulogne] where there is an exhibit of women's portraits from 1870 to 1900." Rilke's compassion for women who appear to be unloved makes itself known over and over in poems such as "A Woman's Fate" and "The Wilted One." He would notice certain women in the streets of Paris and speculate on their situation. As he writes to Lou Andreas-Salomé in July 1903: "And then those women who pass swiftly by one in the long velvet cloaks of the eighties, with paper roses on out-of-style hats under which the hair hangs as if the strands of it were melted together."

Dame vor dem Spiegel

Wie in einem Schlaftrunk Spezerein   A
löst sie leise in dem flüssigklaren   B
Spiegel ihr ermüdetes Gebaren;   B
und sie tut ihr Lächeln ganz hinein.   A

Und sie wartet, daß die Flüssigkeit   C
davon steigt; dann gießt sie ihre Haare   D
in den Spiegel und, die wunderbare   D
Schulter hebend aus dem Abendkleid,   C

trinkt sie still aus ihrem Bild. Sie trinkt,   E
was ein Liebender im Taumel tränke,   F
prüfend, voller Mißtraun; und sie winkt   E

erst der Zofe, wenn sie auf dem Grunde   G
ihres Spiegels Lichter findet, Schränke   F
und das Trübe einer späten Stunde.   G

Lady before a Mirror

Like spices into a sleeping potion
into the clear and liquid mirror
she gently releases her weary manner;
and she pours her smile into this solution.

And she waits until all the liquidness
has risen from it, then spills her hair
into the glass, and raises a fair,
wondrous shoulder from her evening dress,

and quietly drinks what the glass has displayed.
She drinks what a lover might in delirium,
testing, distrusting, but won't call her maid

until finding candlesticks, a dresser,
and the last dregs of a late hour that come
to rest in the ground of her mirror.

Rilke here explores the perception of the self through the device of the mirror. Compare the poem to a passage in *The Notebooks of Malte Laurids Brigge* where Malte is contemplating the image of the self: "We discover that we don't recognize the role [we are supposed to play], we long to take off the makeup and the falseness and be real. But somehow a piece of the costume still clings to us. A trace of some embellishment remains in our brow, we don't perceive the declining corners of the mouth. And it is thus that we walk [through life], a travesty and a lonely half: neither being nor actor."

Die Greisin

Weisse Freundinnen mitten im Heute   A
lachen und horchen und planen für morgen;   B
abseits erwägen gelassene Leute   A
langsam ihre besonderen Sorgen,   B

das Warum und das Wann und das Wie,   C
und man hört sie sagen: Ich glaube–;   D
aber in ihrer Spitzenhaube   D
ist sie sicher, als wüßte sie,   C

daß sie sich irren, diese und alle.   E
Und das Kinn, im Niederfalle,   E
lehnt sich an die weiße Koralle,   E
die den Schal zur Stirne stimmt.   F

Einmal aber, bei einem Gelache,   G
holt sie aus springenden Lidern zwei wache   G
Blicke und zeigt diese harte Sache,   G
wie man aus einem geheimen Fache   G
schöne ererbte Steine nimmt.   F

The Old Lady

White-haired girlfriends in the midst of today
eavesdrop and laugh and plan for tomorrow;
these casual people languidly weigh,
aloof from each other, each their own sorrow,

the why and the when and even the how,
and one overhears each say: I believe;
but in her bonnet's old-fashioned weave
she is sure, as if she just seemed to know,

that they mistake themselves, these and all.
And the tip of her chin in its downward fall
rests on the necklace made of white coral
that matches her shawl and her forehead's tones.

But once, upon hearing a laugh, she takes
from her eyelids two watchful keepsakes,
two glances, and hard things of them she makes,
like something from a secret jewel box,
like beautiful, inherited gemstones.

In a letter to Clara Westhoff in 1900 (he was courting her at the time) Rilke remembers an older woman Clara had mentioned who seems much like the one above: "I recall precisely all that you said then. The figure of the old lady who rarely speaks, and then only with reserve, who conceals her hands when a gesture of compassion might stir them, and who with a rare embrace builds bridges to a few people, bridges that disappear when she withdraws her arm and it lies again like an island."

Das Bett

Lass sie meinen, daß sich in privater   A
Wehmut löst, was einer dort bestritt.   B
Nirgend sonst als da ist ein Theater;   A
reiß den hohen Vorhang fort–: da tritt   B

vor den Chor der Nächte, der begann   C
ein unendlich breites Lied zu sagen,   D
jene Stunde auf, bei der sie lagen,   D
und zerreißt ihr Kleid und klagt sich an,   C

um der andern, um der Stunde willen,   E
die sich wehrt und wälzt im Hintergrunde;   F
denn sie konnte sie mit sich nicht stillen.   E
Aber da sie zu der fremden Stunde   F

sich gebeugt: da war auf ihr,   G
was sie am Geliebten einst gefunden,   H
nur so drohend und so groß verbunden   H
und entzogen wie in einem Tier.   G

The Bed

Let them suppose that what one contests there
is resolved in private sorrow afterward.
Nowhere but there exists such a theater;
pull back the tall curtain to see what entered

before the chorus of nights, commencing
its take on a broad, unending song,
as both lay there and the hour slipped along
that accuses itself and tears her clothing,

for that other's sake, for the sake of that hour
that struggles and writhes in the background;
for it could not suckle her of its own power.
But as she bowed to that strange hour she found,

appearing there, within her at last,
what once in a lover she expected to find,
so imminent and so greatly aligned,
and withdrawn as it would be in some beast.

As to the difference between loving and being loved, Rilke wrote the following
diary entry in 1907: "To be loved is to be aflame. To love is to radiate light with an
inexhaustible oil. To be loved is to pass away; to love is to endure."

Der Fremde

Ohne Sorgfalt, was die Nächsten dächten,   A
die er müde nichtmehr fragen hieß,   B
ging er wieder fort; verlor, verließ–.   B
Denn er hing an solchen Reisenächten   A

anders als an jeder Liebesnacht.   C
Wunderbare hatte er durchwacht,   C
die mit starken Sternen überzogen   D
enge Fernen auseinanderbogen   D
und sich wandelten wie eine Schlacht;   C

andre, die mit in den Mond gestreuten   E
Dörfern, wie mit hingehaltnen Beuten,   E
sich ergaben, oder durch geschonte   F
Parke graue Edelsitze zeigten,   G
die er gerne in dem hingeneigten   G
Haupte einen Augenblick bewohnte,   F
tiefer wissend, daß man nirgends bleibt;   H
und schon sah er bei dem nächsten Biegen   I
wieder Wege, Brücken, Länder liegen   I
bis an Städte, die man übertreibt.   H

Und dies alles immer unbegehrend   X
hinzulassen, schien ihm mehr als seines   J
Lebens Lust, Besitz und Ruhm.   K
Doch auf fremden Plätzen war ihm eines   J

The Stranger

Not caring what his neighbors thought right,
which he wearily deemed things without worth,
he lost himself, left, again he went forth,
for he hung upon such a traveling night

differently than on any night of passion.
Superbly he stayed in wakeful attention
underneath stars that were so intense
and bent apart by such narrow distance,
arranging themselves as in battle fashion;

other nights, with hamlets scattered under
the moon, like a heap of hoarded plunder,
had already yielded, or seemed to display
parks with gray mansions, seats of nobility,
which with inclining head he gladly
inhabited for just the briefest stay,
deeply grasping that one remains nowhere;
and past the next bend he saw that there waited,
stretching to cities that seemed exaggerated,
landscape, bridge, and bustling thoroughfare.

And to leave every one of these things behind,
all undesired, seemed to outpace renown,
possessions, and a life that was fortunate.
Yet in strange plazas the fountain of stone,

täglich ausgetretnen Brunnensteines   J
Mulde manchmal wie ein Eigentum.   K

which through constant use appeared worn down,
sometimes seemed to him like an estate.

The figure of the stranger is the Rilkean ideal of the artist, for the artist is always a stranger to society. Rilke strove for this ideal, but the one figure who he was sure had already attained it is Rodin, of whom he writes to Lou Andreas-Salomé in August 1903: "Oh what a solitary person is this old man who has descended into himself and stands full of sap like an ancient tree of autumn! He has become deep; he has dug out a deep place for his heart, whose beating proceeds from afar as from the core of a mountain." The third stanza, with its "gray mansions, seats of nobility," seems to reference Rilke's habit of taking refuge on the estates of wealthy and noble patrons.

Die Anfahrt

War in des Wagens Wendung dieser Schwung?   A
War er im Blick, mit dem man die barocken   B
Engelfiguren, die bei blauen Glocken   B
im Felde standen voll Erinnerung,   A

annahm und hielt und wieder ließ, bevor   C
der Schloßpark schließend um die Fahrt sich drängte,   D
an die er streifte, die er überhängte   D
und plötzlich freigab: denn da war das Tor,   C

das nun, als hätte es sie angerufen,   E
die lange Front zu einer Schwenkung zwang,   F
nach der sie stand. Aufglänzend ging ein Gleiten   G

die Glastür abwärts; und ein Windhund drang   F
aus ihrem Aufgehn, seine nahen Seiten   G
heruntertragend von den flachen Stufen.   E

The Approach

Was it in the coach's turn, this great sweep?
Was it in a glance at those baroque figures,
those angels standing among green pastures
of bluebells, in the memories they keep,

embraced, accepted, then left to dissipate
as the park enclosed the end of the journey,
striped with shade by each overhung tree,
and suddenly released–for there was the gate,

that now, as if calling to this thing inbound,
forced the long coach-front to turn as it neared,
and steered to a halt. All agleam the sliding

glass door descended, and there appeared
from the opening, slim and striding
down the shallow carriage steps, a greyhound.

Rilke had seen the approach to many great estates where he stayed as a guest as he wandered penniless through Europe. He described a visit to Janowitz Castle in Bohemia thus: "Through the gateway to a park, and it was an ancient park, hemming us in tightly with damp autumn. Until after a number of turns there were bridges and vistas, and bordered by an old moat the castle arose… covered with windows and coats of arms, balconies and oriels, and enclosing court-yards as though they were never to be glimpsed by anyone." The greyhound that emerges from the carriage is perhaps meant to suggest Rilke himself, for the family crest of the knights of Rülko, with whom Rilke claimed kin, bore a promi-nent greyhound. And the poet might even have been treated like some exotic pet by a few of his wealthy hosts.

Die Sonnenuhr

Selten reicht ein Schauer feuchter Fäule   A
aus dem Gartenschatten, wo einander   B
Tropfen fallen hören und ein Wander-   B
vogel lautet, zu der Säule,   A
die in Majoran und Koriander   B
steht und Sommerstunden zeigt;   C

nur sobald die Dame (der ein Diener   D
nachfolgt) in dem hellen Florentiner   D
über ihren Rand sich neigt,   C
wird sie schattig und verschweigt–.   C

Oder wenn ein sommerlicher Regen   E
aufkommt aus dem wogenden Bewegen   E
hoher Kronen, hat sie eine Pause;   F
denn sie weiß die Zeit nicht auszudrücken,   G
die dann in den Frucht- und Blumenstücken   G
plötzlich glüht im weißen Gartenhause.   F

The Sundial

Rarely a shiver of moist rot reaches
from garden shadows, where falling drops
hear each other and a wandering bird cheeps,
to the sundial posted among the swatches
of marjoram and coriander that keeps
the tally of the summer's hours;

but as the one in the Florentine bonnet
(followed by her maid into this vignette)
bends herself over the edge of its contours,
then how shadowed and secret it appears.

Or when suddenly comes a summer rain
out of billowing undulations that strain
the tall canopy, then it seems to pause,
for it cannot convey the kind of time
that in each fruit and every flower stem
suddenly glows in the white garden house.

The sundial described here can only count each hour as it dies, it cannot count
hours of life, and therefore it "cannot convey the kind of time / that in each fruit
and every flower stem / suddenly glows in the white garden house." Rilke wrote
to Paula Becker in 1900: "It was at that moment that the thought first occurred
to me that every hour we live is an hour of death for someone else, that there
are probably more hours of death than of living. Death has a dial with infinitely
many numbers upon it."

Schlaf-Mohn

Abseits im Garten blüht der böse Schlaf,	A
in welchem die, die heimlich eingedrungen,	B
die Liebe fanden junger Spiegelungen,	B
die willig waren, offen und konkav,	A
und Träume, die mit aufgeregten Masken	C
auftraten, riesiger durch die Kothurne–:	D
das alles stockt in diesen oben flasken	C
weichlichen Stengeln, die die Samenurne	D
(nachdem sie lang, die Knospe abwärts tragend,	E
zu welken meinten) festverschlossen heben:	F
gefranste Kelche auseinanderschlagend,	E
die fieberhaft das Mohngefäß umgeben.	F

Opium Poppy

Aloof in the garden blooms that sleep so grave,
in which those who secretly probed its edges
discovered the love of emerging images
like willing flowers, open and concave,

and dreams, which emerged in feverish masks,
rising gigantically on the buskin –
all of this stagnates atop the husks
of slender stems, which carry their seeds in

nodding buds that wither in the air,
lifting tight-shut seed-urns in surrender:
shattering fringed calyxes asunder
that feverishly embrace the poppy jar.

A quintessential thing-poem, this portrait of the opium poppy begins off cen-
ter: with its effects on those who might take it. These effects are then condensed
back into the substance from which they came, which resides in the flower bud
after the flower has wilted. The stems nod sleepily as though they themselves
were under the spell of the drug. And finally Rilke grounds the opium bud in the
space that surrounds it, in the calyxes that embrace it as the addict embraces
the opium jar. In twelve lines the poet has named the thing called *Papaver som-
niferum* so that we cannot fail to recognize it.

Die Flamingos

Jardin des Plantes, Paris

In Spiegelbildern wie von Fragonard   A
ist doch von ihrem Weiß und ihrer Röte   B
nicht mehr gegeben, als dir einer böte,   B
wenn er von seiner Freundin sagt: sie war   A

noch sanft von Schlaf. Denn steigen sie ins Grüne   C
und stehn, auf rosa Stielen leicht gedreht,   D
beisammen, blühend, wie in einem Beet,   D
verführen sie verführender als Phryne   C

sich selber; bis sie ihres Auges Bleiche   E
hinhalsend bergen in der eignen Weiche,   E
in welcher Schwarz und Fruchtrot sich versteckt.   F

Auf einmal kreischt ein Neid durch die Volière;   G
sie aber haben sich erstaunt gestreckt   F
und schreiten einzeln ins Imaginäre.   G

The Flamingos

Jardin des Plantes, Paris

As Fragonard's reflected image does,
they give of their white and crimson color
nothing more than someone might offer
when he says of his lady friend: She was

still soft with sleep. For when they rise gently
against the green with a gossamer turning
and stand on pink stems together, blooming
as if in a flower bed, more alluringly

than Phryne; they lure even themselves until,
necks bending, they tuck pale eyes and dark bill
into feathers in which black and fruit-red hide.

Suddenly envy screams through the aviary;
but astounded they stretch themselves and stride,
each one separately, into the imaginary.

This is one of a group of poems inspired by trips to the Jardin des Plantes, where Rilke was accustomed to walk while in Paris, that city in which he experienced so much ambivalence. Other poems in this group are "The Panther," "The Gazelle," and "Parrot Park." Phryne was a fourth-century B.C.E. Greek courtesan who was the embodiment of female beauty. She was probably the model for the Cnidian Aphrodite by Praxiteles. Though the original did not survive antiquity, Rilke could have seen a very good Roman copy at the Museo Pio-Clementino, one of the Vatican's collections.

Persisches Heliotrop

Es könnte sein, daß dir der Rose Lob   A
zu laut erscheint für deine Freundin: Nimm   B
das schön gestickte Kraut und überstimm   B
mit dringend flüsterndem Heliotrop   A

den Bülbül, der an ihren Lieblingsplätzen   C
sie schreiend preist und sie nicht kennt.   D
Denn sieh: wie süße Worte nachts in Sätzen   C
beisammenstehn ganz dicht, durch nichts getrennt,   D
aus der Vokale wachem Violett   E
hindüftend durch das stille Himmelbett—:   E

so schließen sich vor dem gesteppten Laube   F
deutliche Sterne zu der seidnen Traube   F
und mischen, daß sie fast davon verschwimmt,   G
die Stille mit Vanille und mit Zimmt.   G

Persian Heliotrope

Perhaps to your taste the rose's cachet
seems too loud to suit your lady friend;
choose this lacy flower and transcend,
in heliotrope's urgent whispered bouquet,

that bird which among her intimate haunts
praises her loudly yet knows not her heart.
For see how sweet words scent each sentence,
closely in the night, never far apart,
with what wakeful, violet voices have said,
perfumed by the silent canopy bed:

and thus, above quilted leaves, lucid stars
enclose themselves within silken clusters,
almost blurring themselves, an infusion
of silence with vanilla and cinnamon.

Rilke was a consummate observer of natural features, especially of flowers, which he found during his walks through the parks and estate grounds of his many patrons. In 1902 he wrote Clara from Schloss Haseldorf in Holstein: "Flesh-colored azaleas reach out with their fragrance, and the magnolias are already leafing out beside great lotus-like blooms." Here again Rilke's focus shifts skillfully from the object, a flower, to the woman who wears its fragrance, and finally out into the cosmos.

Schlaflied

Einmal wenn ich dich verlier,   A
wirst du schlafen können, ohne   B
daß ich wie eine Lindenkrone   B
mich verflüstre über dir?   A

Ohne daß ich hier wache und   C
Worte, beinah wie Augenlider,   D
auf deine Brüste, auf deine Glieder   D
niederlege, auf deinen Mund.   C

Ohne daß ich dich verschließ   E
und dich allein mit Deinem lasse   F
wie einen Garten mit einer Masse   F
von Melissen und Stern-Anis?   E

Lullaby

Comes the time when I lose you,
how would you lay yourself down
to sleep unless, like the linden's crown,
I sprinkled myself over you too?

Unless I watch over you,
raining down words, eyelids almost,
over your limbs, upon your breast
and your mouth the whole night through.

Unless I shut you in, unless
I left you alone with what is yours,
like a garden with a mass of flowers
of melissa and star anise.

This poem perfectly illustrates Rilke's belief that what one should value and respect most in a friend or lover is that person's solitude. On February 12, 1902, the poet wrote to Paula Becker: "I consider this to be the highest duty in the relationship of two people: for one to stand guard over the solitude of the other. If the very nature of both indifference and the mob consists of the lack of respect for solitude, then love and friendship exist so that new opportunities for solitude will come forward."

Der Pavillon

Aber selbst noch durch die Flügeltüren	A
mit dem grünen regentrüben Glas	B
ist ein Spiegeln lächelnder Allüren	A
und ein Glanz von jenem Glück zu spüren,	A
das sich dort, wohin sie nicht mehr führen,	A
einst verbarg, verklärte und vergaß.	B

Aber selbst noch in den Stein-Guirlanden	C
über der nicht mehr berührten Tür	D
ist ein Hang zur Heimlichkeit vorhanden	C
und ein stilles Mitgefühl dafür–,	D

und sie schauern manchmal, wie gespiegelt,	E
wenn ein Wind sie schattig überlief;	F
auch das Wappen, wie auf einem Brief	F
viel zu glücklich, überstürzt gesiegelt,	E

redet noch. Wie wenig man verscheuchte:	G
alles weiß noch, weint noch, tut noch weh–.	H
Und im Fortgehn durch die tränenfeuchte,	G
abgelegene Allee	H

fühlt man lang noch auf dem Rand des Dachs	I
jene Urnen stehen, kalt, zerspalten:	J
doch entschlossen, noch zusammzuhalten	J
um die Asche alter Achs.	I

At first glance "The Pavilion" seems to belong among the architectural poems of the first volume. But in the encounter with this seemingly abandoned building Rilke shows us how the physical–"the door that hands no longer touch"– evokes the emotional states that we find in ourselves. Observe how an essential

The Pavilion

But even yet, through the double-winged doors,
through the green, rain-stippled glass, appear
reflections of all the smiling allures,
a single glance of happiness, these spoors
of what existed, what no longer endures—
all that was hidden, praised, forgotten here.

But even yet, in those garlands of stone
above the door that hands no longer touch,
a quiet bias to secrecy is shown
and also a compassion for it, such

that they shiver like pond reflections will
when the wind overtakes them with shade,
even the door's crest, like a letter too glad,
too hastily pressed with a seal, speaking still.

How slight are all those things that we displace,
everything pale, painful, and weeping yet.
And going forth through a tear-stained place,
a solitary street,

one feels like one of the cold urns that rise
from the roof's cornice, cracked by the weather,
but still determined to hold together
around the ashes of old sighs.

sadness is built here out of the double-winged doors, the garlands of stone, and the
row of urns along the roof. In the end we are left with only "these spoors / of what
existed, what no longer endures."

Die Entführung

Oft war sie als Kind ihren Dienerinnen   A
entwichen, um die Nacht und den Wind   B
(weil sie drinnen so anders sind)   B
draußen zu sehn an ihrem Beginnen;   A

doch keine Sturmnacht hatte gewiß   C
den riesigen Park so in Stücke gerissen,   X
wie ihn jetzt ihr Gewissen zerriß,   C

da er sie nahm von der seidenen Leiter   D
und sie weitertrug, weiter, weiter...:   D

bis der Wagen alles war.   E

Und sie roch ihn, den schwarzen Wagen,   F
um den verhalten das Jagen stand   X
und die Gefahr.   E
Und sie fand ihn mit Kaltem ausgeschlagen;   F
und das Schwarze und Kalte war auch in ihr.   G
Sie kroch in ihren Mantelkragen   F
und befühlte ihr Haar, als bliebe es hier,   G
und hörte fremd einen Fremden sagen: F
Ichbinbeidir.   G

The Abduction

As a child she fled any watchful servant
in order to view the wind and the night
out of doors, at their very site
of origin—indoors they are different;

still never a stormy night full of thunder
had torn the enormous park to pieces
as now her conscience tore it asunder,

as he bore her down the silken ladder
and carried her off, farther and farther...

until the coach was all.

And she smelled the black coach as it rolled,
and around its journey hovered pursuit
and even peril.
And she found that it wore a lining of cold,
and the blackness and cold were within her too.
Beneath her collar she felt so chilled,
and touched her hair as to bid it adieu,
and strangely hearkened as a stranger called:
Iamwithyou.

This piece continues a theme that began in volume one in the poem "Orpheus, Eurydice, Hermes." But although Eurydice rejects her abduction by Orpheus and returns to death, which is a sort of liberation for her, the abductee in this poem seems overwhelmed by the experience, and the cold of the carriage suggests that she is leaving life, the life of her individuality, behind.

Rosa Hortensie

Wer nahm das Rosa an? Wer wußte auch,   A
daß es sich sammelte in diesen Dolden?   B
Wie Dinge unter Gold, die sich entgolden,   B
enttröten sie sich sanft, wie im Gebrauch.   A

Daß sie für solches Rosa nichts verlangen.   C
Bleibt es für sie und lächelt aus der Luft?   D
Sind Engel da, es zärtlich zu empfangen,   C
wenn es vergeht, großmütig wie ein Duft?   D

Oder vielleicht auch geben sie es preis,   E
damit es nie erführe vom Verblühn.   F
Doch unter diesem Rosa hat ein Grün   F
gehorcht, das jetzt verwelkt und alles weiß.   E

Pink Hydrangea

Who could understand this pink or deduce
how in these blooms it has gathered?
Like gilded objects whose gilt has weathered,
they gently unred themselves, as if from use.

That for such a pink they require nothing.
Does it remain here like a smiling glance?
Do angels fondly gather it in passing
before it fades, nobly as some fragrance?

Or perhaps they abandon it, hoping
that it never knows it is wilted and mean,
yet beneath this pink there hearkens a green
that withers now, and knows everything.

This poem is a companion piece to "Blue Hydrangea," which is found in the
first volume of *New Poems.* Rilke's fascination with flowers of every kind is evi-
dent from his letters and diaries. He writes Clara in 1902 describing the blooms
of chestnut trees: "The white of the blossoms grew splendidly mysterious and at
times the bloom-pyramids had the look of hands raised in prayer extending from
the sleeves of a dark mantle."

Das Wappen

Wie ein Spiegel, der, von ferne tragend,　　　　　A
lautlos in sich aufnahm, ist der Schild;　　　　B
offen einstens, dann zusammenschlagend　　　A
über einem Spiegelbild　　　　　　　　　　B

jener Wesen, die in des Geschlechts　　　　　C
Weiten wohnen, nicht mehr zu bestreiten,　　D
seiner Dinge, seiner Wirklichkeiten　　　　　D
(rechte links und linke rechts),　　　　　　C

die er eingesteht und sagt und zeigt.　　　　E
Drauf, mit Ruhm und Dunkel ausgeschlagen,　F
ruht der Spangenhelm, verkürzt,　　　　　　G

den das Flügelkleinod übersteigt,　　　　　E
während seine Decke, wie mit Klagen,　　　　F
reich und aufgeregt herniederstürzt.　　　　　G

The Coat of Arms

Like a mirror, taking things from afar
and quietly assimilating their pose,
the coat of arms was open in days of yore,
then slammed shut over reflections of those

creatures who dwell within the dynasty's
reaches, everywhere extending its might,
from right to left and left to right,
unchallenged in its works and realities,

which it avows and affirms and shows.
Above it, lined with glory and darkness,
rests the helmet with its iron flanges,

foreshortened under a crest that billows,
while its cover, as if with cries of sadness,
richly and feverishly thereunder plunges.

Malte Laurids Brigge describes several coats of arms in his notebooks; indeed,
he seemed obsessive about the heraldic lions and unicorns that he found on
various crests and on old tapestries. Rilke lived through the waning years of the
Hapsburg and Hohenzollern dynasties, whose coats of arms stood for the power
of life and death over millions of Europeans. Once open, when new conquests
could add to its devices and insignias, now it was simply a force unchallenged.
As Rilke would find out when drafted into the Austrian army during World War I,
the Hapsburg dynasty's power extended everywhere.

Der Junggeselle

Lampe auf den verlassenen Papieren,	A
und ringsum Nacht bis weit hinein ins Holz	B
der Schränke. Und er konnte sich verlieren	A
an sein Geschlecht, das nun mit ihm zerschmolz;	B
ihm schien, je mehr er las, er hätte ihren,	A
sie aber hatten alle seinen Stolz.	B

Hochmütig steiften sich die leeren Stühle	C
die Wand entlang, und lauter Selbstgefühle	C
machten sich schläfernd in den Möbeln breit;	D
von oben goß sich Nacht auf die Pendüle,	C
und zitternd rann aus ihrer goldnen Mühle,	C
ganz fein gemahlen, seine Zeit.	D

Er nahm sie nicht. Um fiebernd unter jenen,	E
als zöge er die Laken ihrer Leiber,	F
andere Zeiten wegzuzerrn.	G
Bis er ins Flüstern kam; (was war ihm fern?)	G
Er lobte einen dieser Briefeschreiber,	F
als sei der Brief an ihn: Wie du mich kennst;	H
und klopfte lustig auf die Seitenlehnen.	E
Der Spiegel aber, innen unbegrenzter,	I
ließ leise einen Vorhang aus, ein Fenster–:	I
denn dorten stand, fast fertig, das Gespenst.	H

Rilke was a natural bachelor, as we may gather from his letter to Emanuel von Bodman of August 17, 1901: "A conjoined life for two people is an impossibility, and where we find one it is a limitation that steals the fullest sense of freedom from one or both partners." The Rilkes were also curious, like the bachelor in the poem above, about ancestral ties. Rilke's uncle Jaroslav petitioned Emperor

The Bachelor

A lamp on the desolate documents,
encompassing night reaching even inside
the wood of cabinets. And he could thence
dissolve himself in his forebears, and bide
within them, the more he read the more sense
that he had their and they had his pride.

Arrogantly, the chairs stood stiff as stone
before the wall, and pure ego slouched alone,
lounging there; from above the night spilled
where the clock's heavy pendulum shone,
and his time flowed from the golden millstone,
all atremble and very finely milled.

He rejected it. As if he might wrest
other times away, feverishly he jerked
on the shrouds of the corpses of his descent.
Until he whispered: *What then is distant?*
To one of those correspondents he remarked,
How you know me–as if it were a post
to him alone–thumping on the armrest.
But the mirror, seeming limitless within,
softly released a window, a curtain;
and there, all but finished, sat the ghost.

Franz Joseph for a knighthood and Rilke himself touted his connection to one
Otto Rilke, hero of the *Cornet,* who according to the preface to the first edition
was the son of Appel Rilke, Lord of Langenau. Otto is the Rilke ancestor who is
supposed to have fought against the Turks in the seventeenth century.

Der Einsame

Nein: ein Turm soll sein aus meinem Herzen   A
und ich selbst an seinen Rand gestellt: B
wo sonst nichts mehr ist, noch einmal Schmerzen   A
und Unsäglichkeit, noch einmal Welt.   B

Noch ein Ding allein im Übergroßen,   C
welches dunkel wird und wieder licht,   D
noch ein letztes, sehnendes Gesicht   D
in das Nie-zu-Stillende verstoßen,   C

noch ein äußerstes Gesicht aus Stein,   E
willig seinen inneren Gewichten,   F
das die Weiten, die es still vernichten,   F
zwingen, immer seliger zu sein.   E

The Lone One

No—a tower shall rise up from my heart,
I myself from its outer edge unfurled:
where nothing else exists, once again hurt
and the unsayable, once again the world.

Yet one thing alone, vast in extent,
which tends to light and then to darkness,
yet one ultimate and yearning face,
cast among the never-to-be-content,

yet an outermost stone countenance
heeding its inner sense of the ponderous,
compelled to an even deeper bliss
by the calm annihilation of distance.

W.H. Auden called Rilke "the Santa Claus of loneliness," a name perhaps meant
to question the authenticity of his fellow poet. But Rilke truly felt that loneliness
was the inescapable lot of the artist. As he wrote to Paula Modersohn-Becker in
March 1907: "Solitude is really an interior affair, and to recognize this and live
accordingly is probably the best and most useful form of progress."

Der Leser

Wer kennt ihn, diesen, welcher sein Gesicht A
wegsenkte aus dem Sein zu einem zweiten, B
das nur das schnelle Wenden voller Seiten B
manchmal gewaltsam unterbricht? A

Selbst seine Mutter wäre nicht gewiß, C
ob *er* es ist, der da mit seinem Schatten D
Getränktes liest. Und wir, die Stunden hatten, D
was wissen wir, wieviel ihm hinschwand, bis C

er mühsam aufsah: alles auf sich hebend, E
was unten in dem Buche sich verhielt, F
mit Augen, welche, statt zu nehmen, gebend E
anstießen an die fertig-volle Welt: G
wie stille Kinder, die allein gespielt, F
auf einmal das Vorhandene erfahren; H
doch seine Züge, die geordnet waren, H
blieben für immer umgestellt. G

The Reader

Who knows this one who turns his face
away from his own being toward this thing
that only a page, by hastily turning,
sometimes forcibly seems to erase?

Even his mother might not be persuaded
it is he, reading what soaks in his shadow.
And we, who have hours, how could we know
just how much of him had already faded,

lost since he wearily looked up from the page
lifting the heavy substance of his book,
with eyes that do not grasp but gently nudge
the full and finished world they have just ranged—
as quiet children who play in some lone nook
grow suddenly adept with what is at hand—
but his expression, in his tight command,
remained forever and ever changed.

Compare the poem above to a letter Rilke wrote to Lou Andreas-Salomé on August 10, 1903: "Perhaps it is just a kind of awkwardness that prevents me from working... for I am equally confused when it comes to gleaning those things that are mine from books or from encounters. For weeks I have sat in the Bibliothèque nationale and read the books I had long wished to read; but the notes I made to help me along are useless to me; for while I read, everything seemed new and momentous to me, and I was tempted to copy out the whole of each one since I couldn't take it with me."

Der Apfelgarten

Borgeby-Gård

Komm gleich nach dem Sonnenuntergange,   A
sieh das Abendgrün des Rasengrunds;   B
ist es nicht, als hätten wir es lange   A
angesammelt und erspart in uns,   B

um es jetzt aus Fühlen und Erinnern,   C
neuer Hoffnung, halbvergeßnem Freun,   D
noch vermischt mit Dunkel aus dem Innern,   C
in Gedanken vor uns hinzustreun   D

unter Bäume wie von Dürer, die   E
das Gewicht von hundert Arbeitstagen   F
in den überfüllten Früchten tragen,   F
dienend, voll Geduld, versuchend, wie   E

das, was alle Maße übersteigt,   G
noch zu heben ist und hinzugeben,   H
wenn man willig, durch ein langes Leben   H
nur das Eine will und wächst und schweigt.   G

The Apple Orchard

Borgeby-gård

Come shortly after the sun has gone under,
see the green turf of the eveningtide;
is it not as if this scene we ponder
were long ago gathered and stored inside,

so that now, from feelings and things we recall,
from promise and half-forgotten elation,
still mixed with a darkness from within us all,
we might strew it before us in contemplation

beneath the trees, as in Dürer's art,
bearing the weight of a hundred workdays
in overstuffed fruit; humbly it stays
full of patience, seeking its counterpart,

exceeding all measure, yet waiting still
to be raised up and sacrificed, if only one,
willingly throughout a lengthy life span,
but held this silent growing as one's will.

Rilke connects art and trees and human patience in *Letters to a Young Poet,* letter 3: "To be an artist means not figuring and counting but ripening like a tree that does not force its sap, and stands poised in the storms of spring, unafraid that summer may not come. It comes. But it comes only to the patient ones, who stand as if eternity is spread before them, unshaken, silent, and immense. I learn this lesson every day of my life, learn it painfully, and I am grateful to patience for everything!" Franz Kafka, who was a contemporary of Rilke, also born in Prague, once maintained that the only sin is impatience.

Mohammeds Berufung

Da aber als in sein Versteck der Hohe,	A
sofort Erkennbare: der Engel, trat	B
aufrecht, der lautere und lichterlohe:	A
da tat er allen Anspruch ab und bat	B
bleiben zu dürfen der von seinen Reisen	C
innen verwirrte Kaufmann, der er war;	D
er hatte nie gelesen – und nun gar	D
ein *solches* Wort, zu viel für einen Weisen.	C
Der Engel aber, herrisch, wies und wies	E
ihm, was geschrieben stand auf seinem Blatte,	F
und gab nicht nach und wollte wieder: *Lies.*	E
Da las er: so, daß sich der Engel bog.	G
Und war schon einer, der gelesen *hatte*	F
und konnte und gehorchte und vollzog.	G

The Calling of Muhammad

But since Divinity found him despite
his hiding place, the angel appearing
loud-voiced, erect, and blazing with light,
he relinquished all his claims, pleading

that he himself might somehow remain
as he had been, the bewildered merchant,
illiterate; yet now he was sent
these words too much for even a wise man.

But the masterful angel pointed, indeed,
kept pointing to what the page displayed
and would not give in and further willed: *Read.*

Then he read, so that the angel bowed its head.
And already he was one who *had* read,
and *could* read, and was fulfilled as he obeyed.

Concerning the Arabian prophet, Rilke wrote to Marie von Thurn und Taxis in 1921: "Since my visit to Córdoba I have become almost aggressively anti-Christian. I am reading the Koran, which in certain places takes on a voice inside of me that I inhabit with as much power as the wind in a pipe organ." Rilke goes on to say that the Christian religion no longer allows one to speak directly to God. "Surely the best alternative was Muhammad, breaking like a river through prehistoric mountains toward the one god with whom one may communicate so magnificently each morning without this telephone we call 'Christ' into which people repeatedly call 'Hello, who's there?' although there is no answer."

Der Berg

Sechsunddreißig Mal und hundert Mal A
hat der Maler jenen Berg geschrieben, B
weggerissen, wieder hingetrieben B
(sechsunddreißig Mal und hundert Mal) A

zu dem unbegreiflichen Vulkane, C
selig, voll Versuchung, ohne Rat,– D
während der mit Umriß Angetane C
seiner Herrlichkeit nicht Einhalt tat: D

tausendmal aus allen Tagen tauchend, E
Nächte ohne gleichen von sich ab F
fallen lassend, alle wie zu knapp; F
jedes Bild im Augenblick verbrauchend, E
von Gestalt gesteigert zu Gestalt, G
teilnahmslos und weit und ohne Meinung–, H
um auf einmal wissend, wie Erscheinung, H
sich zu heben hinter jedem Spalt. G

The Mountain

Thirty-six times, then a hundred times
the artist had portrayed that single mountain,
thirty-six times, then a hundred times,
snatched away from it, then driven back again

to the unknowable volcanic landscape,
blissful, unswayed, full of its own allure,
while that thing attired in its own shape
held back none of its looming grandeur:

a thousand times during each day's immersion,
allowing unequaled nights to slope away,
all of them as if too short to convey
how every image was at once undone,
shape raised up to shape, vast, impassive, bereft
of all meaning, that he might suddenly
become aware, climb to epiphany,
and lift himself up behind each cleft.

The artist portrayed in the poem above is Hokusai (1760–1849), the Japanese master of ukiyo-e or woodblock prints of the so-called floating world of actors and courtesans. Hokusai produced two series of prints, *Thirty-Six Views of Mount Fuji* and *One Hundred Views of Mount Fuji,* working intensely until he felt that he had gotten it right. As Rilke admonishes Franz Kappus, the correspondent of his *Letters to a Young Poet:* "Everything depends on bearing for the full time and then bringing forth. Every impression, every seed of a sensation should be allowed to wax in the darkness, in the ineluctable, the unconscious, in that area inaccessible to one's own understanding, and the moment of a new clarity must be anticipated with deep humility; that alone is what it is to live as an artist: in awareness as well as in creation."

Der Ball

Du Runder, der das Warme aus zwei Händen   A
im Fliegen, oben, fortgiebt, sorglos wie   B
sein Eigenes; was in den Gegenständen   A
nicht bleiben kann, zu unbeschwert für sie,   B

zu wenig Ding und doch noch Ding genug,   C
um nicht aus allem draußen Aufgereihten   D
unsichtbar plötzlich in uns einzugleiten: D
das glitt in dich, du zwischen Fall und Flug   C

noch Unentschlossener: der, wenn er steigt,   E
als hätte er ihn mit hinaufgehoben,   F
den Wurf entführt und freiläßt–, und sich neigt   E
und einhält und den Spielenden von oben   F
auf einmal eine neue Stelle zeigt,   E
sie ordnend wie zu einer Tanzfigur,   G

um dann, erwartet und erwünscht von allen,   H
rasch, einfach, kunstlos, ganz Natur,   G
dem Becher hoher Hände zuzufallen.   H

The Ball

You round one above us, in your flight
bearing the warmth of two hands blithely
as if it were your own, that which is too light
and untroubled, which we cannot see,

not thing enough, yet enough of a thing
not to slip suddenly unseen into us
out of the string of the nebulous;
it slipped into you, between the fling

and the undetermined fall, that quality
which in rising, as if raising you higher,
abducts and sets the act of throwing free,
and bends and hovers and shows each player
some new location, moving them till they
seem like dancers arranged for a ball,

simple, artless, natural, and spry,
awaited below and desired by all,
falling into the cup of hands held high.

Rilke here concentrates not on the physical ball but on the essence that passes from hand to ball, "not thing enough, yet enough of a thing": that elusive quality that seems to exist only in immersion in the world. He writes in his diary in 1914: "There is only a single task: to connect oneself in some way to nature, to that which is robust, striving, and vivid with unhesitating readiness, and then, without cunning or calculation, to move forward in one's endeavors, even when one is engaged in the most trivial and everyday activities."

Das Kind

Unwillkürlich sehn sie seinem Spiel   A
lange zu; zuweilen tritt das runde   B
seiende Gesicht aus dem Profil,   A
klar und ganz wie eine volle Stunde,   B

welche anhebt und zu Ende schlägt.   C
Doch die Andern zählen nicht die Schläge,   D
trüb von Mühsal und vom Leben träge;   D
und sie merken gar nicht, wie es trägt–,   C

wie es alles trägt, auch dann, noch immer,   E
wenn es müde in dem kleinen Kleid   F
neben ihnen wie im Wartezimmer   E
sitzt und warten will auf seine Zeit.   F

The Child

Involuntarily, for a long while
they watch its play; sometimes the circular
living face appears from the profile,
clear and whole like a fully lived hour,

which rises and rings till the end unfolds.
Yet the others do not count its toll,
dulled by their lives and dreary from toil,
and do not even see how it holds,

how it holds all; and then beside them,
even then, dressed in its tiny garments,
wearily in waiting-room moments,
it sits there awaiting its own time.

In 1902 Rilke wrote: "One can certainly say that good parents as well as bad ones, that good schools as well as bad ones are wrong with regard to the child. Basically they all misapprehend the child by beginning with the false premise of adult-hood—of one who feels superior to the child. Instead they should recognize that the greatest individuals have always, at specific times, striven to become equal to and worthy of the child."

Der Hund

Da oben wird das Bild von einer Welt A
aus Blicken immerfort erneut und gilt. B
Nur manchmal, heimlich, kommt ein Ding und stellt A
sich neben ihn, wenn er durch dieses Bild B

sich drängt, ganz unten, anders, wie er ist; C
nicht ausgestoßen und nicht eingereiht, D
und wie im Zweifel seine Wirklichkeit D
weggebend an das Bild, das er vergißt, C

um dennoch immer wieder sein Gesicht E
hineinzuhalten, fast mit einem Flehen, F
beinah begreifend, nah am Einverstehen F
und doch verzichtend: denn er wäre nicht. E

The Dog

Above him a world he sees in glances
is endlessly renewed and made genuine.
But sometimes, secretly, something chances
to plant itself by him, and when within

this image he noses, lowly as he is,
not spurned yet not included, different,
and as if in doubt he gives up his present
reality to it and forgets this,

again and again he seems to twist
his face toward it, almost begging,
then abandons it so close to knowing,
for otherwise he would not exist.

As Rilke states in the poem "Childhood," children experience things the way an animal does. The artist also experiences things in this way. Mathilde Vollmeyer, on accompanying Rilke to the Salon d'automne in 1907, had the following to say about Cézanne and his work: "He sat before it like a dog and simply looked, without any anxiety or ulterior motive." The artist becomes absorbed in the subject almost like the dog portrayed here.

Der Käferstein

Sind nicht Sterne fast in deiner Nähe   A
und was giebt es, das du nicht umspannst,   B
da du dieser harten Skarabäe   A
Karneolkern gar nicht fassen kannst   B

ohne jenen Raum, der ihre Schilder   C
niederhält, auf deinem ganzen Blut   D
mitzutragen; niemals war er milder,   C
näher, hingegebener. Er ruht   D

seit Jahrtausenden auf diesen Käfern,   E
wo ihn keiner braucht und unterbricht;   F
und die Käfer schließen sich und schläfern   E
unter seinem wiegenden Gewicht.   F

The Scarab

Are the stars not almost like things that are near;
and what to you is so completely unknown
that you cannot encompass the subtle core
of carnelian within each dense stone,

within these scarabs, without also bearing
that very space that anchors their wing-shields
within your bloodstream—never was a thing
more gentle or more near in the way it yields.

For thousands of years in these beetles its fate
has been to rest, where no one can hinder
or need it, and folding their wings under,
the scarabs sleep beneath its cradled weight.

The image of the scarab also appears in volume one of *New Poems* in "Tombs of
the Hetaerae." Here Rilke writes a sort of love poem to the scarab in which he
dwells less on the art object and more on the space around it, in other words, on
its mode of being in the world. The scarab is an image of resurrection in Egyp-
tian mythology, but Rilke is more interested in the physical presence, the thing-
ness of this object, the weight of it in the hand, not in any metaphysics we might
ascribe to it.

Buddha in der Glorie

Mitte aller Mitten, Kern der Kerne,	A
Mandel, die sich einschließt und versüßt, –	B
dieses Alles bis an alle Sterne	A
ist dein Fruchtfleisch: Sei gegrüßt.	B
Sieh, du fühlst, wie nichts mehr an dir hängt;	C
im Unendlichen ist deine Schale,	D
und dort steht der starke Saft und drängt.	C
Und von außen hilft ihm ein Gestrahle,	D
denn ganz oben werden deine Sonnen	E
voll und glühend umgedreht.	F
Doch in dir ist schon begonnen,	E
was die Sonnen übersteht.	F

Buddha in Glory

Center of centers, core of all cores,
almond, that encloses itself and grows sweet,
this universe, unto the farthest stars,
is the flesh of your fruit: it is you we greet.

See how you sense that nothing more verges
on you; your shell is a thing without end,
and there the potent sap of you surges.
And an outer radiance seems to attend

it, for at the zenith your every sun
shall revolve, massive and blazing ones.
Yet within you has already begun
that which shall surely outlast the suns.

As noted before in this text, when Rilke worked as Rodin's secretary his window looked out on the gardens of Meudon-Val-Fleury, in the middle of which was a large Buddha. The "Center of all centers, core of all cores" is analogous to the great work—in the artist, to the great artistic work. As Rilke wrote to Robert Heinz Heygrodt in 1921: "As soon as an artist has found the vital center of his action, nothing will be more important than for him to continue within this center (which is certainly the center of his nature) and never move any further away from the inner walls of his quiet and ever-widening accomplishment."

About the Translator

Joseph Cadora's stories have appeared in various literary journals, including *Southern Humanities Review* and *The Montserrat Review,* whose editors nominated him for a Pushcart Prize. His reviews of literary fiction have appeared in the *San Francisco Chronicle* and online at the University of Rhode Island. His literary awards include the Roselyn Schneider Eisner Prize in Prose, the Judith Lee Stronach Prize for both prose and poetry, and a prize from the Academy of American Poets.

Index of Titles in English

Index of Titles in German

Poetry is vital to language and living. Since 1972, Copper Canyon Press has published extraordinary poetry from around the world to engage the imaginations and intellects of readers, writers, booksellers, librarians, teachers, students, and donors.

WE ARE GRATEFUL FOR THE MAJOR SUPPORT PROVIDED BY:

THE PAUL G. ALLEN
FAMILY FOUNDATION

THE MAURER FAMILY
FOUNDATION

NATIONAL
ENDOWMENT
FOR THE ARTS

WASHINGTON STATE
ARTS COMMISSION

Anonymous
Arcadia Fund
John Branch
Diana and Jay Broze
Beroz Ferrell & The Point, LLC
Janet and Les Cox
Mimi Gardner Gates
Gull Industries, Inc.
on behalf of William and Ruth True
Mark Hamilton and Suzie Rapp
Carolyn and Robert Hedin
Steven Myron Holl
Lakeside Industries, Inc.
on behalf of Jeanne Marie Lee
Maureen Lee and Mark Busto
Brice Marden
New Mexico Community Foundation
H. Stewart Parker
Penny and Jerry Peabody
Joseph C. Roberts
Cynthia Lovelace Sears and Frank Buxton
The Seattle Foundation
Dan Waggoner
Charles and Barbara Wright
The dedicated interns and faithful
volunteers of Copper Canyon Press

To learn more about underwriting Copper Canyon Press titles,
please call 360-385-4925 ext. 103

The Chinese character for poetry is made up of two
parts: "word" and "temple." It also serves as pressmark
for Copper Canyon Press.

The interior is set in ITC Bodoni™ Twelve Book and
Six Book. ITC Bodoni was designed by Sumner Stone,
Jim Parkinson, Holly Goldsmith, and Janice Fishman
in 1994 after research into Bodoni's original steel
punches. Book design by VJB/Scribe. Printed on
archival-quality Glatfelter Author's Text at
McNaughton & Gunn, Inc.